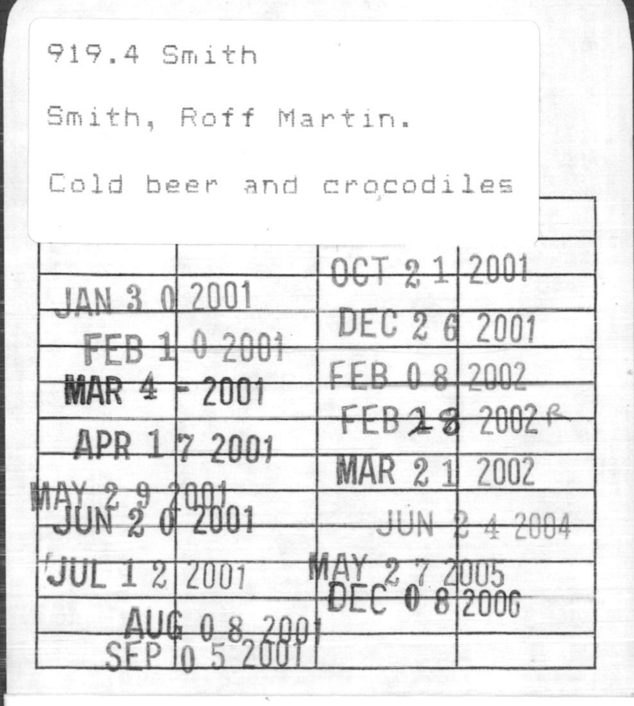

JAN 5 2001

Vestal Public Library
Vestal, New York 13850

COLD BEER AND CROCODILES

COLD BEER AND CROCODILES

A BICYCLE JOURNEY INTO AUSTRALIA

ROFF SMITH

ADVENTURE PRESS

NATIONAL GEOGRAPHIC
WASHINGTON, D. C.

Published by the National Geographic Society
1145 17th Street N.W., Washington, D.C. 20036

Copyright © 2000 Roff Smith

All rights reserved. Without limiting the rights under copyright reserved above, no part of this publication may be reproduced, stored in or introduced into a retrieval system, or transmitted in any form, or by any means, (electronic, mechanical, photocopying, recording, or otherwise) without the written permission of both the copyright owner and the above publisher of this book.

First Printing, August 2000

Library of Congress Cataloging-in-Publication Data

Cover Design by newearthmedia and Marianne Koszorus
Interior Design by Suez Kehl Corrado

Printed in U.S.A.

THE WORLD'S LARGEST NONPROFIT scientific and educational organization, the National Geographic Society was founded in 1888 "for the increase and diffusion of geographic knowledge." Since then it has supported scientific exploration and spread information to its more than nine million members worldwide.

The National Geographic Society educates and inspires millions every day through magazines, books, television programs, videos, maps and atlases, research grants, the National Geography Bee, teacher workshops, and innovative classroom materials.

The Society is supported through membership dues and income from the sale of its educational products. Members receive NATIONAL GEOGRAPHIC magazine—the Society's official journal—discounts on Society products, and other benefits.

For more information about the National Geographic Society and its educational programs and publications, please call 1-800-NGS-LINE (647-5463), or write the following address:

NATIONAL GEOGRAPHIC SOCIETY
1145 17th Street N.W.
Washington, D.C. 20036-4688

Visit the Society's Web site at www.nationalgeographic.com.

CONTENTS

"Bicycles were ridden or driven or ploughed or dragged wherever men could go, and not infrequently where men could not go with safety. But the bicycle got through—if the man did."

—Charles Edwin Woodrow Bean, *On the Wool Track*

"There are no mountains in the outback, only ridges on the floors of hell."

—Henry Lawson, *The Bush Undertaker*

Timor Sea
Darwin
STUART HIGHWAY
Katherine Gorge
Katherine
Mataranka
Larrimah
Dunmarra
Wyndham
Kununurra
VICTORIA HWY.
Kimberley Plateau
Ord River
Turkey Creek
Halls Creek
Derby
GREAT NORTHERN HWY.
INDIAN OCEAN
Broome
Shamrock Station
Bidyadanga
Anna Plains
GREAT SANDY DESERT
Sandfire
Port Hedland
Pardoo Roadhouse
DeGrey
Karratha
Fortescue
NORTHERN TERRITORY
Nanutarra Roadhouse
Alice Springs
AUSTR
Minilya Roadhouse
Gascoyne
Carnarvon
WESTERN AUSTRALIA
Wooramel Roadhouse
Murchison
Billabong Hotel
GREAT VICTORIA DESERT
Northampton
Geraldton
Dongara
Nullarbor Plain
Eneabba
Kalgoorlie
Eucla
Eucla Pass
EYRE HWY.
Coolgardie
Mundrabilla
New Norcia
Ceduna
Caiguna
Cocklebiddy
Norseman
Swan
Perth
Balladonia
Salmon Gums
Great Australian Bight
Ravensthorpe
Esperance
Margaret River
Jerramungup
Prevelly
Pemberton
Cape Leeuwin
Walpole
Albany
INDIAN OCEAN
Author's route
0 miles 400
0 kilometers 600

afura Sea
Gulf of Carpentaria
CORAL SEA
Great Barrier Reef
GREAT DIVIDING RANGE
Cooktown
Port Douglas
Cairns
Michaelmas Cay
Atherton Tableland
Innisfail
Ravenshoe
Ingham
Townsville
Gilbert River
Staaten
Dorunda
Karumba
Burketown
Normanton
Croydon
Mount Surprise
Norman
Gregory
Camooweal
Avon Downs
Mount Isa
Charters Towers
Birricannia
Muttaburra
Fairfield Station
Longreach
Alpha
Drummond Range
Anakie
Emerald
Fitzroy River
Rockhampton
CAPRICORN HWY
Gladstone
Miriam Vale
Rosedale
Bundaberg
Fraser Island
Hervey Bay
Maryborough
Gympie
Cooroy
Sunshine Coast
Glass House Mts.
Brisbane
Gold Coast
Coolangatta
Nimbin
Murwillumbah
Casino
Grafton
Coffs Harbour
New England Range
Armidale
Tamworth
Singleton
Blue Mts.
Windsor
Sydney
Start/Finish
Goulburn
Gundagai
Canberra, A.C.T.
Albury
Wodonga
Snowy Mts.
Australian Alps
Tasman Sea
QUEENSLAND
NEW SOUTH WALES
Darling
SOUTH AUSTRALIA
Simpson Desert
Iron Knob
Port Augusta
Melrose
Gladstone
Murray R.
Barossa Valley
Adelaide
Mannum
Murray
Tintinara
Naracoorte
Penola
VICTORIA
Coleraine
Bonnie Doon
Melbourne
Geelong
Port Phillip Bay
Queenscliff
Warrnambool
Port Campbell
Shipwreck Coast
Bass Strait
Devonport
TASMANIA
Hobart

PROLOGUE

Stopping to Smell the Wattle

THE RAYMOND was, and is, one of those art nouveau apartment blocks on Elizabeth Bay Road, the kind they built back in the 1920s when Elizabeth Bay was the fashionable face of bohemian Sydney. It was late on a Saturday night and I was lying awake on a makeshift bed of sofa cushions in the dining room of a friend's flat on the second floor, listening to the throb of 12-bar blues drifting up the sidewalks from a club in King's Cross. The room was dark, except where the glow of the night-lit street filtered through the curtains and touched the high spots. Everyone else had gone to bed hours ago. I couldn't sleep for thinking about the bold moves I'd been making over the last few weeks, and the adventure that would begin at daybreak.

For the past 15 years I'd lived in Australia without ever settling in, a sort of accidental expatriate who often spoke of going home but lingered on from not-too-uncomfortable inertia. The wonder that had drawn me here in 1982 had long since faded, replaced by bland familiarity and the day-to-day middle-class routines of going to work, paying bills, and doing weekend chores. I neither liked nor disliked the place. Australia was pleasant, sunny, and suburban, but I felt no emotional bond to it.

The years slipped by, permeated by a vague and restless understanding that I'd eventually go "home" to New England—but not just yet. Eventually I reached one of those crossroads in life where you're obliged to stop and take stock. What I came to was this: I would soon be 38 years old. If I was serious about returning to America, I should do it now. If I was going to remain in Australia, I should find a better reason to do so than shrugging indifference.

Weighing Australia's pros and cons, I realized with embarrassment that I knew surprisingly little about the country. Sure, I had traveled a bit, but always on assignment for some magazine or Australian newspaper, and almost invariably bound for one of the country's seven state capitals. In my haste to reach each destination and return, I had never taken time to stop and smell the wattle—after 15 years, I wasn't even sure the national flower had a scent—hear the voice of the people, or feel the rhythms of the land.

So I decided to take to the road, to look for answers there—or at least to find the purpose and direction that were missing from my life. At dawn I was going to get on my 21-speed touring bicycle, start riding out of town and keep riding, northbound for the tropics, on a journey I hoped would eventually take me counterclockwise all the way around Australia.

I decided to travel by bicycle partly because of the ornery freedom it gave me—self-propelled, slow, and exposed to all the sights, sounds, and smells along the way. I craved this immediacy. I wanted to experience Australia, not view it vicariously through a smudgy windscreen in an air-conditioned cocoon. Then, too, a bicycle suited my financial circumstances perfectly. Having just rashly quit an extremely good job at *Time* magazine,

I was gloriously unemployed—and, as Mark Twain described Huckleberry Finn, I possessed "a troublesome superabundance of that sort of time which is *not* money." I would travel alone, carrying everything I needed in my saddlebags, camping out at night and buying food at shops along the way. I would follow no schedule, simply a personal brief to tread lightly and experience Australia at its own pace. The goal: to come to some kind of terms with the country I'd lived in as a stranger all these years.

That was the idea, anyway, and it had seemed reasonable enough—even noble, in its picaresque way—a few weeks earlier, when the journey was still just an office daydream over glossy road maps. But now, on the night before departure, with my good-byes said, my resignation submitted and accepted, and my final paycheck looking inconsequential in a world of high unemployment, it seemed like madness. I wasn't particularly fit, I wasn't all that young, and for a six-foot-tall journalist I tipped the scales at a much-too-comfortable 14 stone (196 pounds). I hadn't been on a camping trip in years. I had never traveled in the outback—nor, for that matter, had I ever strayed too far out of the suburbs. Everything I knew about what lay beyond that sea of red-tiled roofs could be chiseled on an aspirin tablet.

The bars were closing now and the streets were growing silent. An occasional slither of tires on pavement—a taxi, probably—and once a peal of laughter from a group of revelers—sailors, perhaps, leaving the X-rated neon of Darlinghurst Street for the short walk back to the waterfront. Later still, I heard a man's plaintive wail: "Bill! Oh, Bill! Bill!" His melancholy echoed among the darkened buildings. I was wondering if Bill was his mate or his dog when I finally drifted off to sleep.

When I woke, a feeble light was sifting into the room—enough for me to make out my bicycle and a pile of saddlebags, water bottles, and camping gear leaning against the far wall. It was a little after six o'clock. It was time to go.

CHAPTER 1

Shaky Pedaling

I HEARD THE VOICE of the people, all right, as I was picking my way out of Sydney's suburban tangle. A battered Kingswood sedan ran a red light and came careering straight at me. Behind the wheel crouched a middle-aged harridan—Grendel's mother on a bad hair day. She came within inches of skittling me, took one paw off the wheel to flip me the finger, then screeched *"Asshole!"* out the window in a frontier voice that would have made a sea gull wince. The burning cigarette stub never budged from those sweet lips.

That near-death experience—not the last adrenaline rush I would get in the saddle—tore me from a reverie in which I had been envying the jazzy sophistication of travel writers to whom departure is as simple as an airy spin of a globe. An autumnal melancholy settles over London or Manhattan and suddenly, two pages later, we're living in an adorable peasant's cottage in Umbria or making a literary homage to Joseph Conrad on a pearling lugger through the Moluccas. Their smooth prose paves a delightful fiction that it is all so easy: Pack your grip, face the sun, and go. Money, visas, and adorable peasant cottages will tumble into your lap like dominoes.

And maybe it works that way, for them. Me, I would start out on a cold and cracked inner-city sidewalk, on a dead-quiet Sunday morning when everyone else was sleeping in, full of doubts and misgivings and wondering what in the world I was playing at.

Reality hit home once I loaded my bicycle with its full complement of gear: paired panniers on both the front and rear wheels, a handlebar bag, a sleeping mat, a spare tire, and four water bottles. I hefted the bike experimentally, fascinated and dismayed by its weight and strange balance, marveling that anyone—let alone me—would contemplate pedaling it to such faraway places as Darwin, 4,000 miles distant and diagonally on the other side of the continent.

I clambered onto the saddle and tentatively pushed off, giddy to discover that the bike moved so easily. I flicked the gears and glided through the quiet streets. The overburdened bicycle practically steered itself. I held the handlebars anyway, for form's sake.

I followed the long, curving descent toward Woolloomooloo Bay, the streets deserted but for an occasional cab prowling for a fare and the odd nighthawk who hadn't made it home yet. I rolled along the edge of the harbor, past the bay's silent navy yards, where a string of lights hung on the battle cruiser *HMAS Darwin,* then through leafy parkland along Mrs. Macquarie's Point. It was just before dawn. Lights twinkled in Neutral Bay, and the water in the harbor shone a dull, gunmetal blue. I rode easily, flickering in and out of dense shadows thrown by huge Moreton Bay fig trees lining the footpath. I could almost taste the freedom of the open road stretching out before me.

I was rolling through the Botanic Gardens, pedaling around the quiet waters of Farm Cove toward the Opera House, when the sun's first rays spilled across the sleeping city, lifting its glass-and-steel skyline out of shadow. Soft golden light danced on the iron suspension cables holding up the Harbour Bridge and gave texture to its stone pylons. The Opera House shimmered like a pearl. A stream of sea gulls burst from the footpath in front of me, rising like spirits, their wings dazzling white in the sun.

At that moment it was easy to see why people fall in love with Sydney. It is breezy, brash, infectiously optimistic. Gaze over the red-tiled sprawl of the north shore's Spanish Mission mansions on a sparkling morning, let a lung full of fresh harbor air fill your sails, and you believe anything can happen. If somebody hasn't already made you CEO, agented your screenplay, or put your face on the cover of *Vogue,* they will any day now.

Circular Quay was just waking up. Sunday-morning joggers and walkers burned calories, sightseers snapped sunrise photographs of the Opera House and Harbour Bridge, and the usual retinue of jugglers, buskers, bagpipers, pavement artists, and clowns limbered up for a day of pleasing the crowds. I squeezed the brakes and brought my 55-pound juggernaut of a touring bike to a gentle stop in front of the ferry terminal.

This was the first fork in my road. I could catch a boat here across the harbor or ride through Sydney's old quarter, known as the Rocks, and cross the Harbour Bridge. I liked the idea of starting my odyssey with a ride across the bridge, its pylons a gateway to northbound adventure along the Pacific Highway, while the magnificent harbor spread out beneath me in all its glory. But a couple of practical considerations sold me on the ferry.

For starters, the Pacific Highway is a scary road; narrow, potholed, pitiless, and buzzing with fast, aggressive traffic. It is one of Australia's busiest trucking corridors, 600 miles of white-line fever from Sydney to Brisbane. Live in Sydney and almost every morning you'll turn on the radio to hear about the latest fatal crash somewhere along it. On the scenic front, although a name like "Pacific Highway" implies sweeping ocean views, the highway actually runs tediously inland. From my point of view, there was just no percentage in taking it. So I had already decided to head west out of the city, cross the Blue Mountains, then turn north through the grazing country of the New England Range, rejoining the coast near the Queensland border. That in itself did not preclude a ride over the bridge. I could always cross, then get off the highway and work my way through the labyrinth of busy streets in Milson's Point and North Sydney and head west that way.

But the short ride from Elizabeth Bay to the quay had brought another matter to my attention: A fully loaded touring bike is heavy. And as I knew from having done it before, getting onto the Harbour Bridge walkway requires a climb of 266 steps. Pushing the heavy bike up the stair-side ramp—not to mention coming down again on the other side—was going to be nasty work. So the ferry looked good.

I bought a ticket to Hunters Hill, a prosperous suburb on a leafy peninsula a few miles west of the city. The ferry had just left—I could see the little green-and-yellow craft puttering beneath the bridge toward the tacky waterfront clutter of Luna Park, Sydney's answer to Coney Island. The amusement park's huge grinning clown's face leered at me across the harbor.

The next ferry wouldn't leave for 40 minutes. I leaned my bicycle against a retaining wall and sat on the sun-soaked concrete facing the city skyline. The dazzling reflections on the mirrored façade of the National Mutual Building caught my eye and warmed my face. I found myself thinking how that building was new since my time, and from there I began to count the other skyscrapers that had sprouted since I first laid eyes on Sydney in 1982. Besides the National Mutual Building there was the Renaissance Building, the ANA Towers, Grosvenor Square, and another dozen or so whose names I didn't know. Still more seemed to be new, but I couldn't be sure. A lot of water had flowed under this bridge since the day I lobbed in with my shiny new American passport. This town and I had both changed a lot over those years. Lines had blurred. It was getting hard to recall precisely what either of us had been like back then.

Passersby noticed my loaded touring bike. A few stopped to ask me where I was heading and wish me luck. That's one of the nicest things about cycle touring—your vulnerability makes it possible for strangers to feel comfortable opening up a conversation, and allows you to approach them without the usual urban defenses being thrown up. I tried to sound casual and confident as I reeled off my spiel about circumnavigating the continent, but I felt like a dandy with my spiffy new gear and my pasty office pallor. I marveled that they believed me. Nice somebody did. That spanking-new bedroll lashed to my rear rack irritated me, though. I wished I'd thought to dirty it beforehand.

My plan to ride around Australia was unusual, but by no means unique. The first cyclist to do it was an adventurer named Arthur Richardson, who set out from Perth in June of 1899 and finished the journey—detailed in *Story of a Remarkable Ride*—eight months (!) later. A lot of long-haul cyclists traveled Australia in those early days, their exploits recorded in musty bicycling journals. Richardson had already accomplished the first bicycle crossing of the Nullarbor Plain, taking just 31 days to follow a string of faint camel tracks from Coolgardie to Adelaide in 1896. In 1893, riding over old stock routes, cyclist Percy Armstrong had pedaled from Croydon (in far northern Queensland) to Sydney in six weeks. And in 1895, a doughty adventuress named Sarah Maddock had cycled from Sydney to Brisbane and back along a coastal track of rough gravel, topping her own exploit of a one-way ride from Sydney to Bega in 1893.

Although bicycles never evoked the romance of a camel train or captured the poetic imagination the way noble stockhorses did—Andrew Barton "Banjo" Paterson lampooned the "cycling craze" in his 1896 ditty "Mulga Bill's

Bicycle"—the humble two-wheeler played a key role in opening up the outback. Bicycles required no water and were easy to fix, making them the favored transport of independent men who had to travel vast distances through arid scrub: shearers, prospectors, stock agents, outback preachers, and commercial travelers. "It is extraordinary in what unlikely places one found those tyre tracks," wrote veteran Australian newspaper correspondent Charles Edwin Woodrow Bean in his turn-of-the-century outback classic *On the Wool Track*. "They straggled across the very center of Australia. We crossed them in paddocks as lonely and bare as the Sahara. Bicycles were ridden or driven or ploughed or dragged wherever men could go, and not infrequently where men could not go with safety. But the bicycle got through—if the man did."

The sign that shearing season was under way, wrote Bean, was the number of bicycles to be seen heading into the bush. "The shearer set out on these trips exactly as if he was going from Sydney to Parramatta. He asked the way, lit his pipe, put his leg over his bicycle and shoved off. For precisely the same trip, at that period, the average European would probably requisition a whole colonial outfit, compasses, packhorses, puggaree, sun-spectacles and field-glasses. The native Australian took it like a ride in the park. If he was city-bred, as were many shearers, the chances were that he started in a black coat and bowler hat, exactly as if he were going to tea at his aunt's."

So I was in noble company, even if those hard-bitten, pipe-smoking cyclists could—and often did—cover 100 miles a day through trackless, thorny scrub on threadbare tires stuffed with rope or dead snakes for lack of air. They made riders tough in those days; Ms. Maddock had averaged 80 miles a day on her trip to Brisbane. I would be happy to do half that—and on far better roads than she ever saw—until I found my cycling legs.

BY THE TIME THE *SCARBOROUGH* SIDLED UP to Wharf #5, Circular Quay was noisy with weekend crowds heading off to the zoo, or over to the beach at Manly, or out to Darling Harbour on the fast catamaran. Tourists queued for sightseeing cruises on paddle steamers, tall ships, and floating restaurants. Crowds milled. The waterfront cafés bustled, selling overpriced cappuccino and croissants to folks who reckoned their real cost in greenbacks, sterling, or yen. A little way farther along the retaining wall, a haggard derelict cast one of his rheumy eyes in my direction, malevolently, as though I was crowding his turf and he might have to do something about it.

A deckhand banged down a gangplank and fresh arrivals spilled onto the terminal, bright in T-shirts and sunny expectations. As the last of them came ashore, I wheeled my bicycle up the ramp and claimed a prized corner on the bow. A few minutes later both the *Scarborough* and I slipped our moorings to Sydney and drew away—the ferry to return in 40 minutes, but I not for many months.

Gliding under the bridge, I caught myself wistfully trying to pick out the building in Milson's Point that housed the Australian offices of *Time* magazine, my newly former employer. Until a couple of weeks ago, I had been somebody—a name, a face, a payroll number. I thought about the colleagues I had stayed with in Elizabeth Bay—imagined them lounging over second cups of coffee, perusing the Sunday paper, going out to lunch somewhere before returning to the warm, familiar sanctity of their flat. I saw them doing the odd jobs that needed doing: cutting up vegetables for dinner, watching the evening news, battening down the psychic hatches for another week at the office. Instead of wondering where I might be sleeping that night—or the next night, or the next—I tried to conjure up the picaresque freedom of the outback: the early starts, the wide-open road ahead of me, the light bush camps, the night sky full of stars. Living life straight from the stanzas of "Clancy of the Overflow."

That garish, rictus-faced clown at Luna Park said: Phooey!

THE *SCARBOROUGH* PUTTERED under the Harbour Bridge, past the leafy peninsula of McMahon's Point on the north shore and the gritty docks and loading cranes on the south, then nosed its way toward Hunters Hill. Valencia Street Landing has an almost countrified setting with its shady gum trees and manicured parkland, although it overlooks the industrial sprawl of wharves, cranes, and docked freighters. Sydney's north shore somehow manages to keep aloof from all that. From here the ugly docklands seem more like an expensive landscape feature—an urban-chic view of an authentic working harbor.

I rolled off the landing and along Valencia Street, a quiet thoroughfare of upper-middle-class homes sheltered from view by well-trimmed hedges. I was getting used to the weight of the bicycle now, pedaling it with greater confidence as I rolled along these prosperous back streets. In one sheltered driveway I glimpsed an older-model Rolls Royce, a distinguished Burgundy color, resting in the sun. But this well-ordered hush did not last long. Within a couple of miles Valencia Street emptied into the chaos of Victoria Road, the clogged artery that runs into the heart of Sydney's sprawling western suburbs.

THERE'S NO EASY WAY out of Sydney, whichever way you look at it. Australians believe that big leafy backyards are a part of their birthright and so, as their cities grow, they simply clap new suburbs onto the outer fringes. High-rise housing isn't in the picture. Consequently Sydney covers an area nine times larger than that of Paris. Although I had ducked the manic pace and aggression of the Pacific Highway, I still had to pick my way through a snarl of mean streets, angry drivers, black-spot intersections, inner-city truck routes, and bus exhaust. This megalopolis stretches almost 50 miles west, right to the foothills of the Blue Mountains.

Before I had gone a mile, I began to think I might have made a poor choice. The driver of a delivery van zoomed by so close that his rear-view mirror literally gave me the nudge. I skittered off the road, out of control, and by chance happened to come to a stop in a McDonalds' parking lot, my mouth open in a silent scream, my hands trembling violently, the back of my neck cold with sweat. Okay, lunch time! I dawdled shakily over a burger and Coke, thinking traffic might calm down in the afternoon.

All I accomplished was to delay myself long enough to roll into Parramatta just as the Rugby was letting out. League is a religion in New South Wales, and when church lets out they don't exactly go in peace. Cars with football scarfs fluttering out the windows roared past me, their drivers either putting their feet down with punch-in-the-air abandon or grimly muscling their way through traffic, wanting to make somebody pay. I held my breath and melded with the traffic flowing past the high sandstone walls of the old Parramatta Jail, then headed toward Windsor.

When I set out that morning, I had optimistically imagined myself bedding down for the night somewhere west of Windsor. There was no way that was going to happen now. Here I was only in Parramatta, with the sun nesting low in the branches of the trees and the sky the fragile translucence of approaching dusk, and a wide sprawl of suburbs still lay ahead.

I pushed on, already saddle sore and achy from the day's exertions. Within half an hour some of the saner drivers began putting on their lights. Their glowing taillights receding into the gloom made me think of home and hearth and dinners waiting on the table. By then I was riding on hard, cold gravel on the shoulder of the road, bouncing in ruts I could no longer see. It grew darker. Headlights flared in my face. If I had been older in the ways of the road I would have pulled over, found the darkest patch of shadow I could in bushes well away from the road, grumbled over getting stuck in the suburbs, and bivouacked. Anyone rousted me would have been their bad luck. But I was green. I spent the night in a motel somewhere west of Baulkham Hills.

CHAPTER 2

Escape Route

MY FIRST SUNRISE on the road brought a blinding shaft of light through the curtains of a cheap motel room and the muffled hum of Monday-morning traffic along Windsor Road. Here I was with 30 miles under my belt and only 9,970 more to go. I lay in the tangled sheets, reliving yesterday's last few nightmarish miles—the blinding glare from oncoming cars, the treacherous crumbling edge of a darkened highway, the cars zooming past my elbow every few seconds. No more night riding for this little black duck!

But who knew what the day would bring? I clambered groggily out of bed and brewed myself a cup of lukewarm instant coffee from one of the packets the management had left in a basket on the TV. It tasted like saltpeter. I risked a few nasty gulps, splashed the dregs in the sink, then took a steamy shower, hoping to unravel the knots in my shoulders from gripping the handlebars so tightly through the gantlet of western-suburbs traffic.

Traffic was humming along as feverishly as ever when I hit the road again about an hour later. The morning air was soft and cool, a carbon copy of yesterday. But no sparkling harbor this time—only the tedious spread of new housing developments that looked as though they'd sprung up after the last rain. As the miles passed, I began to pull free of the frenetic gravitational tug of Sydney. Traffic grew quieter. The fields around the houses grew larger. Some of the older houses had hand-painted signs in their front yards spruiking home-ripened tomatoes, pumpkins, or farm-fresh eggs.

A couple of hours of pedaling bought me a hilltop view of Windsor, a pretty and very English-looking village on the banks of the Hawkesbury River. Sydneysiders don't trumpet it now, but 200 years ago their city was the poor dockside cousin of prosperous farm towns such as Windsor and Parramatta along the Hawkesbury. All that is water under the Harbour Bridge: Sydney's voracious, amoeba-like sprawl engulfed Parramatta long ago. Windsor, by contrast, still has a countrified feel—and just enough gentlemanly cachet left over for city suits to want to come out here and buy weekend hobby farms. As I pedaled Windsor's streets, past the graceful old courthouse, I felt that I had finally shaken the suburbs. Exuberant at being out in the sticks at last, I crossed the Hawkesbury and rode out of town on a quiet, sunny country road.

THERE IS PROBABLY SOMETHING TO BE SAID for getting fit on the road, but I can't imagine what it would be. Back when I was dreaming up this trip on the wall map above my desk, I picked a thin and palsied red line running through the Great Dividing Range as my escape route to the west and north. It was called Old Putty Road, and it stretched nearly 100 lonely miles through the wilderness of Wollemi National Park to the town of Singleton. I expected there to be some hills and steep grades along the way—I would be crossing the Great Dividing Range, after all—but we're not exactly talking the Rockies here. The coastal mountains in this part of the range are not all that great—a couple of thousand feet high at most. You can see them from the top of Centrepoint Tower in Sydney: a low line of bluish-gray hills, made smudgy by the haze of eucalypt oil given off by their thick forests of gum trees. No worries.

Had I taken the trouble to crack a history book before going bush, I would have learned that these mountains are so steep, dense, and wild that early explorers spent 25 years finding a way through them. As it was, I became the poster child for the old adage: Those who fail to learn history are condemned to repeat it. By midafternoon, my learning curve on what lay west of Sydney was nearly as steep as the heartbreaking hill I was trudging up beside my bike.

When I finally got to the top of the grade, red faced and sweaty, I leaned my bicycle against a road cut, took a long pull from a water bottle, and dug out my map. I had covered about a thumbnail's worth of Old Putty Road. Another three or four inches to go—about three days' hard slog at this pace. Even then I'd be only in Singleton, a two-hour drive for any smart-aleck city slicker who took the freeway up to Newcastle, then cut inland. My heart sank. And I was planning on riding 10,000 miles? Already the ligaments in my right knee were twanging like guitar strings. I thought of all the people I'd boasted to about my grand adventure. Darwin—what I reckoned to be the minimum distance for a respectable failure—was still 3,900 miles away. From the top of that first sweaty grade, Broome, Carnarvon, and the Nullarbor Plain seemed as remote and unattainable as the Southern Cross.

CHAPTER 3

A Fantom Encounter

I RODE THE NEXT 350 miles on sheer Yankee mulishness, puffing and blowing up the hills, the throbbing ligaments in my right knee resisting each crank of the pedals. Despite the discomfort, I stubbornly ground out 30 or 40 miles each day, stopping to treat my knee periodically with ice cadged from pubs or packets of frozen peas purchased in grocery stores.

Dying railroad towns such as Quirindi and Werris Creek came and went, slipping by like troubled dreams. When I hit Tamworth it was raining—a cold, slanting rain—and a few snowflakes swirled in the wind as I rode across the high plateau toward Armidale. On to the rain-forest town of Dorrigo, wrapped in high fog when I arrived, then down through the mountains and back to the coast, heating up my brakes on a descent that plunged 2,000 feet in a series of switchbacks to Coffs Harbour.

It was warmer here, sultry, with banana plantations on the hillsides, purplish thunderheads, and little seaside hotels. I sat on the end of the pier, watching the fishing boats unload, listening to the deep growl of thunder back in the hills, and felt an agreeable sense of remove from Sydney. But that was all. It seemed shallow reward for so much pain, angst, and effort. I'm not sure quite what I had expected: sudden flashes of perception, a cavalcade of interesting characters and meaningful experiences that would effortlessly and intuitively reveal Australia to me, making sense of 15 years. It wasn't happening. Hell, I wasn't even having fun; this was just one long, hard slog. "Travelling is a fool's paradise," Emerson had written in his essay *Self-Reliance,* and after a fortnight on the road I was beginning to agree with him.

I pushed on and hit Grafton two days later, rumbling across the long, narrow bridge over the Clarence River just ahead of a cattle truck. I could sense it on my tail, and imagined the smoldering impatience emanating from its driver. My ears burned with resentment, a little at him, but mostly at me. I'd had enough. At the corner of Fitzroy and Prince I called a halt. I was beat and this nonsense was getting me nowhere. Feeling like a right mug, I plopped down on a sidewalk bench as weary and dejected as I have ever been in my life. I was still sitting there half an hour later—glumly sorting my eights and aces and trying to figure how to play my hand—when I saw him.

He was ambling along Prince Street, coming up from the river end of town. There was no particular reason for me to have noticed him: just another scruffy guy with a duffel slung over his shoulder, probably on his way to or from the druggie town of Nimbin, a little farther down the line. It was a busy time of day—Grafton's a bustling town of 20,000—and the sidewalks were crowded. He was anybody anywhere. But I knew with heart-sinking certainty that this guy was going to sit on my bench. And talk. I wanted company right then the way I wanted a bout of malaria, but I was too tired to move. Sure enough, he plopped down on the opposite end of the bench. He tucked the duffel between his feet and sat quietly, watching the cars shuffle through a couple of light changes.

I eyed him carefully. He was pale and slight, about five-seven for a guess. Angular face, a little gaunt, framed with long, stringy hair. He was young. I put him at 17, but I was to learn later that he was 25. He wore a tatty black hat, a frumpy coat that looked like it came from the missionary box, and a handful of bright slogan buttons on his lapel. He reminded me of the Artful Dodger. I made him as a panhandler. After a while he shook his head slowly and turned to me: "Hi. This is going to sound strange, but I saw you here and I had this feeling that for some reason I was supposed to come over here and talk to you."

"Yeah?" I scanned those slogan buttons, looking for "Jesus Saves," but all they urged me to save was the old-growth forests (not to mention abolishing nukes and supporting Greenpeace).

"Yeah. Funny, isn't it? Don't know why." He produced a pouch of Drum and carefully rolled himself a smoke. He started to offer me one, then flicked his eyes at the bicycle and back to me. He grinned. "Guess not, huh?"

I cracked a thin smile and shook my head.

He lit up. Leaned back. "Going far?"

I began to recite my stock reply, but I was too frayed at the edges to hold to the script anymore. That spiel had sounded tinny way back at Circular Quay. Now it really annoyed me. Like hell I was having fun. I was tired, disillusioned, and cranky. Sick of eating on cold concrete picnic tables, using dirty gas-station toilets, and drinking out of whatever public tap I could find, unless I sat at some counter and shelled out money I didn't have for an overpriced cup of coffee I didn't want. And I said so.

Once I started, the words just poured out. Here was a guy I didn't have to impress with any song-and-dance about taking a nifty journey of self-discovery. I was miserable, confused, and free to own up to it. He listened patiently, sometimes with the ghost of a smile on his face, putting in a word now and then, but pretty much letting me have the floor. As I rambled on, my pent frustration lost its heat. I found myself chortling over the memories of getting out of Sydney: the maelstrom traffic, the harridan in the blue Kingswood, the sweaty grind over the Great Dividing Range on Old Putty Road—the world's meanest shortcut.

Somewhere in this monologue I took on the role of spectator, instead of being the weary, thrashing combatant with rubbery legs and feet of clay.

We sat together for about half an hour. Then he looked at his watch and said he had to push on. He slung his duffel, nodded: "I just knew I was supposed to sit here. I'm glad I did. Have a good trip. I have a funny feeling we'll meet again somewhere along the road."

He mixed with the pedestrians on the sidewalk, then faded out of sight. I never saw him again. All I know about him is that he said his name was Robert Fantom; that he had lived rough on the streets of Sydney and now drifted up and down the coast, doing odd jobs and picking tobacco. And helping troubled strangers on a sidewalk bench see the absurd side of existence.

I sat on the bench a while, soaking up the morning sunshine, noticing colors, sights, and sounds that hadn't seemed to be there before. Watching Grafton go about its business, a pleasant restlessness came over me—the kind of gentle spurring of curiosity I'd imagined would drive me when I dreamed up this journey. I wheeled my bike to the edge of town, along a warm sidewalk shaded with jacaranda trees, then headed north on a quiet, narrow road. I camped that night in a wood about 45 miles north of town, watching a shimmering gibbous moon rustle the treetops. It would be several more days yet before my knee limbered up, but as I drifted off to sleep my mind felt comfortably settled in to the rhythms of the open road. I may have started pedaling in Sydney, but for me the real beginning of my journey will always be that park bench in Grafton, at the corner of Fitzroy and Prince.

CHAPTER 4

Numb in Nimbin

THEY LET ME TAKE A SHOWER at the fire station in Casino and lock my bike beside the pumper while I went shopping for supplies. It was a fine morning, with a nice slant of sunlight filtering through the trees over the sidewalks and magpies warbling in the leaves. Casino is an old meat-packing town and railroad hub, with wide streets, a false-front main street, and deep verandas around the pubs. On the way back to the station I called in at a white goods store and bought a cheap transistor radio to liven up my evenings. It was early August. The winter sun set not long after 6 p.m., leaving me little else to do at night except sit in the tall grass and wait for it to grow late enough to go to sleep. Buying the radio made me feel as though I was settling in, putting up the curtains in my new life on the road.

When I got back to the station, a pot of coffee was brewing and the guys were talking pig-shooting: Somebody's mate had just lost one of his best dogs to a tough old boar, which had nearly killed the man himself. We sat around drinking coffee and talking into the afternoon, when I said my good-byes and pushed off for the rain-forest country around the Nightcap Ranges.

It was a pretty ride through here, mountainous with the hillsides cloaked in remnants of the dense rain forests the early settlers called "The Big Scrub." Little dairy farms nestled in the hollows. Their weather-beaten barns had a settled look, as though they'd been in the family for generations. It was milking time when I drew up at one and asked the farmer if I could pitch my bivvy in one of his paddocks. He was a big, bluff man in muddy overalls and gumboots and looked tired after a long day. When he stretched I fancied I could hear the vertebrae cracking like knuckles along his spine. He gave me a hard, appraising eye while his cows ambled around him. After a long moment he nodded, reluctantly, but then pointed across the way to an old track and a barely visible wooden bridge and said in a more neighborly voice: "The creek over there is where our kids used to camp." I thanked him for the tip.

"No worries." He closed the gate behind the last cow to enter the pen.

The bridge was about half a mile from the farmhouse. I set up camp in the tall grass on the bank of the creek, made a sandwich out of a slice of ham I'd bought from a butcher shop in Lismore, and ate it listening to the birds twitter in the gathering dusk. There were no prizes for guessing why the farmer had been leery of me. A few miles farther up the road lay the hippie town of Nimbin, with its annual Marijuana Harvest Ball and its twilight society of drifters, dropouts and aging Aquarians. Among them, I hoped, would be Robert Fantom. He had mentioned he was heading up that way, and I wanted an opportunity to thank him again for hearing me out back there in Grafton.

The sun dropped behind the hills. The light deepened to a rich, shadowy blue. I tried out my radio and listened to the ABC news as the first few stars sifted out of the gloom. Half a mile away, a light shimmered on in the farmhouse. From my camp I watched the distant headlights of cars gliding noiselessly up the valley, then heard the faint sizzle of tires on bitumen as they passed by and disappeared around a bend. The night was clear, starry, and cold. I slept well.

MORNING BROUGHT RAGGED MIST in the hollows and heavy dew that soaked the grass and beaded up in large, cold drops on my bivvy sack. I shook it out, rolled it up, and was on my way, with the moon fading in a pale sky. Thirteen miles brought me to the turnoff for Nimbin. I rolled up Cullen Street a little after eight. It was a tawdry line of wooden false-fronts that somebody a long time ago had painted in rainbow motifs and psychedelia and decorated in early Captain and Tenille.

Nimbin had been just a fading dairy town in 1973 when it was chosen as the site for the Aquarius Music Festival, a sort of antipodean Woodstock, except that here a lot of the audience never went home. Now the place had the creepy fustiness of a haunted attic. At the Rainbow Café a sign boasted that over one million joints have been smoked on the premises. A lone middle-aged man opened up the Hemp Embassy, which campaigned for legalization and sold souvenir shoulder bags made out of hemp. A gaunt, leathery woman in her 40s nursed a baby in front of the frowsy Nimbin museum, crammed with garish 1970s ephemera. The place seemed as fresh and full of life as month-old bong water. I asked around if anybody had seen Robert Fantom. Nobody seemed to know him. Somebody suggested he might have friends in one of the communes scattered out in the hills; he could be hanging out there.

I was in no hurry; I'd linger a while. If he was around, he might drop in. I perched on the boardwalk and watched a lazy weekend unfold around Nimbin. Shopkeepers in paisley tights, scarves, and floppy sweatshirts set out sidewalk displays of incense, beadwork, crystals, and chimes (it was Saturday, and the tour buses would roll up soon). Nimbin was a whistle stop on the Byron Bay tour circuit—a musty curio for nostalgic baby boomers and something a little more for wistful backpackers too young to remember Vietnam.

Battered Volvos drew up to the curb and fathers wearing graying ponytails and Icelandic sweaters stepped past me into the deli to pick up a carton of milk and the weekend paper. I drifted into a shop and had a cup of coffee with a guy who was stirring a kettle of tie-dye. He was sturdy and blond, about my age, with a healthy tan and a ponytail; he looked like a surfer.

"I used to be a model," he said. "But then I went into drag for 17 years. I was growing breasts. It just killed me for the men's swimwear market."

"I'll bet."

"I'm Truly de Vyne."

"Beg yours?"

"Truly de Vyne." He spelled it out for me. "I used to do a drag act in King's Cross as Truly de Mented, but I feel I've reached a more peaceful stage in my life now, so I've changed my name to Truly de Vyne."

THE SIDEWALKS OUTSIDE WERE BRIGHT with aging boomers, fresh off one of the tour buses. I recalled what Robert Fantom had told me about Nimbin; how the town's gentle pot culture was being challenged by the ugly smack culture from Sydney's meanest streets, turning the town against itself. I could see what he meant. The other side of Cullen Street was where the rot set in. A knot of dark-garbed punks drifted in and out of the shadows, sidling up to anyone who wandered close and murmuring out of the sides of their mouths. They were hard and scruffy, obvious thugs, with "H-A-T-E" tattooed on their knuckles and black knit caps pulled low on their skulls. They leaned on lampposts and picked their teeth with stilettos. (No they didn't. I made up that part up about the stilettos. But they conveyed that impression.)

"Lovely, isn't it?" groused a guy in tattered overalls who had stepped out of the deli with the *Sydney Morning Herald* under his arm and noticed me studying the goings-on. "Scum dealing smack right on the street." He shook his graying, shaggy head. "I mean, there were always a few users around here. Everyone knew who they were, and they pretty well kept their troubles to themselves. They didn't bring their habit to town." He sighed. "That there's not the real Nimbin, but what can you do? Yah!" He unlocked his 20-year-old mustard-colored Mercedes, tossed the paper in the passenger seat, and drove off, glowering at the smack dealers.

I wondered what the real Nimbin was.

There was still no sign of Robert Fantom. I felt myself growing restless, irritated at Nimbin's almost religious affectations: the bare feet, the roach clips and tie-dyes. This was a town shuffling toward old age, afraid to move on, clutching counterculture totems as though they were articles of faith. I like a little dip in the waters of nostalgia as much as anyone, but who wants to spend his life in a cobwebby attic? I needed some air. I saddled up and rode.

Nothing becomes Nimbin like the leaving of it. The crackling mutter of Cullen Street ceased behind me like someone had lifted a gramophone needle. And then birds were singing and the sunshine felt as though it had some warmth to it, instead of offering merely light. The road drew me on; through the Nightcap Ranges with their volcanic crags and rain forests, past macadamia-nut plantations, and into the town of Murwillumbah, with its wooden tropical houses high on stilts, rioting bougainvillea, and tea plantations. Early the next morning I rode up to the beach at Tweed Heads. It was bright and warm; sunlight danced on the Pacific. The beach town was quiet, sleeping in on a Sunday morning. I tiptoed past the small sign on the street that marked the Queensland border.

CHAPTER 5

Gold-Coast Gantlet

GOLD COAST FM—92.5 on the FM dial—was hosting a breakfast sausage sizzle at a beachside park in Coolangatta, an old coastal resort town that blurs with Tweed Heads. A small crowd, mostly locals, had turned out for free sausages, cartons of flavored milk, and promotional T-shirts. I veered joyfully into the park, drawn by the warm, summery smell of hot dogs by the beach. I hadn't had a hot meal in two days, and this one wasn't going to cost me a dime. I leaned my bike against a retaining wall and queued for my sausage, casting a sly eye around at those who were already eating for indications that seconds might be a possibility. It looked promising. A couple of joggers, a woman walking some kind of a spaniel, and two young mothers with four kids between them drifted up behind me.

The sausages hit the spot. I devoured six of them, lounging on the wall, dangling my feet, and liking Queensland just fine. Satisfied with myself for making it as far as the border, I was in a mood to admire the clean lines of the apartment blocks along the beach and the quiet, sun-drenched streets. The cars along the curb seemed to be dozing in the warmth. Palms threw sharp shadows. The Pacific Ocean sparkled bright blue. There was a pleasing simplicity to it all, like California in the 1950s. It exuded the same sort of myths, too: your pick of jobs, 300 and something days of sunshine a year, affordable eight-room houses with beachfront and pool.

When a deep recession hit Australia in the 1990s, thousands of families decamped and headed north, chasing prosperity and sunshine up the Pacific Highway. It became the Mother Road. Even if you couldn't find a job here, what a great place to be unemployed: miles of golden-sand beach, a creamy surf on a deep blue sea, and endless summer. I had written some stories about this great fin-de-siècle migration when I worked for the *Melbourne Sunday Age*. Newspaper travel budgets being what they were, I saw only the dreary, rust-belt end of things: a moving van drawn up before a nondescript suburban house, the moody skies, a husband and wife offering distracted observations as they watched the glassware being loaded.

This was my first glimpse of where they'd been headed; the Queensland miracle. Sign me up, Scotty. A couple of hundred yards after I'd rustled across the border, hungry and dirty, I was kicking back with a full belly, sporting a bright new T-shirt, and enjoying the protection of some sunblock donated by a local woman who had cautioned me about those never-ending rays of Queensland sunshine. I had arrived.

They were still serving sausages when I pushed on at the crack of eleven, easing along beachy streets, past old-fashioned budget motels and more sun-splashed apartment blocks, time-shares, and retirement units. Coolangatta is the quietest of the string of resort towns along this stretch of sand. The tempo picks up quickly as you head north. By the time I hit Broadbeach a few miles down the road, I was running a riptide of traffic. Sporty, open-topped Sierras driven by tanned young things with spiky hair and surfboards overtook older-model executive sedans steered by sun-seeking pensioners. Sharky men and women—real estate agents, no doubt— purled by in gleaming BMWs. There were nifty, self-contained camper vans driven by Swiss or German or English tourists, and big, smooth, air-conditioned charter buses crammed with sightseeing church groups or hung-over conventioneers or Japanese honeymooners, their noses pressed to the cool, tinted glass. There were rent-a-cars, airport limousines, and taxis. And floating 1,000 feet up in the warm, thick morning air, there was a Qantas 737 on final for the Gold Coast's Bilanga Airport.

In the distance ahead of me, the beachfront high rises at Surfers Paradise shimmered like pearls in the seaside haze. I was coming into Australia's Costa del Sol, its Ipanema, its Miami Beach—a glittering strip of condominiums and giant resort hotels, hard-partying nightclubs and karaoke bars, 35,000 motel rooms, 500 restaurants, a glitzy casino, and a swag of South Florida-style theme parks. This strip of sun-kissed beach has been a popular getaway spot for more than a century, but until a generation ago it was just a tacky sprawl of low-slung auto courts, shimmering neon, and boardwalk amusements—an antipodean Asbury Park. Fellow thirty-somethings I'd known in Sydney and Melbourne often waxed nostalgic about the bucket-and-spade holidays they'd enjoyed up there as kids; driving up the Pacific Highway, surfboards on the roof of the old Holden, summers as open as the dazzling Queensland sky. Then came the rapacious 1980s. A school of spiffy carpetbaggers known as the White Shoe Brigade floated in on the high tide, bringing boatloads of junk-bond dollars with them and transforming the Gold Coast into what it is today: something Bugsy Siegel might have dreamed up had he been Australian.

AMONG THE MOST COLORFUL of these Gatsby-esque figures was a man named Christopher Skase, now one of Australia's most passionately wanted fugitives. He was a prince among Australian entrepreneurs, his sleek, suntanned profile a regular feature in glossy business magazines and society columns. He owned a national television network, developed magnificent luxury resorts, and threw extravagant parties that were the last word in conspicuous consumption. But when everything went pear-shaped after the stock-market collapse, Skase packed his bags and fled to Mallorca, where he could safely blow raspberries at his creditors while polishing his tennis game behind the walls of a handsome Mediterranean villa.

Over the years, Skase's gloating untouchability—the Spanish declined to extradite him—has so infuriated his fellow Australians that he has become almost a cartoon villain, a national piñata that everyone from the prime minister on down wants to hit with a stick until the candy spills out. And nobody doubts there is plenty of candy there. A few years ago, a late-night TV comic launched a telethon—"The Chase for Skase"—to bankroll American bounty hunters who would kidnap the fugitive and gun-walk him back to a Queensland court. The station switchboard lit up with donors. Thousands of dollars were raised. Finally, with contributions nearing the fund-raising goal, the Australian attorney general put in a good-natured appearance on the TV show to explain that—tempting as it was—the Australian government would never sanction kidnapping, not even to capture Skase.

The bounty money went to charity. Sighs went out and hands were thrown up in frustration in parlors around Australia and a few dogs probably got kicked.

THE GOLD COAST HIGHWAY WAS A DRAG of nightclubs, gas stations, motels, real estate offices, fast-food outlets, high rises, and tourist traps. Surfers Paradise was waking up or stumbling home; nursing hangovers, gazing with bleary disbelief into empty wallets, gingerly sipping double espressos or the hair of the dog, wondering if food would help and thinking about lunch. A local cyclist, a sandy-haired man in his 40s, drew up beside me at a stoplight in front of Jupiter's Casino. He nodded and said hello. At the next light we exchanged names; his was Paul. We talked while dodging traffic, and three lights later—with what I would come to know as typical Queensland hospitality—he invited me to a barbecue that afternoon.

I tailed Paul through a labyrinth of back streets, each seemingly smaller and quieter than the last, until we came to a peaceful, working-class neighborhood of gaunt frame houses, shaggy mango trees, and bougainvillea running rampant. It was a pleasant, drowsy place, about half a century away from the fast-money glitz along the beach. We stopped in the driveway of a weather-beaten Queenslander—those old-style tropical bungalows raised on stilts to let the air circulate beneath the floor. It baked quietly in the soft heat, wooden louvers open to catch any moving air. A radio crackled inside. We rested our bicycles against a shed and went up the stairs.

Paul was a commercial diver, divorced and between jobs just then, sharing digs with his 80-year-old father. The rooms had the unbuttoned easiness of two blokes baching together. Paul opened an old fridge and thrust a cold beer in my hand. We drank and listened to the rugby game on the radio. Paul said his family had been one of the first to settle here, in the 1870s, but most of them—at least the younger ones—were now looking at their cards, trying to figure whether or not to pull up stakes. "We all hate what this place has become. You should have seen it a few years ago, when it was just a nice little string of family holiday towns and blocks of retirement units. Everybody knew everybody. Then everything went crazy. Hordes of people came up from down south, hustling jobs, and bringing all the sleaze and crowding and crime of the city with them. Every time you turned around there was a new resort or theme park going up. A block of scrub you couldn't have given away before suddenly became red-hot real estate. House prices and council rates have shot through the roof—locals who have been here all our lives can hardly afford it anymore."

A flow of out-of-state money had transformed working-class pubs into "bistros," all brass and ferns and five-dollar boutique beers, or sent them sliding the other way, into noisy dives that catered to the party-hardy backpacker crowd with wet T-shirt contests and limbo dancing. There were no jobs anymore, other than part-time work flipping hamburgers or turning down beds in motel rooms. "You can't even sunbathe in the afternoon now," said Paul, "because the high-rises along the beach block out the sun. Most of my friends got fed up and left. I'm thinking of doing the same thing. I hear they're screaming for tradesmen over in Western Australia, in the iron mines and out on the offshore rigs in the Timor Sea. Got a letter from a friend of mine the other day and he tells me you can clear a thousand a week there—easy. I figure I'll hang around here another few weeks, see if anything pops up and then, if nothing does, make my way to Port Hedland. Forget this place."

The barbecue was at his aunt's place, another old-style bungalow built for the tropics, with a big mango tree in the backyard. A lot of family was there, the occasion being a rare visit home by another aunt, who had married an American serviceman after World War II and gone to live in Kentucky. It was the classic Aussie barbecue: plenty of charred snags and chops, fresh-cut salads, bread and butter, music and laughter and cold beer. Everyone had a good time. It was late when we got back to the house, the streets dark and empty, a counterpoint to the distant urban glow of Surfers Paradise. I slept in the spare bedroom.

CHAPTER 6

Twilight Time in Brisbane

AFTER BREAKFAST I SET OUT for Brisbane, battling the frenetic Monday-morning traffic through the suburban corridor that reaches toward the Gold Coast like a Sistine touch. I hit Brisbane in the shank of the afternoon, traffic humming and a warm western sun raking the city, sparkling on the tinted-glass skyline and casting shadows in the suspension beams of the Story Bridge. They rippled over my face as I tooled across the Brisbane River and into the heart of town. More than 700 miles had passed beneath my wheels since Sydney, and if this graceful span of Depression-era ironwork happened to bring the Harbour Bridge to mind, it wasn't just retrospection talking. The same man—an Australian civil engineer named John Bradfield—designed both bridges. This one was his encore.

I rolled down the ramp at the north end of the bridge and followed the flow of traffic downtown, taking the turns as they came. Office blocks and grand old Victorian buildings threw angular patches of shade over the streets. The heart of the city is cradled in a bend in the Brisbane River, with the lush, tropical Botanic Gardens at the tip. I lay my bicycle down and sat on a lawn overlooking the river, grateful for the tranquillity after dodging traffic all day on the run up from Southport.

It had taken me longer to reach Brisbane than I had planned. When I set out that morning I had hoped to ride straight across the metropolitan area in a day, nonstop, and camp in the bush somewhere north of Caboolture. It would have been my longest day's mileage yet, but with a dawn start I had thought I might do it. I hadn't reckoned on grumpy back-to-work Monday drivers, miles of gravelly construction, and my own rat-in-a-maze attempts to find quieter side roads (which succeeded only in adding 15 pointless, infuriating miles to the ride). Now, with the shadows growing longer, there was no point in going farther. Another couple of hours and the evening rush hour would start. If I tried to push on now, I'd only get stuck somewhere in the suburbs when darkness fell. Recalling what that had been like in Sydney, I decided to get a bunk at a backpacker's hostel and head out early in the morning.

That easy decision gave me the rest of the afternoon free. Strangely enough, it also made me feel guilty. After so many years the Protestant work ethic isn't easy to shuck. Somehow even life on the road can assume shop hours; *Easy Rider* meets John Calvin. At least two hours of daylight remained and here I was, self-indulgently knocking off early.

After a while, feeling like I ought to do something with this stolen sunshine, I ambled down to the Eagle Street ferry landing. I took my time. By then the sinking sun had happily taken the issue out of my hands, and there was no arguing: It was too late to push on.

I leaned my bike against a wall, sat on the warm, pebbly concrete, and watched the city close down for another day. Cool, dark shadows stretched over the promenade, the sky softened, and the sandstone cliffs along Kangaroo Point, on the opposite bank, glowed like honey. The ferry soon bustled with homeward-bound commuters, dressed Brisbane-casual with briefcases, rucksacks, foil-wrapped bouquets of flowers, newspapers, and department-store shopping bags. Crowded blue-and-white City Cat ferries motored through the water. The Story Bridge streamed with homing traffic, the lights on its ironwork shimmering softly against a violet dusk.

I, too, needed somewhere to go.

CHAPTER 7

Cross Cultures in Sugar Country

THE TRAFFIC WAS BRISK and reckless on the arterials through Brisbane's sprawling north. I experimented with a few strategies for circumventing the rush, poking around hilly side streets and cul-de-sacs but always ending up back on Gympie Road, a clamorous truck route that blazed a corridor through the rapidly spreading suburbia. Eventually I just followed it, hoping that Brisbane could not expand faster than I could pedal.

Thirty harrowing miles brought me to Caboolture, a one-time dairy and pineapple-growing town, now a satellite city in Brisbane's outer sprawl. On the edge of town a quieter-looking road promised to lead me north into the sugar plantations around the Glass House Mountains, a series of spectacular volcanic necks that reminded Captain Cook of the glass furnaces in his native Yorkshire. I followed it. I made camp that night in a secluded spot of bush near the roadside and dreamed of pink cement mixers booming past my elbow, racing to the next foundation pour.

THE OLD GENTLEMAN IN COOROY didn't like the look of me. He stood on the veranda of the general store, scowling as though I was some sort of walking bylaw infringement. It was early morning. I had pulled up stakes at my campsite, just west of Noosa, half an hour earlier. Cooroy was where I joined the main coastal highway. I was two days north of Brisbane and, with the exception of that respite by the Glass House Mountains, it had been hellish.

Some of it had been bad judgment on my part. I had veered back to the coast in order to follow a road that—on my map, at least—appeared to hug the seashore. Instead of a breezy ride through a chain of prosperous beachside communities, the road along the Sunshine Coast had turned out to be a gantlet of heavy, aggressive traffic, construction sites, new housing developments, and metastasizing shopping centers, car yards, and fast-food joints. I could have been in Alice Springs for all the view of the ocean I got. When I asked a road-crew foreman if I was on the right road—after all, my map showed a red line running hard on the coast—he laughed and told me the ocean was only a couple of hundred yards to my right, over the line of sand hills.

It had been another 30 miles, nearly to Coolum Beach, before I got to enjoy any ocean views. But the run from there to Noosa had been delightful, everything I had hoped the Sunshine Coast would be—and probably once was, before the developers went open slather. Noosa was, and is, a fashionable resort town and surfing mecca, with a row of trendy shops along Hastings Street and a building code that forbids any building to rise higher than the trees.

The only trouble with this short, pleasant, breezy stretch is that it ends here; anyone heading farther north pretty well has to follow the Bruce Highway. And so I had broken camp that morning, ridden over the pain-and-pleasure hill I was told was popular with Noosa's triathletes, and rolled into Cooroy—and the imperious gaze of the old codger at the general store. Since no one else was about, I asked him what the road ahead was like.

He nearly bit my head off. "What do you mean? That's our national highway! Of course it's a good road, a fine road."

"I'm sure it is. I was just wondering if there were any shoulders on it."

"Absolutely not! I tell you that is a beautiful fine road. They're working on it all the time! No, you won't find any shoulders there."

Served me right for asking such a foolish question. I don't know what I'd hoped to gain by it, unless it was some kind of hand-holding reassurance that things would not be as scary as they had been farther south. It wasn't as though I had much choice, if I wanted to push north in a hurry and get away from Queensland's built-up southeast.

In any event, all the worthwhile road advice I'd received so far on this trip could have been wrapped in a tire patch; motorists and cyclists just don't see things the same way. But the old goat in Cooroy, at least, was dead accurate on two points: there were no shoulders, and they were working on it all the time.

That pitiless, narrow, broken, and potholed strip of bitumen—25 miles to Gympie—was the most dangerous and frightening I've ever had the misfortune to ride; a suicide run of hammering trucks, heavy construction, muddy detours, and lane closures. When I say the road crews were working on it, it was more a matter of heavy equipment sitting idle, a slalom course of plastic pylons laid out, and knots of gruff men in fluorescent orange vests leaning on shovels, talking and flicking cigarette butts into the tall grass. The morning smelled of hot asphalt. Traffic backed up for miles as we waited for a convoy car to lead us through the muddy mess. Tempers spilled over like radiators in the breathless heat.

And where there was no construction, where the narrow highway was already more patch than road, and where its edges crumbled abruptly into a deep ditch, that was where everyone put the hammer down to make up lost time. Trucks belched plumes of diesel exhaust. Fast sedans took curves high and wide, suspensions squealing, their drivers frantically hunting room. Or they played suicide squeeze, passing an old Bedford farm truck on a short straightaway while oncoming drivers turned ashen gray and flashed their lights—and your diarist skidded frantically into the bush.

Death wore its heartiest hail-fellow-well-met guise in the form of sunshine-bound pensioners towing caravans up the coast on that long-dreamed-of trip around Australia. Stouthearted grandparents who had probably never towed anything in their lives until the morning they set out, splendid in the new Land Cruisers they had bought the previous week with their superannuation-fund payout. They rumbled up the highway at a brisk pace, marveling at the tropical scenery, oblivious to the four-bunk Millard careering out of control behind them. They waved and tooted cheerily as they swept past me, their super-wide towing mirrors fanning my cheek. As I watched them recede, straddling my bike in the weedy ditches where I had screeched to a halt, I couldn't help thinking of my own grandfather's remarkable ability to fill almost any size room with his bony elbows, spidery legs, and size-13 double-A feet—and his open astonishment at the clumsiness of those around him.

It took me all morning to reach the old gold-rush town of Gympie, named from the Aboriginal word for the agonizing stinging nettle that grows along its riverbanks. It was raining steadily when I rolled down the main street, having just survived my closest-ever brush with a truck on the outskirts of town. My nerves were shot. It was lunchtime. I bought a hot chicken at a deli and devoured it in the shelter of the post-office veranda, nodding hello to a steady lunchtime flow of shopkeepers and young mothers come to check their mail, and watching the rain drip from the eaves. I asked around, and worked out an alternate route of back roads that would take me as far as Maryborough—55 miles farther north—without spending much time on the highway. It was complicated and circuitous—even the locals giving me directions couldn't quite agree on its finer points and bickered pleasantly among themselves—and it added a fair bit of distance, but it boosted my chances of surviving to sundown.

The rain tapered off after an hour or so. A few stray sunbeams even cut through the clouds, giving the main street's false-front streetscapes a fresh, bright feel against the darkness of the hills above town. Steam rose from the warm pavement. I threw away the chicken bones, washed my greasy fingers in a roadhouse rest room, and set out again.

Within a few miles I was rolling past steamy cane fields and banana plantations, their rich emerald greens a counterpoint to the sooty clouds. Insects whirred in the breathless late-afternoon warmth. The nightmare of the Bruce Highway was fast receding; this was the way I had imagined cycling Queensland.

At a drowsy crossroads hamlet called Bauple, I pulled up in front of the prettiest Queenslander house I had ever seen. If you've never come across one before, it's a style of tropical architecture unique to Australia; Edwardian-era bungalows raised on stilts, surrounded on all sides with deep verandas, and embellished with fretted balustrades, intricate scrollwork, lattices, ornamental arches, and decorative awnings. Supposedly Queenslander houses have their architectural roots in the colonial homes built in India during the days of the Raj, but in tropical Australia they flourished into a style all their own. I had seen these old-fashioned houses as far south as Murwillumbah, in northern New South Wales, and quite a lot of them around Brisbane, but generally they had some jarring element—a clumsily boarded-up veranda, ugly jalousie windows, an added-on solarium that was totally out of character. This one was perfect: light and airy and nestled in a tropical garden shaded by mango trees and bright with flowers. It called to mind an age of crisp white linen, parasols, and pitchers of iced lemonade. A woman and a couple of kids sat on the veranda. She smiled and said: "Hi."

I realized I'd been staring. I waved back apologetically. "Don't mind me. I was just admiring your house. It's beautiful."

Picking up my accent: "I suppose you don't see many of these where you're from."

I laughed, thinking of a New England winter in a house like that. "Not a lot, no."

"Come on up and I'll show you around."

"Love to, if it's all right."

"Come on up."

I leaned my bike against one of the house's stilts, clambered up the flight of wooden steps, and introduced myself. The woman's name was Deb; the kids were Claire, Tom, and Declan. They were just back from school and the veranda was busy with toys. Deb waved her hand at the clutter. "We practically live out here on the veranda. That's the idea with these old tropical houses: You can be out here all the time. Even when it's pouring down with rain, the kids can come out here and play. They can even ride their bikes under the house."

Deb showed me around. The rooms were bright and pleasantly cool, with high ceilings and ornamental arches above the doorways to let air circulate even with the doors closed. "The house is about 90 years old. We've owned it for 15 years, but we only just moved in here. We've been living way out in the bush and we're still sort of settling in to town life. It's not easy. Until now the kids have always gone to School of the Air, and they're finding it a little hard to adjust to the day-to-day grind of going to school and being with other kids."

I was intrigued. I had never met anyone whose children "attended" Australia's legendary outback school, where lessons are broadcast by two-way radio to outlying sheep stations and lonely ranger posts. I asked what the schooling was like. "It was fabulous," Deb said. "Because it was so much more of a challenge, everyone worked that much harder. School of the Air really stressed excellence, so outback kids wouldn't be left behind compared with town kids. There is none of that urgency in the regular schools. They just cater to the lowest common denominator."

While Deb and I were talking, her husband, Darryl, came home. He was a forester, a lean, nut-brown outdoorsman in olive-green khakis. He smoked a stubby pipe, and his eyes were bright and humorous.

Deb and Darryl invited me to stay for dinner and made up the spare bed for me. We had pasta and vegetables and fresh fruit. The dining room opened onto the velvety tropical night. Moths fluttered in the doorway. It was pleasantly warm, still damp from the day's rain. A cane grower was burning off in a nearby field, and we could see a line of flames licking the sky and smell the peculiar burnt-molasses scent that hangs over sugar country at harvest time. Bits of ash fluttered in the air.

After the dishes had been washed and put away, they broke out the atlas, asking me questions about my trip; what I had seen so far and where I planned to go. We sat around the table, Deb and Darryl skillfully turning the evening into a geography lesson for their kids. This was a family who did things together, partly by long practice of living in outback isolation, but mostly because they were loving, close-knit, and enjoyed one another's company.

Deb and Darryl were subtle and good-humored teachers, finding interesting and creative ways of explaining the geography, history, flora, and fauna of various points along the route. I kept an ear cocked myself; I was learning plenty. Everybody took turns looking things up, scurrying off to bookshelves crammed with well-thumbed field guides and picture books on rocks and minerals, wildflowers, trees, birds, animals, geography, and archaeology—almost anything to do with nature. It was an entertaining evening, but country hours are early hours and it ended at nine.

I WOKE THE NEXT MORNING to steady dripping from the eaves of the old Queenslander house. The sky hunkered in low and gray and damp. Wet leaves on the mango trees glistened darkly. I had breakfast with the kids, who looked neat and combed and fidgety in their school uniforms. Last night's enthusiasm to learn and look up had been replaced by a weary resentment: "I hate school," Declan muttered. "I wish we were still going to School of the Air."

I said my good-byes at the picket fence and set off down a narrow back road toward the old river port of Maryborough. The rain eased back to warm steamy drizzle. Occasionally the sun broke through, making the bitumen glisten and freshening the greens in the cane fields against a charcoal backdrop of cloud. A big farm truck rumbled past, hauling a load of sugarcane, leaving that whiff of burnt molasses in the air eddies behind it. Other than that the road was quiet, just the drone of insects and the soft hissing of my tires on the wet pavement. Twenty miles brought me back to the coast—and to Maryborough. A fresh patter of rain sifted out of the clouds as I snaked through a few side streets, past more of those elegant Queenslander houses and into an old-fashioned downtown district that looked like a faded Chamber of Commerce postcard in the bleary morning light.

BACK IN THE 1870s, Maryborough had been one of the busiest ports on the Queensland coast, flush with gold-rush money from the diggings around Gympie, noisy with immigrants just off the clippers from Europe, its wharves piled high with sugar, timber, and wool shipped down the Mary River. It was also a center of the notorious blackbirding trade—a South Pacific form of slavery in which islanders "conscripted" to work the cane fields were often kidnapped by unscrupulous sea captains, who were paid by the number of workers they delivered—with few questions asked.

It was Thursday. Adelaide and Kent Streets were closed off for the weekly Heritage Market Day, and a mix of tourists and locals browsed the stalls on the rain-slickened streets. I bought a packet of honey-roasted macadamia nuts and ate them squatting in a sheltered doorway, waiting for the showers to pass. They never really did. I pushed on through the rain to the little holiday town of Hervey Bay, arriving late in the afternoon, wet and tired. I took a room in a backpacker's hostel.

ONLY A HANDFUL of other guests were there: a middle-aged English woman; an Irish girl named Una and a New Zealander named Dean who were cruising up the coast in Dean's battered 1969 Valiant and looking for fruit-picking work; and the Germans. There were two of them; as I learned later on, their names were Jurgen and Frank. I met them in the kitchen, where they were using every pot, plate, and utensil to render up some kind of noodle dish. They were twenty-something, shirtless and towheaded, with flat, tanned stomachs and Quicksilver board shorts. Bare feet. Splayed toes for gripping surfboards. A pair of cheap plastic wraparounds dangled from Frank's neck. Jurgen wore a gold chain and had a voice that could pick a lock.

I looked around for a clear place to prepare my dinner. Every counter was strewn with bags of groceries, empty cans of tuna fish, wrappers, or a slick of carrot peelings. Great clouds of steam billowed up from pots on the stove. They were chattering in German. I cleared my throat. "Excuse me."

Jurgen threw me an acid glance over his shoulder. "Go away. Come back when we are finished." He resumed his conversation as though I had already bowed out.

"I think we can share."

Jurgen continued fiddling with the steaming pots; I wasn't there. Frank resentfully cleared away a small patch of onion skins—roughly enough space to put down a tea cup—and indicated I could use that, if I was going to be so petty. I was. I made the area a little bit wider and began to fix my dinner. A moment later Jurgen made a remark in German that must have been exceedingly witty. Frank howled, looked at me, then laughed some more. They finished making dinner and carried their steaming plates into the TV room, leaving behind an ugly pile of dirty saucepans in the sink.

I MADE A MESS of spaghetti in one of their pots after cleaning it out, then joined them in the TV room. They were watching *Dead Man Walking* on the VCR and ad-libbing in German. Evidently it was a comedy. With a hot dinner in him, Jurgen became expansive. He even nodded across the room to me, introduced himself, and made small talk. "Is that your bicycle I saw out back?"

I said it was.

"How long have you been on the road?" He threw his questions down like a challenge; it was just his manner.

"Since Sydney. Yourself?"

"Seven months, but not riding bicycle."

"How do you like Australia?"

He snorted. "Australia is a waste of time." He peeled back the foil top on a tub of instant chocolate mousse and dipped into it with a plastic spoon. He made me think of a pouting Lord Fauntleroy.

"What's wrong with it?"

He shrugged, peeked into the pudding, and tasted another spoonful. "It's just nothing. A stupid, empty country filled with stupid, empty people. There is absolutely nothing interesting here. I mean, it's pathetic, the way they make a big deal about some little stream somewhere and you have to travel 2,000 miles just to see it and when you finally get there that's all it is—some pathetic little stream. Big deal."

"Where was that?"

"Katherine Gorge."

"Oh." There was nothing I could add to that. I'd heard of the ancient gorge in the Northern Territory, with its galleries of Aboriginal rock art, but I'd never seen it myself.

"They keep bragging about how beautiful everything Australian is, but I've seen it all and there is absolutely nothing here that you can't find bigger and better somewhere else. And I mean nothing."

"Been to the Great Barrier Reef?"

"Fiji's better."

"Uluru?"

"A big red rock."

"You must like something about it. You've stayed seven months."

"Cairns is a pretty good party town."

"But let me guess: They party heartier in Berlin, huh?"

A wry grin around a mouthful of pudding. He jabbed at me with his chocolate-smeared spoon. "*Ja.*"

I DID MY DISHES AND DRIFTED out into night, wearing a fleece against the cool of the evening. The rain had eased; a fresh breeze blew in from the sea. I followed the esplanade along the bay. Hervey Bay isn't really a single town, but a chain of five hamlets merging along a crescent of beach. It is the jumping-off place for tours to Fraser Island, the world's largest sand island, with its own unique rain-forest ecosystem. As I walked past the brightly lit pizza joints, cafés, and hostels in Torquay—the touristy focus of the community—I toyed with the notion of staying over a day and visiting the island. But even on short acquaintance I was already resenting all the heavy-handed marketing and the sense of obligation: You *must* take a four-wheel-drive tour of the island, you *must* go on a whale-watching cruise, you *must* try group trekking on the jungle trails. I didn't feel like joining a line of lemmings to purchase a neatly wrapped experience. I made up my mind to push on in the morning.

I swung back through the darkened streets, away from the beachfront. All was quiet on the moody, rain-slickened sidewalks except for the faint sound of a chorus somewhere singing "How Much Is That Doggie in the Window?" It drifted out of the old Memorial Hall. I poked my head in and found ten members of the Hervey Bay Musical Society at their Thursday-night rehearsal. They were arranged along an old-fashioned stage, under the direction of a middle-aged woman who sat at an electric piano. Otherwise the drafty assembly hall was empty. The door closed with a boom behind me. Everyone glanced up. I stepped sheepishly into the light, murmuring apologies. The director half stood, peered from her piano, and pointed to a mustard-yellow plastic chair in the middle of the room. "Have a seat! We'd love an audience."

For the next two hours I sat, front row center, like an impresario, while the Hervey Bay Musical Society rehearsed its way through a medley of old show tunes, Beatles hits, and sing-along numbers. The director's name was Zella Bridle. She told me she was originally English, and had lived for a while in New Zealand where, many years ago, she had placed second in an operatic singing contest behind a then-undiscovered Dame Kiri Te Kanawa. She worked them hard; they had a pageant coming up in September. "No! The sopranos are falling down over there!" They cleared throats, tap, tap, took a deep breath, and started "Rock Around the Clock" all over again. Rehearsal broke up around 10:30 and we spilled out into the damp night. I walked back to the hostel with "Mame" running through my head.

JURGEN AND FRANK were getting tuned up for a big night when I got back. Heavy metal blared from the jukebox. They leaned on the wall beside it, banging their heads, talking loud and sucking on bottles of Fourex. About a dozen empties graced the floor, the counter, and the top of the jukebox. The room reeked of stale beer. A handful of guests who'd been trying to hear the TV glowered at them. If the Germans noticed, they didn't care. At a break in the music, the doughty middle-aged English woman approached.

"Do you two mind? The rest of us are trying to watch the movie."

Jurgen shrugged. "We want to listen to this." He set his beer down and dropped a couple more coins in the slot. A pause, then Metallica's "Enter Sandman" exploded from the jukebox. Jurgen and Frank resumed their head banging. It was going to be that kind of an evening. I went to bed with a pillow over my ears.

DAWN BROKE GRAY AND FLAT, heavy with the promise of more rain. I took a walk along the beach. The bay was dead calm, the color of old pewter, and deserted, except for a woman walking her dog and a fisherman in a yellow slicker surf casting from the rocks. I stopped at a just-opening bakery and bought a few things for breakfast. Back at the hostel there was movement in the kitchen. Frank was subdued, puttering around the toaster, puffy-eyed and bleary, looking like he'd crumble into a million pieces if anyone bumped him. There was no sign of Jurgen. The thought of him suffering the torment of a four-aspirin hangover warmed me to my ankles, but it turned out to be even better than that. I overheard somebody say that Jurgen had wandered down to the pub, pissed off a shearer, and got his nose spread over his face like syrup on a waffle.

That made it a beautiful two-coffee morning, with an extra doughnut. I set out for Bundaberg a little after eight.

CHAPTER 8

Bundaberg Bayou

IT'S HARD NOT TO THINK of old-style Dixie when you travel Queensland's coast. It has the same steamy fecundity, gracious hospitality, insularity, and deep conservatism, with an undercurrent of smoldering racial tension. For many years it was ruled by an iron-fisted peanut farmer named Joh Bjelke-Petersen, a local version of Louisiana's Huey Long, who clung to power thanks to an intricate gerrymander that gave his fellow farmers twice the electoral clout of city folk. That all came to an end in the late 1980s—not in a .22-caliber pistol blast like the one that finished Huey Long, but by the more traditional Australian method of getting dumped in a backroom party ballot.

In the years since then, Queensland has largely rejoined the rest of the country in the early 21st century, but the sultry feel of the Deep South remains. As I rode into the old rum and sugar town of Bundaberg, I had a sense of riding into a small city in the Louisiana bayou. Maybe it was all that humid sunshine, the endless flat miles of rustling cane, or the fundamentalist churches. Maybe it was the carload of rednecks that flipped a firecracker in my face as they swept past me in a shower of grit, squealing rubber and "Yahoos!" on the outskirts of town.

I rolled up Bourbong Street around four o'clock, peevish about the rednecks, hot and sweaty from covering the 82 miles from Hervey Bay in just over six hours. The shops along the mall were winding down for the weekend and the local lads were warming up for a jukebox Saturday night. I sat in the pavilion, munching peanuts and watching the mating ritual. A flock of teenage girls, cigarettes aflutter, preened themselves in front of the milkbar, studiously oblivious to the greasers who cruised four abreast in the front seat of triple-carburetor Kingswoods, fluffy dice dangling from the mirror, radios blaring, and biceps strategically spread on the open windowsill. It was all straight out of the 1950s.

I was glad I had somewhere to go. Earlier that afternoon, stopping at a roadside park for lunch, I had met a church youth group on an outing; two of the adult chaperones, Peter and Beverley, had offered me dinner and a bed when I reached Bundaberg. I had their address in my pocket. They explained that they'd be home about five o'clock. I rolled around at dusk. They made me welcome, and sat me down to a double helping of shepherd's pie.

WE WENT TO CHURCH the next morning, a high-octane, charismatic service at the Christian Outreach Centre on Elliott Heads Road. It was a spacious post-modern hall, with three crosses staked on the front lawn and the fullest parking lot I'd seen since riding past Jupiter's Casino on the Gold Coast. The congregation was young; thirty-something families, mostly. There was no altar up front—just a Bible rock band with electric keyboard, two guitars, an energetic drummer, and a matched set of female vocalists cooing into their microphones. They played nonstop for 40 minutes, a rollicking medley of born-again jazz and blues and rock. They were very good. They got the congregation tuned up, clapping and singing and praising Jesus, and then—just when you were settling in for the concert—the band throttled back and the preacher took the floor, mike in hand. The transition was so smooth you hardly noticed the shift in gears. He was a vigorous 40, ginger haired and balding, dressed Queensland-casual in a gray T-shirt, white linen jacket, and black trousers. He looked like a bandleader but sounded like a football coach at halftime on Grand Final day with his team looking down the barrel of a 66 to 6 scoreline. It was a rousing stir, delivered in a fine declamatory baritone. At the end of it no one was unaware that things were mighty bleak, Satan's team was charging up the field at will, and we all had to do something about it, as in quick; tackle harder, pass more cleanly, stop fumbling so much.

After a fiery half hour or so, the call went out and a few hesitant sinners tottered forward to be saved, looking a little nervously around at the assembly hall full of faces. A tall, lean, dark-garbed man with silver hair stepped up quietly behind them as the pastor held their hands, his eyes tightly shut, face reddening with prayerful effort, then gave them a gentle push. They tipped backward, legs buckling slightly at the knees. The fellow in the dark suit caught them and eased them gently to the ground, where they lay motionless on the carpet, slain in the spirit. Then the dark man moved discreetly along the row, poised to catch the next redeemed sinner. The band cranked up again. More people came up to be healed; bad backs and stiff necks, mostly, and they soon joined the others stretched out on the carpet. There was more witnessing, exchanges of peace, communion, and another long set of Bible rock—that band was really good—before the service let out a little before noon. Just before releasing us, the preacher sounded a warning that witchcraft had been let loose in Bundaberg—evils he'd delve into more fully at the 6:30 session.

I RODE DOWN TO THE PAVILION on Bourbong Street after church and stretched out in the sun, unwinding a little after the morning's revival and nibbling a cut-lunch of ham-and-cheese sandwiches that Beverley had been kind enough to pack for me when she set up breakfast. The mall was quiet, bright with flowers and fresh, clean sunshine. I heard familiar voices call out behind me and turned to see Una and Dean, from the hostel in Hervey Bay, drifting up the sidewalk. They'd driven up that morning in Dean's wheezing Valiant and checked in at a seedy backpacker joint, opposite the tattoo parlor. An hour or so had been enough for them to figure out there wasn't any fruit-picking work to be had, although the guy behind the desk at their flop promised them there'd be plenty any day now if they'd just stick around and wait. Anything from avocados to zucchini—you name it. Una was skeptical. "I think it's just a game he plays to get travelers to hang around as long as possible, paying him 15 bucks a day for his lousy bunks." It sounded funnier when she said it; nothing beats an Irish accent for honing cynicism or telling you to go to hell.

I finished my sandwiches. The three of us ambled down to the riverfront, where a few yachts were tied to the wharf. A round-the-world yachtsman, a deeply suntanned Dutchman named Hans, was scrubbing the hull on his catamaran *Funtastic* and grumbling about the delay in getting his charter certificate. He had dropped anchor in Bundaberg a few weeks ago with the notion that he could easily pick up a roadstake running charters to Lady Musgrave Island, a pretty coral atoll on the Great Barrier Reef, then drift on up the coast. Maybe sail through the Moluccas and on to Sri Lanka. But the Queensland marine authorities were dragging their heels and now he was cooling his here in Bundaberg, shelling out 60 bucks a week in berthing fees. This week, he thought, they might come through and he could start doing charters.

Ears open for opportunity knocking, Dean asked Hans if he needed any deckhands.

"Ja," Hans nodded, "once I get my certificate. This is a 14-berth catamaran, I'll need help all right. You want to stay? Just cost you groceries. Should be any day now and I'll be set."

They were thinking it over when I left, Dean figuring that even if this business with Hans fell through, working on a charter boat might be a good idea. They could always head up to Airlie Beach and try to get work on one of the dive charters there. "Beats hell out of picking fruit," Dean enthused.

I rode across the river on an old iron bridge and took the back road to Gin Gin. Twenty-five miles later I was rolling through lightly wooded farmland in a clear slant of honey-colored evening light. A gray sedan passed me. The occupants—a middle-aged couple—waved cheerfully. A mile later I saw the car parked in front of a small green house with ornamental ironwork around the veranda. The couple was puttering around in their yard. I pulled over and asked if I could camp in their paddock across the road. But Phil and Alva wouldn't hear of it: "I should think we could do better than that!"

Twenty minutes later I was sitting, shaved and showered, on their back deck, with a plate of cheese, crackers, and fresh-sliced green peppers in front of me, a tumbler of good scotch in my hand. Dinner was simmering in the kitchen, which was redolent of rich beef stew. A 1981 Brown Brothers Cabernet Sauvignon was breathing on the table. A gentle flurry of sugarcane ash fluttered in the twilight—"black snow," they call it around here: a cane grower burning off his fields.

It seemed this pocket of Queensland bush has a tradition of hospitality to passers-through. Alva explained: "We're at the foot of a long, tough grade that used to be a challenge to the old steam trains heading north to Gladstone. Back in the Great Depression every swaggie for miles around used to come here for a chance to hop one of the slow-moving freight trains and maybe find some work farther down the line. They were always polite, decent men who'd just hit hard times, and my mother never turned anyone away without a feed. Well, except for one tough-looking guy with curly black hair who was obviously bad. My mother ran him off with her pea gun. She was a good shot; could hit a hawk on the wing. The swagmen used to put a rock on the fencepost of homes where the people were friendly and would give them a feed. We were always proud of the rock on our post. I guess now you can put one there too."

Consider it done. I slept that night on a bunk in an old railroad navvy car they had restored as a sort of guest quarters for visiting grandchildren. Breakfast the next morning was tea, toast, cheese, and Vegemite to the strains of a crackly radio serial, *Dad & Dave,* on the kitchen radio. *Dad & Dave*—a gentle comedy about bush folk struggling to make a go of things on Queensland's scrubby Darling Downs—was one of Australia's most popular shows in the 1930s, and the show still airs occasionally on local country stations. After breakfast I pushed on.

THE ROAD NORTH TO ROSEDALE, Lowmead, and Miriam Vale followed the railroad line, climbing the same long grade that wearied the steam engines of old—and continues to weary cyclists of any age today. Just past the hamlet of Rosedale the bitumen petered out and the road became a stony washboard. It was quiet here, just bright sunlight and birds chirping in the branches overhead. Occasionally I passed a woodcutters' camp, where railway workers had been carving out sleepers for the line. But there was nobody home, just neatly stacked timber aging in the sun.

The miles passed. Lowmead was a simple, quiet crossroads, with a pub and a jacaranda tree and a dilapidated house where a bunch of Aborigine kids played stick cricket in the yard. At the pub a morning drinker exchanged soft banter with the woman behind the bar. I bought an orange juice and sat on the steps, watching the kids play their version of cricket and listening to a kookaburra sound off somewhere in the bush. The sun arced overhead.

A couple of miles past Lowmead I came to a dead end. A barricade sign said the road was closed, torn up by a grader and made impassable in what must have been a prelude to improving it somehow. Another sign pointed down a dirt-track detour that wasn't on my map. I followed it. A few forks in the road later, and with no further signposts, no traffic, and deep in a silent forest, I began wondering where this was leading. I decided to ask directions at the next house I came to.

It was a run-down, sullen-looking place, with no cars in the yard and the only sign of life a snarling Rottweiler prancing along the edge of the property. He wasn't on a chain. I passed by.

The next place, a mile or so on, wasn't any more inviting, with a gloomy, down-at-the-heels setting and signs inviting me to "Enter at Own Risk" and "Beware of Dog." But the car sitting in the overgrown yard looked like it had been driven recently, and I couldn't see any guard dogs. I leaned my bike against the gate and approached the house. As I did, I noticed two nasty-looking mongrels sleeping in the sun next to the garage. Possibly chained—or perhaps that was wishful thinking on my part.

I was too far in to turn around. I stepped lightly, wanting very much for these sleeping dogs to lie. I rapped softly on the door. The dogs woke up and started woofing at the air, but they didn't run around the side of the house. Through a big picture window I could see a sparely furnished living room and a couple of toddlers playing on the carpet. They stopped playing and stared. I smiled. They didn't. The door opened a crack and a man poked a suspicious nose at me.

"Whaddya want?"

I tried to sound cheerful, but probably came across as an encyclopedia salesman trying to get his foot in the door. I explained my situation: "I'm hoping I'm not lost. There was a detour just past Lowmead but no signs since, and I'm wondering if this is still the way to Miriam Vale."

He glanced over my shoulder and saw the bike leaning against the gate. He didn't look any less suspicious, but he nodded slightly. "Keep moving, bud, you'll get there." The door closed in my face.

I went back to my bike, feeling eyes burning into my shoulder blades. The dogs bayed. I saddled up and rode. Behind me I heard a screen door slap shut, then the sound of barking dogs came from all over that big, weedy yard. He had unchained them. No more visitors today, thank you. I wondered what his story was: Witness protection? Drug dealer? On the lam? Whatever—it wasn't any of my business. I kept moving.

The road widened and became more presentable. An hour later I was moving through eucalypt-wooded grazing country, pedaling slowly behind a mob of sheep being mustered by a farmer on a motorbike. It was late in the afternoon. Raking sunlight refracted in the dust and lit the sheep, the narrow lane, and the canopy of gum trees above it in a fine golden mist. I asked the grazier about Miriam Vale and he said it was just ahead. I rolled up to the Miriam Vale pub just on dusk and decided to take a room. All this Queensland hospitality was making me soft.

THE PUB WAS DROWSY with the murmur of late-afternoon drinkers. I was heading upstairs, room key in hand, when I heard a gruff voice call out from the barroom below. "Say, you riding that pushbike around Australia?"

I turned and saw a big, craggy-faced man in his 60s sitting at a table, with a lean, tanned woman who looked to be his wife. I said: "Yeah."

"You're an idiot." He lit his pipe and leaned back in his chair, rather well satisfied with himself, and waited to see what I would say to that.

I recognized the classic Australian shit-stirrer. I grinned. "Smile when you call me that, pardner."

He grinned back, through a cloud of fragrant smoke. "When you get settled in come on down. I'm buying you a beer."

His wife spoke up. "And you'd better do as he says. He's military police."

"I'll report for beer drinking at 17:30."

I went up to my room. Australian pubs are nothing like motels, as their $15-per-night tariffs ought to suggest. They are typically old-fashioned places, built for last century's travelers, with the showers down the hall and cramped guest rooms that are just big enough to squeeze in a sagging bunk, an old dresser, and maybe a wardrobe. In the tropics they usually include a ceiling fan. I tossed my bags on the bed, sorted out some clean clothes, and tottered down the hall to take my shower. When I was cleaned up enough I went downstairs. There was a beer waiting for me at the table. I introduced myself and sat down.

It was an enlightening aperitif, although "Happy Hour" might have been too charitable a term for the conversation. Graham and Coral were as hard-bitten a pair of pensioners as I had ever seen. They were driving up the coast with their two much-loved dachshunds, on their way to the plot of land they'd bought near the Daintree Rain Forest many years ago—in the good old days, that is, before the do-gooders came up from down south and spoiled everything. Everything had gone to hell now, they both agreed, since Joh had been booted out of office.

Coral listened with starry attention, nodding to me helpfully to make sure I was following the drift, while Graham launched into a muscular rundown of all the things wrong with Queensland today: left-wing politicians, greenies, unions, Aborigines, dole-bludgers, Asians, and weak-kneed city folk from Sydney and Melbourne who didn't understand how things worked up here. The parasitic environmentalists had tied up the Daintree Rain Forest in so much protective legislation that Graham and Coral couldn't build roads or string up power lines to their little patch of paradise. "They ought to take those assholes out and feed them to the crocodiles," Graham snorted, relighting his pipe for the umpteenth time. Another nod from Coral. And as for Aborigines: "They ought to declare an open season on them, the way they do with ducks."

I wondered if he truly believed all this or if he was just stirring, gilding a few hard-edged opinions for my sake. A couple of times I caught a glint in his eyes that suggested he was doing just that. Other moments I wasn't so sure. Whatever his politics, I got the feeling that the only bit of the world that really mattered to him was the woman sitting across from him—with perhaps the two dogs waiting in their caravan running an indulgent second. Coral rested a hand on my forearm: "You really should meet them—they're lovely."

CHAPTER 9

In Which I Contemplate Tackling the Capricorn Highway

AUSTRALIANS HAVE NEVER let geography get the better of them. Here at Rockhampton, an enterprising town council nudged the Tropic of Capricorn a few miles north to a brightly painted monument outside the tourism bureau. Visitors can pose with one foot in the "Temperate Zone" and the other in the "Torrid Zone," then trot inside to buy postcards, tea towels, and camera film.

Giggling tourists were snapping pictures of one another doing the "I'm in, I'm out, I'm in, I'm out" routine when I rolled up on a sultry August morning, two days out of Miriam Vale. I leaned my bike against the "Torrid Zone," sat down in the tropical sunshine with a muesli bar and a bottle of water, and went into executive session with my map. It was time to take stock.

I was now 1,000 miles north of Sydney. So far I had pretty much followed the coast, running in the ruts of thousands of Australian sunseekers and foreign tourists. Although I wouldn't quite say Australia was repeating itself, it was starting to rhyme. Every landmark along the seaboard seemed to have been named by Captain Cook. Every inlet had apparently been eye-glassed as a potential site for a penal colony, then explored by runaway convicts and settled by tough, well-connected Scotsmen who made fortunes in wool, beef, or sugar. Every seaside community had its shingle out for holiday-makers, a handsome line of false-front Victorian façades along the high street, and real estate agents who were tripping over their chins spruiking house and land packages only 20 minutes from the beach.

I got the idea; I wanted a change of scenery.

Rockhampton marks the start of the Capricorn Highway, a thin ribbon of bitumen that follows the Tropic of Capricorn westward for almost 500 miles into the dusty Queensland outback. I had probably traced the fragile red line on the map a thousand times in my mind, imagining myself riding into these vast empty spaces, rolling through isolated settlements with names such as Dingo, Comet, and Alpha all the way to aptly titled Longreach. This was the outback of legend, where graziers got about in light aircraft and their children went to school by radio, where Banjo Paterson had penned "Waltzing Matilda" and Big Jackie Howe—outback Australia's John Henry—had sheared 321 sheep in a single day at Alice Downs station in 1892. I spent the night camped along the banks of the Fitzroy River and headed west the next morning.

CHAPTER 10

Into the Outback

THE CAPRICORN HIGHWAY was my first real taste of outback travel. I'd had a few glimpses before, when I was the mining writer for the *Sydney Morning Herald*, but those were just fly-in, fly-out assignments; a day or two of outback novelty, being escorted around a craggy, sun-drenched site by a mine manager, then sent packing back to the city. Long, empty hours looking down at a sunburnt immensity from 39,000 feet—both coming and going—gave me a vicarious sense of desolation, but that was all. This was all going to be at eye level, down and dirty with the heat, the flies, and the dust, earning each mile with hard work, sweat, and perseverance. And I was silly enough to be looking forward to it.

I left Rockhampton in midmorning, riding to the roundabout below town (where the Tropic of Capricorn actually lies) and heading west, past the sprawling cattle yards and along a narrow ribbon of bitumen that stretched out to a fine point on the horizon. It was remarkable how quickly the greenery and bustle of the coast fell away. Generations of Australian schoolchildren may have recited Dorothea MacKellar's outback ode "I Love a Sunburnt Country" as though it was the Pledge of Allegiance, but when it comes to picking a place to live it's pretty clear they want a leafy, well-watered suburb near the beach. Nothing brings home that truth like your first trip west. The landscape suddenly opens up and becomes hotter, drier, and flatter, while the towns get progressively smaller, rougher, and farther apart.

Seventy-five miles of hard riding brought me to the railroad siding town of Duaringa, its hard-bitten century-old pub nestled in a stand of eucalypts half a mile off the road. I coasted in just on dusk. The pub was crowded and noisy, its doors wide open to let in the cool Queensland evening and let out the brassy laughter, sweat, and smoke. I took a seat near the door and signaled for a beer. The bartender had shoulder-length black hair and a ZZ Top beard. He was a couple of inches over six feet, and sinewy. He looked capable, which in a place like this meant he could do a one-hand vault over the bar and deal with anything going on in the room. He drew me a beer, made polite chatter when he took my money, then went back to leaning against the back of the bar, arms folded across his chest, pleasantly aloof; watchful. The cold beer cut the dust in my throat. I settled back, tipped my stool against the wall and tuned in to the conversation. The topic was brawling and brawlers. Half an hour of eavesdropping bought me this:

1) Little scrappy guys can beat the shit out of big tough guys. Generally, or often enough, anyway. Or at least sometimes.

2) There is a scrappy miner over in Clermont who has kicked the shit out of every would-be tough guy from here to Mount Isa. His nasty little fists leave bruises the size of dinner plates.

3) His secret: Go for the ribs. Right over the heart, if possible.

There were bleary nods all around: Yep, tha's right, go for the heart.

Fingers raised for another round. A bloke started in on a story about one time down in Blackall. I finished the last of my beer and slipped unobtrusively out the door, making my way along the veranda to my room. Behind me the haw-haw-haw of a punch line drifted into the night. The thin door and walls muffled it a little, but not very much.

I made a dinner out of a tin of sardines, an avocado, and some dried peaches, and read a few pages of *The Bush Undertaker*—a dog-eared volume by Henry Lawson I had bought that morning in Rockhampton. Although I had seldom taken much interest in Australian literature before setting off on this journey, I began reading it out of curiosity after finding a paperback volume of Banjo Paterson that someone had abandoned in the hostel at Hervey Bay. I enjoyed it. Traveling as slowly as I was, under my own steam, exposed to wind, heat, rain, and the spicy tang of the eucalypts, had brought Paterson's landscapes to life. And I liked his sense of humor.

Lawson I enjoyed even more. His characters weren't jolly swagmen, telling yarns in doggerel verse, with rosy cheeks and a twinkle in their eyes. Most of them were drifters with a sharp sense of irony and a worm's-eye view of the world. A lot like Lawson himself, who roved for years and died a penniless alcoholic in 1922. Not surprisingly, given his dour circumstances, Lawson was disdainful of Paterson's whimsical renditions of a cheery, carefree, sunny, and perpetually wholesome outback. The poetic bushman was a myth, Lawson wrote. Many were "narrow-minded, densely ignorant, invulnerably thick-headed."

As the evening progressed and Duaringa's old pub rocked with drunken laughter, shouting, crashing tables, a throbbing jukebox, and two incredibly overworked obscenities, I had a hunch that while Paterson's outback might prove elusive, Lawson's was alive and well. The pandemonium from the bar sounded like a medieval sacking.

DAWN BROUGHT A CHORUS of snoring and the sound of dry wretching from the toilet down the hall. I gave my key to the publican, who was working a mop in the barroom, and set off down the empty highway. At Dingo, about two hours down the road, I encountered my first road train, a triple, parked along the roadside in front of a diner. I rolled slowly beside it, taking in its massive proportions. Road trains are unique to outback Australia: more than half the length of a football field, weighing up to 170 tons, and a fearsome sight as they thunder down a lonely outback highway, their 62 wheels churning up boiling clouds of dust and gravel. They keep the lonely settlements and stations in groceries, petrol, and dry goods, and bring their wool or beef to market. This one was on its way back from dropping off a herd of cattle at the sale yards near Rockhampton. Its heavily built trailers, thickly coated with fine dust, reeked of livestock.

Back on the coast, well-meaning townsfolk had warned me about cycling with road trains, telling me that the slipstream from the speeding monsters would likely suck me under their wheels, or that their rearmost trailers would swing wide and clip me into oblivion. I'd heard this often enough to be nervous, but now—as I pedaled past this hulking monster—I felt like Bambi sneaking around a dozing Godzilla. No doubt about it, here was the apex predator of the outback highways.

I had already seen signs of their passing—the flyblown remains of scores of kangaroos and even good-sized cattle that had wandered in front of their massive bull-bars. Some of the carcasses appeared to have been hurled a good 50 feet into the bush. Rarely were there skid marks. Evidently the juggernauts just kept on trucking, booming down the desert highways bound for lonely destinations hundreds of miles away. But I needn't have worried. When the road train caught up with me a couple of miles west of Dingo, it thundered majestically—and harmlessly—past, its driver giving me a friendly honk and a generous portion of road.

In fact, over the next few months and thousands of miles of outback travel, I was never to have a single problem with road trains, nor have I ever met a cyclist who did. The drivers were always courteous and gave me plenty of room—there was enough road for everyone out in those vast spaces. Still, I never lost my sense of exhilaration when one of the behemoths rumbled past in a swirl of dust and thundering noise. Seeing them called to mind Huckleberry Finn's impression of a Mississippi barge sliding past him in the night: It *amounted* to something to be a raftsman on a craft such as that.

AS I RUSTLED farther west, the afternoon temperatures climbed into the 90s. I found myself stopping for rest, shade, and water much more frequently. For the first time, I had to ration supplies and calculate the distance to the next settlement. Back on the coast, seaside towns, petrol stations, and general stores had been as plentiful as the greenery. But out here, once I rolled past the town limits, there was nothing but dry scrub for the next 30, 40, or 50 miles.

There was a certain violent majesty to these landscapes—vast, harsh expanses under a flaring sun, the gruesome spectacle of giant wedge-tailed eagles tearing flesh off rotting kangaroos, and at the end of the day a boiling red sun sinking into the bush. Sometimes the eagles thought I was after their flyblown carrion myself; they blocked the road, jealously guarding the carcasses with their six-foot wingspans. I looked in their glittering eyes and gave them a wide berth. Once a deadly king brown snake, which I mistook for a strip of blown truck tire, lashed out at my ankle as I raced by in front of its snout. Sometimes it was easy to think this was the highway to hell.

On my third day I reached Emerald, where I bought food and refilled my water bottles (they now numbered six and held 6.1 liters). I headed out again that afternoon, riding past a line of derelict boxcars, beyond the picked-out cotton fields, all brown and scraggly, and into the scrub toward the old sapphire diggings near Anakie. The day had started out hot, bright, and sultry, but an hour or so out of town I noticed a bank of clouds brooding along the southern horizon, like a mountain of rich, dusky grapes.

It was still sunny where I was, although the air felt cooler and the light not quite so strong. Nervous gusts skittered weeds across the highway. Thunder growled. The breeze, which had been blowing softly from the north all morning, grew restive, then whipped up strongly from the south, chilly and brisk as though someone had just switched on a giant air conditioner. One sudden, sharp, savage gust nearly skittled me. More clouds appeared, flanking me from the east this time, settling low and blotting out the landscape with purplish-black swaths of rain. Lightning snapped like the eerie greenish tongues of snakes.

I pedaled fast, skittering on the road from the force of the crosswinds. Before I could go more than a couple of hundred yards, the first fat tropical raindrops began splashing down around me. Within a mile I was drenched. Then, as suddenly as it had come, the desert storm veered and rumbled off to the north. I pulled up and watched it slide away, still punching the air with lightning and thunder. As I looked on, the sun broke through and a perfect arch of rainbow formed over the plains.

When the sun returned, it had lost its bite; the tenor of the day had changed. Storm clouds continued to scud across the sky, and coolish, desultory breezes kicked weeds across the highway. Thunder was in the air and a gentle rain was falling when I reached Anakie later that afternoon. I found shelter under an empty, tin-roofed structure and made camp for the night.

THE ROAD WEST OF ANAKIE was more desolate than anything I had encountered so far: 80 miles across two craggy mountain ranges to the tiny settlement of Alpha, with nothing in between but a dying railway siding called Bogantungan. Later in my journey I would cherish a crossing of a mere 80 waterless miles, but just then it was a challenge that had me diligently checking my bicycle and pouring water into every container (seven of them by now, holding 7.6 liters in all) that I could lay my hands on. I set out early, grateful for the overcast skies and the cool morning air.

The first stretch—30 miles or so to Bogantungan—went fairly quickly. I had hoped people still lived at the old siding, which would have given me a chance to refill my water bottles, perhaps even buy a carton of cold milk if there was such a thing as a general store. And there was—a tiny, old-fashioned shop painted turquoise blue, with neat gardens and a rainwater tank. It was a homey counterpoint to what was obviously a soon-to-be ghost town. But there was no milk—or much of anything else, for that matter—in the shop; just empty shelves, a few dusty cans of ginger beer and sarsaparilla, and three chocolate bars.

"I haven't bothered ordering stuff," explained Robyn, the shopkeeper, as she carted the last of the tinned goods to her car. "Nobody here to buy it, not since the railroad pulled out. I've been here since 1953 and my mother ran the shop before me, but no more. I'm closing up for good." I bought the last of her chocolate bars. She closed the trunk of her car and locked up the store. "Help yourself to the rainwater."

After she drove away I filled my bottles and took a good, long drink. The derelict town was silent under a dull and overcast sky. A grizzled old man watched me from the doorway of a ramshackle house with an overgrown yard, amiably curious about the new voice he heard on the street. He called out: "Where you headed?"

"West. Longreach."

He shook his head. "Never been there. Emerald is about as far as I go. Don't care much for long car journeys."

His name was Frank and he'd lived in Bogantungan all of his 70-odd years. "This used to be a real lively railroad town, years ago, when I was a boy. In my father's time there were more than 20 pubs here—some were just iron sheds, of course, with a few jugs of rum, but there were some big, proper two-story ones, too, with fancy iron lacework on the verandas. There used to be a real nice one right over there." He pointed to a weedy lot where bougainvillea flourished. "Burned down—oh—years ago."

He looked at my bike, leaning against a tree. "You've got a job ahead of you, if you're going west. There's no water for the next 50 miles and you've gotta cross the Drummond Range—the road's like this." He held his forearm at an acute angle. "I reckon you'll be walking by the time you get to the top."

THE PASS OVER THE DRUMMOND RANGE was only about 1,800 feet high, but it was a pitiless grind of steep switchbacks and broiling sun that brought to mind one of Lawson's laconic observations: "There are no mountains in the outback, only ridges on the floors of hell." There was something apocalyptic about the view from the top: a sweeping expanse of dull, reddish plains, lifeless under a pewter sky, with shadowy blue haze obscuring the distant horizons. The desiccated remains of scores of road-killed kangaroos littered the highway for miles, their mummified skulls leering in death. Flies hummed over fresher carcasses. The air reeked. I wondered what this lonely highway would have been like on a really hot day.

I gulped down a bottle of water at the top of the pass, then rode down the western flank of the range into a nagging headwind that wearied me all the way to Alpha. I was tired and sunburned and hungry when I finally hit town. After the long and lonely crossing, I was looking forward to a good meal and some friendly faces.

Alpha, its wide streets dead quiet late on a sleepy Sunday afternoon, did not look promising. A sheepdog lounging on the veranda of the pub loped out, ears down and growling, to head off my bike. An unfriendly face peered out of the pub. I dismounted, keeping my bike between me and the dog, and walked along the empty main street to a café whose billboard I had seen on the highway a few miles back. The soft murmur of a radio coming from inside suggested it might be open.

I tested the door. It yielded and I stepped inside to the familiar roadside cooking smell of hot grease. A prim, bespectacled girl behind the counter regarded me with a blend of suspicion and hostility. She scribbled down my order for a hamburger, then made for the kitchen as though she had recognized my face from a police bulletin. I plucked a carton of coffee-flavored milk out of the fridge, opened it, and sprawled on a green plastic chair beside a rack of rental videos, pretending not to notice the faces peering at me from the kitchen. It was a man who brought the burger out to me, while the girl watched apprehensively from the background. He took my money without a word and slipped back to his observation post in the kitchen. They watched me eat. I used my Sunday manners. Nobody shot at me.

MUCH AS I WAS RELISHING my time in Alpha, I thought I'd press on. The sun was sinking fast over the railroad yards, but the clouds had dissipated and the clear evening sky still held an hour or so of usable light. I finished my burger, tossed the wrapper in the wheelie bin, and rode out of town, pausing to top off all seven water bottles from a tap at the gas station. I rode ten miles in the cool of the evening and ducked into the bush to make my camp. The sky was blushing mauve and pink and the first stars were out.

Sometime in the night a massive cold front swept across eastern Australia, coming up from the frigid Southern Ocean, thousands of miles away from my little camp, and—according to my radio the next morning—scattering snowflakes as far north as Stanthorpe, in southern Queensland. Snow never fell up here, of course, along the Tropic of Capricorn, but all the same I'd woken up late in the night, shivering, to the moan of an icy breeze through the branches of the eucalypts and a sky full of stars as sharp as needles. Incredulous at this sudden shift in climate, I pulled the Gore-Tex cover of my bivvy bag over my face, greedily, like a trap-door spider in hiding, and nestled deeper into my sleeping bag.

Blinking in the dark, I woke early. The air was frosty, with a chill wind still blowing out of the south. I set off briskly, wearing a fleece, bouncing along the lonely, narrow road through the bush, my breath steaming in the cold morning air.

CHAPTER 11

Getting to Know Ewe

TWO MORE DAYS OF RIDING brought me to Longreach and the end of the Capricorn Highway. Longreach is a classic outback town, nestled in the heart of mythical Australia, with its Royal Flying Doctor Service base and School of the Air and pubs full of shearers. On the edge of town is the original 1920s hangar from which a seat-of-the-pants outback airline known as the Queensland and Northern Territory Aerial Service got its start, and flourished into Qantas.

I stayed in a cheap trailer and spent a couple of days doing a bit of housekeeping: replacing the worn chain on my bicycle, buying a couple more water containers (bringing the total to nine), and catching up on my laundry. Although I had lived in Australia for more than 15 years, I had never actually seen the inside of a shearing shed; Longreach, its population of 3,700 handily outnumbered by the million-odd sheep around it, seemed a good place to address this curious gap in my experience. I asked around and learned that they were shearing out at Fairfield, a 42,000-acre spread that was only 20 or so miles out of town. I called the grazier who owned it—a man named Rob MacIntosh—and he invited me to come out. "Take the Muttaburra Road out of town," Rob told me, "and keep going until you've crossed five cattle grids, counting the one at the edge of town. The house is a mile off the road to your right. The shearing shed is four miles farther back. To get there, you go past the airstrip..."

I knew right then that this was the Australia I had ridden 1,500 miles to see. I set out for Fairfield early the next morning.

IT WAS A ROUGHER ROAD than I had expected, deeply rutted and ankle deep in some places with fine dust. A hot, gusty headwind slowed my progress almost to walking pace. It was late in the morning before I spotted the homestead, shimmering in the dancing waves of heat. Rob had just come back to the house to refuel his truck and collect a mob of rams to bring down to the yards. He was a sandy-haired man in his early 30s, about six feet tall and 13 stone, with humorous eyes. Fine tufts of wool clung to his shirt, which he had rolled up to his elbows. I liked him immediately.

"We're all down at the shed. You can leave your bike by the hangar and hop in." I did, holding the truck's rickety door shut so it wouldn't swing open.

We loaded the rams from a holding pen near the house and bounced down a dusty track four miles to the shearing shed. It was an old, rambling, corrugated-iron structure, baking in the glare of a hot Queensland sun. Hundreds of sheep waited in pens around it, their collective idleness raising a film of dust I could taste. The sounds of voices and movement drifted out of the shed, only to be swallowed up in the vast empty stillness. Rob and I unloaded the sheep from the back of his truck—all but one; an old and unlucky ram had suffocated in the crush—and herded them into the sun-drenched yards.

We clambered up the steps into the shed. After the dazzling white heat outside, it took my eyes a moment to adjust to the dimness. The images that materialized could have come straight from a canvas by Tom Robertson, the Frederic Remington of 1890s Australia. Shearing has changed little in the past century—gloomy, heavy-beamed sheds, bent-over shearers toiling with their handpieces, slatted floors, wooden pens where sheep await their turn at the combs, the smell of lanolin, machine oil, and sweat. The family was hard at work. Rob's wife, Margot, was there, tossing the fleeces onto racks and trimming off the dags (the soiled bits of wool around the edges). Her sister Alison was acting as rouseabout, gathering fleeces and driving new sheep into the pens for the shearers. There were three contract shearers; Dave, Doug, and Tolly, a lean, dark saturnine man who was the head of the team.

There was a brief pause for laconic introductions and crushing, callused handshakes, then a few gulps from a water jug and back to work. Rob got busy on the wool press, compacting the fleeces into 400-pound bales, which were wrapped in canvas and then stenciled with the Fairfield name. Out of the way, in a safer part of the shed, the MacIntoshes' four young children played on the wool bales and regarded me curiously, giggling and shy.

As he worked the press, Rob filled me in on the workings of Fairfield. "We're running about 12,000 sheep at the moment. Over the next few days I'm going to bring them all in, drench them, and run them through the sheep dip to make sure they're free of parasites. You're quite welcome to stay and help, if you like."

I said I'd love to.

THE SHEARING TEAM FINISHED—or rather almost finished—by late afternoon. Just before knock-off time, I noticed Tolly exchanging a few quiet words with Rob. Sidelong glances in my direction, followed by low chuckling. Then Rob came up, grinning, put a hand on my shoulder, and said: "The shearers have decided you're not getting out of the shed without shearing a sheep."

I laughed, then blanched. "You're kidding, right?"

"Nope. They've left one for you. Get to it."

Tolly supervised, and the others grinned in amusement while I wrestled with the heavy electric handpiece and the fat old ewe they'd left for me. The sheep knew it was in the hands of a neophyte and kicked up no end of fuss. I clutched desperately at clumps of wool, the handpiece humming noisily and making my forearm tingle. After a month's hard riding I reckoned myself in pretty fair shape, but before I was halfway through shearing that sheep my lower back ached and my thighs burned. Tolly shouted encouragement, instruction, and finally—when he felt I was giving the ewe more of a light trim than a proper shearing—reprimand: "No! Dig in! You're robbing the farmer!"

I had known that shearing was tough, skilled work, but hearing that over a cold beer in a cozy pub ain't the same as bending your back over a struggling sheep and finding out for yourself. When I finally finished and shoved the poor, ungrateful yet freshly shorn creature down the chute—"the moneybox," in shearer's lingo—I asked Tolly how many he'd sheared that day. He shrugged. "Aw, 202." I looked at his tough hands and recalled a bit of advice an old codger had given me in a pub back in Ilfracombe a few days earlier: "Don't ever mess with a shearer, mate, you'll always come out second best."

THE LIGHT WAS FADING when we drove back to the homestead, the setting sun casting honey-colored light through the dusty windscreen and illuminating the face of Mary MacIntosh, who sat on her father's lap and steered the truck. She sang "You Are My Sunshine" and glanced at me regularly to make sure I appreciated her driving skills—which, considering she was all of three years old, were prodigious. "We're coming up to a gate now,

Mary," Rob gently chided her. She corrected course, and we whizzed between the two posts, a plume of dust in our wake.

Rob must have noticed the rigid, pasty smile on my face. "Some day one of us could be hurt and she might be the only one around to drive for help. Kids have to grow up quickly out here."

The day began before dawn, with bowls of oatmeal, fruit, thick slices of fresh baked bread, and steaming mugs of tea. As soon as it was light, Rob suggested a ride in the plane, partly to scout out where the sheep were gathering on the property and partly a hospitable gesture to show me around. We pushed the old Cessna 172 out of the hangar, climbed in, then bounded noisily down the rough dirt strip in front of the homestead, trailing a cloud of dust. The ground lurched away and then the empty Queensland outback spread out majestically, rust red, from one distant, hazy horizon to another.

Down on the isolated homestead, a private world in miniature, the kids spilled out of their little schoolhouse to wave to their daddy. Margot glanced up from hanging the washing on the line, and a few young lambs frolicked in the vegetable garden. There was something magical in the moment; at that instant, for the first time in many years, I felt excited to be in Australia.

BOUNCING IN THE MORNING THERMALS, Rob told me the story of the time back in 1870 when Australia's most daring rustler, Henry Redford, stole 1,000 cattle from the Mount Crawford Station, just north of here. Known as Captain Starlight because he ripped them off under cover of dark, the tough bushman and his men drove the herd across 1,000 miles of uncharted desert to market in South Australia. "Remember," Rob explained, "this was across the same country that had killed Burke and Wills," referring to the heroically ill-fated explorers who had tried to cross the unknown continent on camelback in 1860. "Redford was a real bushman, though, who had learned from the Aborigines how to get about in the desert. He not only crossed it, he brought the whole herd of stolen cattle with him. He might have got away with it except there was a distinctive silver shorthorn bull in the herd that gave the game away."

Redford was apprehended in Melbourne and brought back to Queensland for trial. The case was a sensation, with Redford's daring and bush skills capturing the public's imagination and sympathy. A jury of his outback peers returned a quixotic verdict: Not guilty, but he's got to give the cattle back.

An outraged judge ordered the panel to reconsider. It did: Not guilty, and he can *keep* the bloody cattle! "Being a good bloke can get you pretty far in this country," Rob concluded. He banked steeply, away from the craggy promontory known as Starlight's Lookout, and over a mob of sheep—fattish gray dots scrambling in a line through the richly textured, rust-and-olive landscape a couple of hundred feet below. Later that day, we drove out in the Land Cruiser to start rounding them up.

I spent the next few days at Fairfield, helping Rob muster sheep, repair a windmill, and put up some fencing. It was hot, hard, dusty work that often ended well after dusk. The MacIntoshes ran 12,000 sheep on their property, and I think I met all of them.

We spent one day drenching livestock, wrestling our way through a race crammed with uncooperative sheep that did not wish to have anti-worming medicine squirted down their throats. They bit, gouged, and butted. One particularly sly and evil-tempered beast allowed me to get the medicine into him and then, once I'd turned my back, whirled and charged vindictively up the race, slamming his heavy rack into my knees. I dropped, cursing in pain and surprise at this dirty trick. The ram retreated down the race, his dignity avenged and a smug light in his small, mean eyes.

Another day we drove metal fence posts into the hard, cracked earth under a noontime sun as we built a new yard near the homestead. My back ached. My office-soft hands picked up first a fine set of blisters, then the raw beginnings of calluses.

My favorite chore was mustering—roving the scrub with a mob of sheep kicking up clouds of dust before us—while Rob taught me a little about running a sheep station. Things like how to gather the mob and shift them along at just the right pace, never rushing them, with an eye out for pregnant ewes, slower than the rest and needing more careful urging. Or how to work with Jack, Sarah, and Biddy—boisterous sheepdogs who would walk off the job in protest, retiring disgustedly to the shade by the shearing sheds, if they felt they were getting orders from someone who didn't know his business. I learned how to drive a tractor, how to spot-weld gates and fences, how to haggle a badly placed fence post out of the ground with a front-end loader.

"Know how to work an angle grinder?" Rob asked me over breakfast one morning. "No? Well, you're going to learn today." And we spent the morning cutting steel to fashion a new gate. I realized that Rob was taking me in hand, in the nicest sort of way, not to impress a tenderfoot with how tough and hardy you have to be to survive out here, but because he genuinely loved his life and wanted me to share his enthusiasm. He succeeded, if not beyond his expectations then certainly beyond mine. The work made me tired, achy, sunburned, and often feeling a bit useless. Yet one afternoon, when we were working our way through the scrub, bringing 1,200 sheep back to the yards, I realized that I had rarely enjoyed myself more.

WE HAD A BARBECUE down at the Billagong one evening; Rob, Margot, Alison, the four kids, and I. We drew up just after sundown, a warm evening glow still illuminating the western sky. Overhead the first few stars were emerging from the gloom. We gathered armloads of dead wood in the fading light, dragged over a few promising logs, and soon got a fire crackling.

Margot set out salads and bread, fresh vegetables and dip, on the bonnet of the Land Cruiser. Rob and I drank rum out of pannikins. Lamb chops sputtered on the grill. We ate in darkness, looking out at the constellations reflecting in the pond, greedily licking the grease off our fingers.

Afterward we sprawled comfortably in the dust, looking into that deep eternity of sky, telling ghost stories, exchanging odd bits of trivia about old movies we'd seen, and sorting out the world's problems. As the level of rum grew lower in the bottle, Rob challenged me to sing "The Star-Spangled Banner." I had just enough under my belt to agree to give it a go—provided, of course, that Rob would first recite the entire "Man from Snowy River"—a safe bet, I reckoned, since the famous Banjo Paterson ballad is more than 100 lines long. To my astonishment he hopped up with a delighted grin, declared we had a deal, and launched into the much-loved epic, with verve and flair and without missing a beat. My performance of "The Star-Spangled Banner" was pathetic by comparison.

The fire had died down by this time, the kids all long asleep. The silences grew fatter as we too drifted off, comfortable on the warm, soft earth, covered by a blanket of stars. A gentle breeze made the windmill creak steadily, reassuringly, like an old parlor clock.

I SPENT SIX DAYS all up at Fairfield. Nothing extraordinary happened in that time—it was a pretty typical week on a Queensland sheep property, really—but somewhere along the line my whole relationship with Australia had undergone a sea change. I knew when I left that if nothing else came out of the rest of the trip, getting to know the MacIntoshes and sharing their lives at Fairfield—however briefly—had made the whole thing worthwhile.

CHAPTER 12

Rule Birricannia

ONE OF THE GREAT ADVANTAGES of traveling by bicycle is its relaxed pace. You move slowly enough to appreciate the sights and sounds and smells of the countryside: the bright wing of a parrot flitting through the scrub, the whir of insects, the fragrance of the eucalypts. You are exposed to the wind, sun, and rain. You get the full measure of each mile.

These same qualities can also be frustrating disadvantages, particularly if you happen to have taken a lonely 500-mile side trip and now ache to get back on track. Although I had been weary of the tourist trail by the time I reached Rockhampton, I still wanted to ride north to Cairns and the lush tropics of the Atherton Tableland. That meant returning to the coast. The obvious solution was to ride back along the Capricorn Highway, but the prospect of back-pedaling through the same towns and over the same ranges I had crossed only a fortnight earlier wasn't very appealing. Neither was the idea of taking the bus or train back—my purpose in setting out on this trip had been to lead a life of chance and circumstance on the open road, not to buy distance over the counter and settle into the comfortable certainty of a timetable.

It was Margot who came up with a solution: I could post myself on the mail truck that swung by Fairfield a couple of times a week. The truck went on to some of the other lonely stations, farther down the road, and could take me as far as Muttaburra. From there, well, I could just see what happened. "I'll call up Nobby and see if he can take you," she said. The postman was agreeable. The next morning the family came down to the gate to see me off.

I was sad to go. In a few short days I had come to feel that I'd known the MacIntoshes all my life. While we said our good-byes, Nobby—a nuggety, deeply tanned bloke—nestled my bicycle in his cargo of mailbags, wire coils, posts, fencing, cartons of beer destined for Muttaburra's pub, and some tinned food for its grocery store. It was a dusty and circuitous drive to Muttaburra, calling in at isolated sheep stations along the way to pick up or drop off packages and exchange a few words of gossip with the owners.

We finally hit town just before two o'clock. The streets were dead quiet beneath a taut blue sky. The taste of dust was everywhere.

Almost all of central Queensland had been in the grip of drought for the past few years—almost a normal circumstance out here. All along the Capricorn Highway people had grumbled about it, and every morning Rob and Margot would look north, across their paddocks, hoping in vain to spy rain clouds building on the horizon. But I had never seen anything like the parched landscape around Muttaburra that August afternoon. This was heartbreak country, where the earth was cracked and scoured by the sun for miles around, with just a few blackened leafless sticks jutting up on the plain and, very occasionally, a solitary emaciated sheep tottering through the dust.

Once, on a distant heat-warped horizon, I spotted an emu strutting defiantly through the glare. Otherwise the landscape was lifeless, apocalyptic.

Later that afternoon, an old man at the Exchange Hotel put it to me succinctly: "Out here," he said, "a wealthy grazier is a man who can still afford the petrol and bullets to drive out and decently shoot his sheep."

Muttaburra was a shearing town, but most of its shearers—hard-living New Zealand Maoris—had packed up and left weeks ago, looking for work as far afield as New South Wales, even Western Australia. The streets had an eerie, vacant feel.

I helped Nobby unload his consignment of beer at the Exchange Hotel and asked around for a ride north or east. The publican shook his head: "Nope. Hardly anybody ever goes up that way." I tried the grocery store and the post office and got the same answer. Nobby asked if I wanted to head back to Longreach with him, but I didn't like to quit. I'd said I'd wait. "See you in a few days then," he remarked grimly, as he clambered back into his truck. "You can probably camp in the scrub behind the pub."

I watched him rumble out of town. Silence fell on the street. A crow cawed. The sun grew big and brassy overhead. I thought about trying to ride on, but the road was too deep in bulldust; I'd only end up walking. I leaned my bike against the pub's veranda, then ambled into its cool dimness to buy a beer and wait.

It was quiet in the pub; an old man shooting a game of eightball by himself. A yellowed map of Queensland adorned one wall. There was a bullet hole in it. The old man pocketed his final ball and asked if I fancied a go. We shot a couple of games, drank a couple of beers, and the hands on the clock advanced a couple of hours. He left. Others drifted in and out. A pair of tough-looking graziers talked drought in loud voices on the veranda; a bank sale on a 70,000-acre spread and the busted-out farmer had been lucky to get ten bucks an acre. Bloody banks.

I was nursing another beer when a young guy named Pete wandered up to my table and said he'd heard I was looking for a lift out of town. "I'm heading out to Birricannia after I finish this beer."

"Where's that?"

"Oh—cattle property, about 75 miles from here. Don't know where you want to go after that, but at least you'll be 75 miles farther than Muttaburra."

"You're right there. I've got a bicycle with me, though. That okay?"

"Sure. Chuck it in the back of the truck."

We left a couple of beers later.

PETE WAS A FAST DRIVER. On these dusty tracks, his ute kicked up a plume of dust that must have been visible miles away. A builder who had worked on sites all over central Queensland, he was on his way to Birricannia to see some mates.

"Say, tomorrow morning we're all going over to the horse-racing carnival in Townsville to blow a month's wages. If you want to get back to the coast, we could give you a ride in the back of the truck. It'll be one hell of a bumpy ride, but at least you'd get there. What do you reckon?"

I couldn't believe my luck.

"Better than sitting in Muttaburra, ain't it?"

"I was going to buy property and retire there."

"Last January you could hardly have squeezed into that pub. It was packed; you wouldn't have had to wait five minutes for a lift to anywhere. Because of the drought everybody's gone looking for work someplace else. Wait another couple of weeks and there won't be anyone left. A pity. Muttaburra's a nice town."

"The bullet hole in the map was a homey touch."

"Notice that, did you? Somebody got murdered in there oh, about ten, twelve years ago—over a dart game, I think. Guy shot from outside, through the window, then came in and—blam!—fed him one in the head for good measure. No fooling around there."

Pete drove in silence for a few minutes, then chuckled. "That is one crazy place. Did you notice that new repair work next to the bar? A guy thought that some guy inside was chatting up his girl so he rammed his car right through the wall of the pub. Came to a stop in the women's rest room, engine still running."

"What did the girlfriend say?"

"Nothing, mate! She wasn't even there! He had it all wrong! The blokes in the bar dragged him out of the car and beat the shit out of him for being such a dickhead. Of course it cuts both ways. Did you see that girl up at the bar, the foxy one chatting with the bloke with the harelip? Now she is one wild thing. A few months ago she made dinner for that guy and he got the wrong idea. Figured there was something doing. So—after they finished eating, he reckoned it was time to saddle up, but she wasn't having any of it. Just friends, see? Well, he got pissed off and strangled a kangaroo she'd been keeping as a pet. She went wild and gave him the biggest hiding of his life. He almost lost an eye."

"What a sweet story. They seemed pretty friendly now."

"Oh yeah, that was months ago."

Forget it, Jake, it's Muttaburra.

The coppery sun was creeping low in the sky, low enough for the pebbles in the road to cast shadows, when we came upon a road train half in the scrub, its drivers grumpily changing a tire. Pete pulled over to see if they needed a hand—you're pretty well obliged to stop on these lonely tracks—but they were fine. We lingered for a while, Pete swapping gossip with the drivers about mutual acquaintances in towns and stations scattered across central Queensland. It is a small world. When we started again, the sun had just sunk below the horizon. A few kangaroos foraged beside the road in the fading light.

A PALE FULL MOON SHIMMERED low in the pink-blue sky as we rumbled through the gates of Birricannia Station and drove up to the homestead. Pete had called ahead from the pub to say that he had given me a lift. The grazier, Tom Kendall, and his son John met me at the bougainvillea-decked archway that led into the yard. Tom was a craggy, sunbaked grazier in his 50s, dressed in well-worn khakis. He had a lined and kindly face. His son, well muscled and brown, was a youthful version of himself. Tom thrust out a broad, callused hand and said: "Welcome to Birricannia." It was said with such sincere formality that I felt like an ambassador calling at court.

Indeed, Birricannia was its own aloof kingdom: 120,000 acres, tucked in the most remote pocket of outback I had ever—until then—visited. Somehow, though, the Kendalls made their home feel as if it sat at the center of the universe.

We went inside, where cans of cold beer were passed around, and we were shown to our rooms. Pete effectively had a permanent room there; as one of John's oldest and best mates, he was virtually a member of the family. The homestead was big, rambling, and old-fashioned. It had been in the Kendall family since 1917. Well-used guns hung on the walls, and the bookshelves were crammed with old hardback novels—a legacy of several well-read generations of Kendalls whiling away long, hot, isolated evenings in the outback.

Dinner had the same gentle gravity I had witnessed at the gate. Tom sat at the head of the table and served the crumbed cutlets, while Wendy, his wife, dished up salad and vegetables and poured the tea. We sat around the big polished table, drinking and talking well into the night.

We set out the next morning after breakfast. Pete and John and a jackaroo from a neighboring station crammed themselves into the cab of John's ute, their swags and beer-filled eskies in the back. I chucked my gear on top and sprawled on an old mattress that Wendy had dug up to make my ride more comfortable.

And we were off. With a pocketful of wages and a beery weekend at the horseraces ahead, they wasted no time in transit. John thundered through the scrub like the front-runner in the Paris-Dakar road rally. I peered in through the rear window, bumping my nose on the glass, and saw the speedometer needle wobbling at 80. We left an awesome corkscrew of dust boiling in our wake.

The cattle grids were the worst: Hit those at high speed and you get some major air, slamming back to earth with a bone-jarring crash. I don't know what the ride was like in the cab, but I was bouncing around the back like a rag doll, terrified, clinging to the sides for dear life. The load shifted, half crushing me; several times I had to snatch at loose belongings as they flew through the air on their way out of the truck. Eyes wide shut, I kept telling myself that at least I was getting back to the coast.

Things got a little better when we hit the paved highway west of Charters Towers a couple of hours later. As we burned up the smooth bitumen, I even fell asleep.

When I woke up we were coming into Townsville, with big tropical thunderheads building on the horizon and the Coral Sea spread out before us. The guys pulled up at a motel, got out, and stared in mute wonder at the hurricane of gear in the back—and at me. My eyes were rimmed with red, my face was sooty, my windblown hair was so caked with bulldust that it stood on end. Dazed from sunburn, exposure, and exhaustion, I looked like a grotesque parody of Don King.

John shook his head. "Geez, mate, I'm sorry. Why didn't you pound on the roof and tell me to stop being such a dickhead?"

CHAPTER 13

Effin' Q

I TOOK A ROOM above the Townsville bus station and drifted down to the seafront, soaking up the sun on a park bench and watching a distant ferry putter its way across the bay, bound for Magnetic Island, hazy and blue in the warm, salty air. It was pretty along the Strand, with its landscaped gardens, banyan trees, and retirees walking Maltese terriers.

After a fortnight of dust and empty horizons, it felt odd being back in the ocean-bred humidity of the coast and the hustle, concrete, and sparkling-chrome traffic of a city of 140,000. Townsville is a nice enough place, a short-back-'n'-sides military town on the Coral Sea, with noisy flocks of rainbow lorikeets in the mall to remind you that the bush is not far away. It isn't what many people expect to find in Far North Queensland—or FNQ, in local-speak. Because it is touted as the capital of tropical Australia and is such a major jumping-off point for cruises to the Great Barrier Reef, it's generally assumed that Townsville is surrounded by the same lush rain forests that cloak the mountains around Cairns, farther north. In fact, Townsville sits on a drab and scrubby coast; the beautiful greenery doesn't begin for another 100 or so miles north, where the mountains tumble down to the sea.

I'd been here once before, back in 1987; an over-nighter to cover the opening of a gold mine near Charters Towers. A bunch of us had made a big night of it at the Breakwater Casino. Around midnight I found myself talking to an American executive of the mining company, a square-built Texan with half a bottle of Bundaberg Rum under his belt. We were standing by the Two-Up pit, where a rowdy knot of cane cutters—big, beery men flush with cash—were betting a few hundred bucks a throw on the tossed coins. The joint was rocking with yelling, laughing, and back-slapping. The Texan looked around, smiled, leaned over, and yelled in my ear: "You know, Ah somehow kinda thought Australia might be a little crude, but this here is real nahsss!"

I set off for Cairns the next morning, riding out of the city through a glary corridor of concrete works, BOC Gasses, electrical contractors, and truck-repair shops. I passed the Royal Australian Air Force base and rode into the shimmering heat rising from the James Cook Highway, which runs up the north Queensland coast to Cairns. I'd been off the bike for more than a week now, but drafting (sorting) all those sheep and building all those fences at Fairfield had made me noticeably fitter: I logged the first century, or 100-mile day, of my journey.

That milestone brought me into the tropics, where steep mountains plunge down to a palm-fringed coast and broad acres of sugarcane fill every valley. It was hot and steamy and sunny by day, while the heavy dews that soaked my bivvy bag at night were as cold and dense as any rain. I rode into Cairns midmorning on my third day out of Townsville.

COMING IN TO CAIRNS was another trip down memory lane. I had been here once before, early in 1982, just a few weeks after moving to Australia as a freshly minted geology graduate taking part in a University of Sydney archaeology expedition; we were looking for old gold-mining camps from the 1870s Palmer River gold rush on the Atherton Tableland. Cairns, our jumping-off point, had been a sleepy holiday town then—a clutter of family motels, a profusion of palm trees, and an airport that handled commuter-sized Fokkers.

Naturally, I had expected to find Cairns changed, but I wasn't prepared for the hard-partying city of 100,000 that spread out before me when I looked over the tangle of hillside suburbs on the outskirts of town. A skyline of cranes and resort hotels stretched along the lazy curve of Trinity Bay, and as I rode into the urban sprawl I noticed a steady stream of Qantas jumbo jets descending through the haze, coming in nonstop from Asia and North America.

I found my way to the Esplanade, the touristy heart of Cairns, with its jumble of not-so-cheap but nasty nonetheless backpacker hostels, T-shirt shops, cafés, and a gantlet of budget-priced tour operators spruiking reef cruises, diving lessons, bungee jumping, skydiving, rafting, snorkeling, and mountain biking. The sidewalks were bright with tanned and sleek twenty-somethings, all diamond nose studs, faux-Bolle sunglasses, and airily waved cigarettes. Stomachs as flat as the palm of my hand. Their sunburned shoulders sported the latest tattoos; backpacker chic. They nattered in Danish, German, Swedish, Dutch, and London English, sipped cappuccinos under café umbrellas, or ate cheap kebabs. With market-stall cunning, they studied the fine print on tourist brochures or calculated exchange rates to the nearest pfennig. They bragged, boasted, laughed, and flirted with each other. Cairns was a lousy town to be 38 in.

I ate a burger at a sidewalk table, found a quiet hostel a little way off the Esplanade, and checked in. The place was almost deserted; everyone was putting in face time at the Esplanade or diving the reef. Cairns is, or rather was, the fashionable embarkation point for the Great Barrier Reef—a distinction it has ceded lately to trendier and more exclusive Port Douglas, 40 miles farther up the coast. Cairns' size and international airport, however, mean that just about everyone passes through here. The city thrives on the reef, feeding on the tide of yen, deutsche marks, and dollars in much the same way its corals prosper in the warm, clear currents.

And the corals do prosper. Aficionados claim that the reefs between Cairns and Port Douglas are the most dazzling anywhere along the Queensland coast—perhaps even the world. I wouldn't know. In all my years in Australia, I had hardly ever been to the beach, let alone dived or snorkeled on the Great Barrier Reef—or dived or snorkeled anywhere else, for that matter. It's not that I'm afraid of the water, or that I can't swim, or that I burn like a lobster; it simply never occurs to me to go.

Maybe it's because I grew up in the White Mountains of New Hampshire, a two-hour drive from the boardwalk tackiness of Maine's Old Orchard Beach. My mental touchstones were all in the forest, or along trout streams or high on granite ledges. If we wanted to go swimming, we splashed around in a lake, river, or even a beaver pond. Seven years in Sydney and I had been to Bondi Beach just three times—and two of those occasions were when I had done the City to Surf, a fun run that finishes on the beach. I was as likely to learn to surf or dive as I was to buy a season ticket to the ballet. And now that I was in Cairns, the brooding, jungle-clad mountains above the city—not the coral reefs that lay somewhere over the watery horizon—captured my imagination.

Indeed, if not for the South Africans, I might never have visited the reef at all. There were three of them traveling together: Claire, Jaxson, and Neil. I'd met them briefly at breakfast at the hostel in Townsville and bumped into them again on the Esplanade here in Cairns. We fell to talking, and drifted around the corner to a pub. They said they were going out on a dive boat the next morning. Why didn't I come along? I made some lame excuses. They persisted, astonished by my admission that I had never snorkeled. A few pitchers later, joshed on by their beachy camaraderie, I decided to give it a go.

I'll always be grateful they drank me into it. The next morning we motored to Michaelmas Cay, about two hours out of Cairns. The dive-master went through the rules and, for neophytes like me, explained the rudiments of snorkeling. Faintly nauseated at this business of spitting into one's face mask, I slipped over the side, plunged my face into the waves, and nearly spat out my snorkel in stunned amazement. A technicolor dreamscape burst in front of me, more sensuous and lurid than anything I could have imagined: a slow-motion kaleidoscope of reds, golds, blues, and oranges; intricately patterned coral beds; plunging crevices where the light shifted from brilliant emerald green to deep indigo. Kicking along the surface, face down, and floating over one of these precipitous drop-offs made me feel as though I was flying. Below me, torpedo-like fish, schools of rainbow-colored darters, and a species patterned with garish blue-and-yellow stripes maneuvered amongst the corals. Farther below, in the cool blue depths, a giant Maori wrasse—an enormous bass on steroids—idled in the current. A huge sea turtle wafted by.

I loved every second of my time out there and resolved to do more of it—maybe even learn to dive—some day. But life is short and the world is full of great things, and on the way back to shore I found myself captivated once more by the jungly mountains soaring above the city. At that distance, their steep flanks and mile-high summits made Cairns' expensive resort hotels look like tiny white sugar cubes along the coast. That's when I fully understood that there are beach people and there are mountain people, and once the mold has set it can't be recast. By the time the catamaran berthed in Cairns, my day on the reef had settled into memory, a glorious novelty to remember and cherish. My forward thoughts were already up in the hills. The next morning I set out.

CHAPTER 14

Kentucky on the Coral Sea

A CENTURY AGO, only the hardy (or foolhardy) ventured into these highlands, seeking fortunes in tin or gold along its hidden jungle streams. The hostile volcanic junglescapes of the Atherton Tableland were some of the last pockets of Australia to be explored by Europeans. Over the years, settlers found their way up the slopes and discovered that they could grow tobacco and corn in the rich volcanic soil. But the Atherton Tableland remained aloof; the small rain-forest towns up here kept an old-fashioned insularity, a sort of tropical Appalachia.

The road from the coast is steep, winding, and narrow, turning back on itself in dozens of tight switchbacks and elbow bends. Pedaling up it was sweaty work. The sun shone hot. Insects whirred and birds twittered. My pannikin, loosely hooked on my rear saddlebag, jingled softly, rhythmically, the sound calling to mind a prospector's mule.

I paused at a lookout about halfway up the range to take a last backward glance at the Coral Sea and an aerial view of the palm-shaded rooftops sprawled around Trinity Bay. From here it seemed as still and as hazy as an old postcard. The tame part of my journey was drawing to a close; even the loneliest stretches of the Capricorn Highway would be a sweet wish compared with what was coming.

On the far side of the tableland and the Great Dividing Range, I knew, the land dips into a vast, empty savanna stretching to the Gulf of Carpentaria. Upon hitting the gulf near Karumba, I planned to cross the great spinifex plains in the center of the continent, then press on to the craggy remoteness of the Kimberley—an ancient mountain stronghold that is Australia's last frontier—on the northwest coast.

Assuming I survived that trek, I would turn south, through the burning desolation of the Great Sandy Desert. The next town of any size I'd see would be Darwin, more than 2,000 miles away, and the next big city I'd strike would be Perth—a good 5,000 miles, and several months, distant. In between those far-flung points was a lonely archipelago of roadhouses, one-horse settlements, rough mining towns, Aboriginal communities, and cattle stations—most of them separated by one or two days' hard riding. This was the Australia I was longing to see; the ride to Longreach and my time at Fairfield had only whetted my appetite for more.

But traveling by bicycle meant I would have to earn it. It was September now. Soon the Buildup would start for the summer monsoons, a time of killing heat and humidity—and then, if I was unlucky enough to be still in the tropics when the monsoons came, torrential rains and flash floods. The distances between settlements meant I'd have to pack plenty of water and food and self-reliance. The "rivers" marked on my map were typically bone-dry gullies, which could turn into treacherous cataracts once the monsoons hit. Those that held water year-round also tended to harbor huge, man-eating crocodiles.

I had chanced on a reflection of myself in a display window at one of the boutiques on Orchid Street in Cairns. It startled me. Seven weeks earlier, when I had been waiting for the Hunters Hill ferry on Circular Quay, I had felt like something of a dandy, with my crisp new gear, shorts and T-shirt bought for the occasion, and my shiny bicycle. It had irritated me, this candied freshness, making me feel as though I were somehow playing a part: modeling a cycling holiday for a glossy fashion magazine. That squeakiness was gone now, worn off by 2,000 miles of hard riding. Both my bicycle and I were well broken-in, and looked it: saddlebags worn and sagging, the waxed canvas ingrained with an honorable testimony of trail dust. My much-rinsed-out T-shirt hung loosely on my shoulders, and the older, leaner, browner face that looked back at me from the polished shop-front window had a few creases that hadn't been there before.

Something in my eyes had changed, too. Somewhere along the line they'd lost their office-bound hesitancy and acquired the clarity that comes from gazing into distant horizons, as human eyes were meant to do, rather than focusing on a glowing computer screen nine inches away. They were healthier eyes. Since I had taken to the road, the headaches that had badgered me at work had ceased. In fact, I couldn't recall the last time I'd suffered one. My hands were lightly callused from gripping the handlebars and brake levers, my reflexes and survival instincts had been honed by erratic drivers, and my expectations had relaxed to meet the plodding pace of my pedals. I knew the true value of 100 miles now: It was a hard day's travel—possibly two, if the wind and heat and hills were against you.

THE ATHERTON TABLELAND was warm and pleasant, the road winding through dense green jungle. I rolled into Tolga late in the afternoon, long cool shadows raking the main street. I stopped at a gas station to buy yet another water bottle (bringing my aquatic arsenal to eight) and to contemplate where I might camp for the night. I fell into conversation with a 19-year-old petrol-pump attendant named Doug. With the kind of delightful small-town hospitality that belonged more to the 1950s than the cusp of the 21st century, his face lit up with a suggestion: It was Saturday night; he and a few mates were going to the drive-in over to Mareeba to see Demi Moore in *Striptease.* "Why don't you come along? Sure. You can leave your bike at the house, and spend the night."

We sat three abreast—Doug, his mate Steve, and myself—in the front seat of Doug's old bomb, greasy KFC boxed dinners on our laps. Some more of his mates were parked in a panel van beside us. They were all about 19, making me feel a bit like somebody's old man along for the ride, but they were good-natured about it. Mareeba's old drive-in was packed. Demi Moore loomed large and grainy on the screen, noisy scuffles and teenage laughter spilled from the popcorn stand, and the night air was filled with insects and the redolence of a joint being smoked two cars down.

We got back to Doug's house a little before midnight. His girlfriend, Irena, was just back from her shift as a waitress. We sat up talking until late; movies, money, macadamia nuts—whatever came to mind. Irena was designing a tattoo for herself, and she showed me some of her ideas—mostly Celtic motifs. Doug warned me about the drug-growing hardcores hereabouts, who hid out in densely jungled hollows like old-time West Virginia moonshiners: "Don't kid around with these guys. I mean it. They are scary."

I HAD A PLEASANTLY OLD-FASHIONED EVENING of a different sort two nights later in the offbeat rain-forest town of Ravenshoe. I had hit town about three o'clock, rolling past the pub and coming to a halt outside a feedstore called Northland's Agencies. Fate must have been singing a siren song, because I certainly had no logical reason to stop there; I didn't need horseshoe nails, chicken pellets, or baling wire. It must have been the same prodding finger that had nudged Robert Fantom along Prince Street, back in Grafton, toward my concrete bench. While I was idling on the sidewalk, perusing the local bulletin board and wondering why I didn't just ride on, an old Englishman sidled up to me and began to talk.

His name was Arthur West, and the sight of my loaded touring bike unleashed some poignant memories from the 1930s, when he and his wife, Ivy—young and fit in those days—had taken long cycling tours of Wales on their tandem. "We were together 61 years, Ivy and me. She died a few months ago. Seeing you standing here with your bicycle just brought so many things back. We had such fun."

WE WENT OFF to an early dinner at a café down the street. Arthur told me he came from Leicester, England but had migrated here in the late 1950s. He was 83 years old; his son Grahame owned the feedstore where I had stopped. After the meal, we continued talking over cups of tea. When it came time to go, the old gentleman wouldn't hear of my camping out that night; instead, he invited me back to his house—where, he said, we could talk some more. I was delighted. I had been given so much on this trip—from Robert Fantom's kindly ear to the hospitality of the MacIntoshes to a Saturday night at the drive-in with the lads. It felt good to be returning something. Arthur—a good raconteur with a keen memory and a sharp eye for detail—made this an easy task.

We sat up late in Arthur's parlor, a quaintly prewar English sitting room with its dark furniture, its ticking clock, and its jumble of old glassware, knickknacks, and faded photographs. He told me a love story. It began back in 1932, when Arthur was 19 and managing a haberdashery on the high street of Leicester. "Silk ties had just come into fashion," recalled Arthur, "and I was arranging a display in the shop window. I had my head down, but out of the corner of my eye I saw a slim, green, high-heeled shoe step past the window. I liked the look of it. I liked it very much. But it was such a quick glimpse. It was lunch hour and the sidewalks were busy and by the time I looked up, the crowd had passed on. I spent my lunch hours the next four days looking out the window, and sure enough I saw the green shoe again. This time I got a look at the rest of the girl as well. I asked around and found out that her name was Ivy, that she was a ballet dancer, and that we had a few friends in common. Better yet—Ivy told me this herself later—she had noticed me and had been asking around to find out who I was." Sixty-odd years on, his delight at discovering that the pretty ballerina liked him too still made his eyes dance like a schoolboy's.

They met and fell madly in love. At that time Arthur was a keen bicycle racer—road and track—but suddenly even cycling seemed a little hollow without Ivy. So he hunted down an old wreck of a tandem that had been rusting in the shed of a friend's house, bought it for ten shillings, and set about restoring it. "I had a job getting it home, trying to steer and balance my own bicycle with one hand guiding that rusty tandem beside me. I can still remember coming through the traffic in the roundabout in the center of Leicester."

Arthur got up, rummaged around the room, and returned with a glass souvenir paperweight showing a clock tower set in a busy thoroughfare. "That's it. Imagine trying to control two bicycles through there in the busiest time of the afternoon. But I managed to get it home and fix it up. Ivy's father had been a courier in the Bicycle Corps during the war, and he still had some of his old racks and panniers. We fastened them on the bike, added a fisherman's creel of woven cane, and set off for Wales. We toured the countryside for a week. It was lovely."

The courtship lasted six years, during which they went on many bicycle excursions—and, later, exhilarating rides on the 1925 Norton motorcycle he bought. I imagined him cutting a jaunty figure on the motorbike: tall, lean, crisply English, his pretty fiancée snuggled up behind him. They married just before the War. He served in the Army, then came home to a big hug from Ivy and a decent job managing the botanic gardens. He and Ivy started a family and grew middle-class prosperous. The Norton was traded up to a small Vauxhall car.

But life in postwar Britain could be grim and gray; Arthur and Ivy saw better opportunities elsewhere. In the late 1950s, they talked it over and decided to emigrate to Australia. Brightly colored immigration posters promised jobs and sunshine, and the Australian government was so keen for settlers that it was paying steamship passage and relocation expenses. For ten pounds administration costs, you could buy a new life Down Under.

I sipped my Earl Grey tea as I listened, examining the framed photographs as Arthur handed them to me one by one. Long past midnight, I caught him yawning, but he seemed pleased by the discovery. He stood up, stretched, and collected my empty teacup and saucer. "You know," he said, "I think I'm really going to sleep well tonight."

I SWUNG BY THE FEEDSTORE the next morning on my way out of town. It was early; Ravenshoe was just waking up. But the store was already open, an array of garden implements on the sidewalk and laughter drifting out the open door—Grahame in noisy banter with a farmer trying to drive a hard bargain on baling wire. For all his Englishness, Grahame had the expressiveness of a vaudevillian, talking with his hands, joking and cajoling.

His son Benjamin was there too, helping out at the shop before heading off to school. I knew from what Arthur had told me the evening before that Benjamin was a fanatical mountain biker; now I noticed him looking a little wistfully at my machine, loaded up and ready for the road. My heart went out to him, facing the prospect of a warm, sunny day cooped up in a classroom. I remembered being 17 and dreaming of all the bold adventures I would have one day. It had taken me another 20 years and a huge leap—if not of faith, of desperation—to get this far.

Benjamin asked me a few questions about handling and hills, hefted the bike, and cast his eyes over the brake and shifter cables, chain, chainrings, and freewheel. I was glad he did, for his sharp and curious eyes spotted a problem I had overlooked: The anchor bolt that tensioned the derailleur cable along the frame had worked its way loose. Benjamin fetched a wrench, but when we went to tighten the bolt, it crumbled and broke.

"They call this shit metal," Grahame murmured, running his thumb over the crumbling end of the cheap alloy bolt and shaking his head. I could see what he meant, and it irritated me: The bicycle had set me back $1,000. I could press on in a single (though hard-to-pedal) gear, but Darwin—the next town likely to boast a bicycle shop—was nearly 2,000 miles distant. Or I could ride 100 miles back to Cairns, get a replacement part, then ride back up the range again.

Grahame came to the rescue: "No problem. We can order that part through one of the bike shops in Cairns and get them to put it on the truck. Be here in a couple of days. It'll cost you something in shipping, but in the meantime you can stay with us and I can show you around. This is a pretty interesting part of the world. I think you'd like it. What do you say?"

I said thanks. I spent the next three days helping out around the shop and making the rounds with Grahame on his truck, delivering grain and hay and supplies to the tiny communities scattered around the Atherton Tableland. I learned how to operate a forklift, stack grain sacks properly, and lash them onto a flatbed with wire-taut trucker's knots.

Grahame was an interesting man. The former art director of a well-known advertising firm who had turned his back on the button-down scene in 1973, he had come north into the rain forest, where he built himself a home of mud bricks, grew organic produce, and raised a family. As we rambled along the back roads, dropping off our goods, I realized that these secluded tropical highlands had been havens for a host of other freedom-seeking eccentrics who couldn't or wouldn't fit the mold of the late 20th century. There was Carl, an irascible Luxembourger who'd come to Ravenshoe two years earlier in a clapped-out Gypsy wagon that he had somehow driven across the continent from Fremantle, Western Australia. There was the former Lady MacDonald, who 30-odd years ago had discarded her title and ancestral estate on the isle of Skye in favor of running a shark boat in the waters off Cairns (she now farmed in the highlands nearby). And, in the hamlet of Herberton, there was an artist named Sherry Vincent. She had grown up on the Nullarbor Plain, the daughter of a rabbit shooter; although she had never attended school, she painted spectacular outback murals on walls and shop fronts.

One sultry afternoon, Grahame and I took tea with Dr. Harry Bromley, a stout old-school British Army medical officer well into his 80s. He had been stationed all over the Far East in Empire days—Shanghai, Hong Kong, Singapore—and had escaped on foot from Burma to India ahead of the invading Japanese Army. In 1951, Dr. Bromley won a Member of the Order of the British Empire award for his work with lepers in the Seychelles Islands. Sitting in his neat tropical garden, it struck me that if Dr. Bromley did not exist, he would have been invented by Agatha Christie.

CHAPTER 15

Emus and Me

ON FRIDAY MORNING, as promised, the replacement bolt arrived. I fixed and loaded the bike, said my good-byes, and pedaled out of town, bound for the Gulf Country.

For much of the past fortnight, I'd been with other people. Much as I had enjoyed the hospitality of these friendly strangers, I itched to get back on the road—aloof, alone, beholden to no one. The warm breeze and sunshine on my face felt particularly good that morning when I rode out of Ravenshoe, grateful for my time there but glad to be on the move again. I followed the lonely bush highway 30 hilly miles to Mount Garnet, where I refilled my water bottles—they totaled nine by now—before setting off on an even lonelier and more arid 75-mile leg through the scrub toward Mount Surprise.

It was a fine day. The sun arced high overhead; the hot, empty miles rolled by. The landscape was drier here on the lee side of the Great Dividing Range; the rain forests on the tableland had yielded to olive-drab scrub that would soon give way to wide-open savanna. I camped that night in a stand of sweet-smelling eucalypts about 30 miles shy of Mount Surprise, taking pleasure in solitude as I watched the first stars venture out of the evening gloom.

The next couple of days passed quietly. I pedaled from dawn to dusk along a nine-foot-wide ribbon of bitumen that stretched into an infinite shimmering horizon, a slowly moving speck across a flat and dusty immensity of savanna. The tawny grasses on either side of the road were brittle and dry, the landscape dotted with thousands of termite mounds resembling weathered tombstones on an ancient battlefield. The air was still, dry, and very hot. There was little traffic; an occasional road train or Land Cruiser and once, in the predawn grayness, an army convoy on maneuvers that rumbled past my secluded camp. Another time I crested a low rise and surprised a family of emus—a sort of Australian ostrich—standing in the center of the road. They turned and trotted away at my approach, but stayed on the bitumen. We went along for a mile like this, the three emus jogging in front of me, not much more than an arm's length away, glancing over their shoulders every now and then to see if I was still there. Eventually one of them veered into the scrub, and the others followed.

Mostly, though, I had the road to myself.

In camp each night, I worried about neither strangers nor snakes. For starters, there's hardly anybody out here. What I generally did was ride into the dusk, stopping when there was still just enough of a glow in the sky to pick my way through the bush without needing a flashlight. Then, with a final glance to be sure the road was empty of prying eyes, I'd duck into the scrub and find a well-concealed spot, maybe a couple of hundred yards back. There, hidden in the shadows, I'd roll out my bivvy bag, make myself a dinner of long-life cheese and crispbreads, dried fruit and nuts, and listen to my transistor radio if I could get a station. If enough light was left in the sky, I'd knock off another dozen pages or so of Tom Cole's rousing autobiography, *Hell, West and Crooked;* the life story of this crocodile hunter, buffalo-shooter, cattleman, explorer, and adventurer had been recommended to me by Rob MacIntosh back at Fairfield. Then I would hang my T-shirt on the handlebars to dry (and get a dew rinse in the morning), set a bottle of water within easy reach of my bedroll, and unwind as the stars came out.

I felt safe. My camp was low-slung and hard to see, even from 30 feet away—and even if you knew where to look. My bivvy shelter was a deep midnight purple that blended flawlessly with the shadows, and the rest of my gear was dark blue, purple, or black. Anyway, we're not talking about a war zone here; Australia, with a murder rate about that of Switzerland, is a very safe country.

That's not to say it's immune from sordid crimes. One of the most gruesome in recent years was the torture and murder of seven backpackers by a deranged outdoorsman named Ivan Milat, now spending the rest of his days in a maximum-security prison in Sydney. After picking up a hitchhiker on the city's outskirts, Milat would take him or her to a remote campsite in Belanglo National Forest in New South Wales, where he used the victim for target practice. The lucky ones he wounded to death with various small-caliber firearms. The less fortunate he stabbed between the vertebrae, paralyzing them but keeping them conscious for the ensuing torture. One backpacker, a young German girl, was beheaded with a samurai sword.

Milat's nickname, "Ivan the Terrible," often cropped up in conversations with curious passersby, together with the chief detective's disquieting notion that Milat had an accomplice—as yet uncaught. Back in Murwillumbah, in northern New South Wales, an elderly gentleman had sought to put me at ease: "Don't worry, after you're murdered I'll remember I saw you and tell the police."

As for the deadly crawlies—well, they are out there, all right. As outback documentary makers love to point out, Australia is home to the world's most poisonous snakes—taipans, death adders, king browns, tiger snakes—all of them armed with venom more toxic than a cobra's. A taipan packs enough neurotoxin to kill a quarter of a million mice. Some species, such as the tiger snake, can also be extremely aggressive, rearing up and lashing out at a camera lens (or bicycle spokes) at the slightest provocation—or none at all.

All this makes for pulse-pounding viewing—which means, of course, that you can dine out for years on the tale if you happen to stumble across one in the bush. Who's going to know that it slithered harmlessly back into the scrub? Which is what it will almost certainly do. Unless they feel cornered, even ill-tempered snakes generally steer clear of humans. Snakes are pragmatists: What's the upside in tangling with people?

In fact, unless you're filming one of those nature documentaries yourself, your odds of seeing a snake are slim. And your chances of being bitten are even slimmer—provided you don't do something idiotic such as thrusting your hand in a hole or under a rock. The mother of all herpetological mistakes is to try to kill a snake: Eighty percent of snakebites are inflicted on people in the act of attempting to kill one of these reptiles. In months of traveling through the outback, I chanced across only a handful of snakes, and most of those were on the road. When it came to camping in the bush, I never lost any sleep worrying about snakes.

Indeed, with all that fresh air, sunshine, and cycling, I didn't lose much sleep over anything. I'd generally listen to my radio and look up at the stars until I grew sleepy. When I woke, the inverted position of the Southern Cross told me whether I had another half-hour or so to laze around until dawn. I liked to get away early, in the cool grayness before the sun could bite. I'd get my camp rolled up and packed on the bike in about ten minutes, enjoy my first—and last—cool water bottle of the day, then push off down the empty highway.

I rode briskly those first few miles, making time while the sun didn't shine. Breakfast was a couple of muesli bars a few miles down the road. By midmorning, when the heat became intense, I'd scout out a bit of shade beneath a tree or in a dry creek bed, then settle in for a few hours' kip during the white-hot part of the day. Maybe read a bit of Lawson or Paterson or Cole, or write in my journal, or just laze in the warmth and listen to the murmur of the afternoon. I'd look up occasionally when a car or road train rumbled by, and listen as its humming tires faded slowly into silence. By midafternoon, when the heat broke and the glare softened, I'd set out again, pedaling into the dusk and looking once more for a secluded place to bed down for the night. The next few days passed like this.

CHAPTER 16

Mates in Paradise

It began in the finest outback tradition, with the offer of a cold beer on a stinking-hot afternoon. I was pedaling steadily across a flat stretch of savanna about 30 miles southeast of the lonely old river port of Normanton. The sky was brassy, the temperature in the low hundreds, my throat as dry and sticky as a strip of roadhouse flypaper. I'd been rationing my water pretty closely all day, but even so I was gulping down a liter every six or eight miles in that heat and looking forward to pulling into Normanton and getting a cold beer in the pub.

It was that anticipation and the relative nearness of town that had kept me going, rather than pulling over and resting in brittle grass as I usually did in the heat of the afternoon. But I hadn't had anything cool to drink in a couple of days, and I was like a horse that smells water. I was just rehearsing that first cold sip of beer when a voice from nowhere said in a broad Queensland drawl, "Geez, mate, I'll bet you'd love a cold stubby along about now."

A pair of hard-bitten Land Cruisers had nosed up slowly beside me, but I'd been so lost in my reverie I hadn't heard them approach. I cocked a wary eye at the cheery-faced, middle-aged man leaning out the window, uncertain if I was being taunted or if a beer was genuinely on offer. "Yeah, I'll bet you're right."

"Want one?"

Waiting for the punch line, I scanned the stranger's sunburned face, but found only openness and amiability. "Are you joking?"

"I never joke about beer, mate. Pull over."

His name was Terry; the fellow beside him was Paul and the two blokes in the other truck were Mick and Thommo. Ice-cold cans of Fourex were broken out of a camp fridge in the back of Thommo's truck (there was a lot of beer in there, I noticed) and eagerly passed around. We drank. That first magical gulp was almost unbearable; the icy liquid stung the back of my throat, then anesthetized it with blessed cool wetness. Another big, cold swig, then another. Before I knew it, I was holding an empty can.

"I reckon that one hardly touched the sides," Terry remarked, slapping another in my palm and getting one out for himself. "Anyone else?"

There were takers all around. Terry was a hearty, ruddy-faced man in his mid-50s, a schoolteacher from Rockhampton on his first trip into the Gulf Country. Paul was smaller, swarthy, part Maltese; a contract builder from Sarina, a small town about 170 miles farther up the coast, he had worked on sites all over the Top End. Thommo was a lean long-distance runner, in his late 20s, who worked for Queensland Rail.

It turned out that Mick, a police constable, was getting married in a fortnight. With the clock running down on his single days, he and Thommo, his best man, and his two uncles had decided to go bush, fishing and pig-shooting in the wild country along the Gilbert and Staaten Rivers.

"Tell you what," said Mick, after a couple of get-to-know-you beers by the side of the road. "Why don't you come along? You want to see Australia, and we're going places you'll never be able to reach on that bicycle of yours. Come on. Chuck the bike in back and we'll leave it at my in-laws' place in Karumba."

It was a generous, spontaneous offer, but I held back for a second. I didn't know these blokes; there were four of them, and the backs of their trucks bristled with heavy-caliber pig rifles. Nobody knew where I was, or was expecting me anywhere; I could easily disappear without a trace. But the canny little voice in the back of my head said: Go, it'll be fine.

As it turned out, the next couple of weeks were among the best of my life. I'll always look back on Terry's offer of a cold beer that afternoon as a turning point in my years in Australia. It was from these guys that I learned the meaning of mateship—that laconic, uniquely Australian brand of friendship that defies easy description. It's a rough-and-ready camaraderie, based on rock-solid loyalty and an ironic tolerance of each other's foibles, and it is usually played out in an outback setting (or in the trenches of World War I). Over the next couple of weeks, we became good mates.

We hit Normanton just at sunset, Mick, Thommo, and I sitting three abreast in the cab of Thommo's cruiser. It was a hot evening. A crowd loitered on the veranda of the Purple Pub, the town's most notorious watering hole, a big old two-story hotel trimmed with ornamental iron lace and famed for its quirky lavender paint job. We drew up in front and went inside to pick up a couple more slabs of beer. It was loud and smoky.

Outside again, the wide, flat street in front of the pub reminded me of something out of the Old West. The dusty town sat on the bank of the Norman River. Just down the street from the pub was a life-size plaster cast of a crocodile that had been shot in the reeds near town in 1957. It was grotesque—a Jurassic Park monster 28 feet 4 inches long, reputedly the largest ever recorded. The croc was set in a snarling pose, as though snapping at the stinging bullet that had ended its life. It must have weighed a couple of tons; those huge jaws could have wolfed down a healthy bullock in a few quick snaps. An Aborigine boy all of four years old sat inside the jaws, watching us rumble down the street.

The sight of that crocodile made me feel a bit like the New England farmer in the old joke; staring at an elephant in the zoo before declaring, "There ain't no such animal!" True: Saltwater crocodiles don't generally come that size any more. Open-slather hunting in the 1940s and '50s killed off most of the century-old monsters, but 20-odd years of protection have swelled crocodile numbers handsomely. "The rivers around here are full of them," Mick remarked as we rattled over the single-lane iron-framed bridge on the edge of town and headed out along the track toward Karumba.

The Norman River shone gunmetal blue in the twilight, its banks thick with reeds. The sun set. The colors faded. It grew dark. Inside the cruiser, we were easy and comfortable, drinking and telling jokes in the dashboard-lit cab as the savanna grasses zoomed past. Garth Brooks' "Boys from the Bush" blared on the cassette deck, Thommo and Mick joining in the refrain. Although I'd known these guys only an hour or so, it already felt like we were old friends.

Mick was probably the all-around nicest guy I've ever met; easygoing, tolerant, a big, gentle bloke. "You have to be being a complete asshole to get arrested by me," he laughed. But clearly Mick was no pushover, either; he had been posted to rough outback towns all over Queensland: Birdsville, Mount Isa, Burketown, Karumba. Now that he was assigned to Sarina, he missed the Gulf Country badly. He let his palm ride the breeze out the window and took in delighted gulps of warm night air: "God, I feel like I'm home again. I'm happy."

I looked into the inky tropical darkness. Dense flurries of moths and insects swirled in the headlights and spattered on the windscreen. After an hour or so a few lights twinkled in the distance, and then we were in Karumba.

Ash Colahan, Mick's future father-in-law, was a former miner from Mount Isa who now ran a fish-and-chips shop on Karumba Point. He was a jovial bear of a man; shortish, with thick brown arms and dense silver hair. After dinner we rolled out our swags and slept on his living-room floor above the shop.

THE NEXT MORNING I STEPPED out onto the veranda—and into air that was warm, steamy, and tropical. Sunlight shimmered on the Gulf of Carpentaria.

We spent the day in Karumba, sorting out supplies before heading into the bush. A travel guide had described Karumba as possessing the atmosphere of a remote Amazon outpost; that description, coupled with Karumba's place on the tropical northern Queensland coast, had convinced me it would be surrounded by lush, pretty rain forest. It had been too dark when we drove up from Normanton to see much, other than tall grass flickering in the headlights. The hard light of morning presented a grimmer picture: a rough-edged trawler port tucked in crocodile-infested mangrove swamps where the Norman River emptied sluggishly into the gulf. Behind it lay a broad, flat expanse of parched and scorching savanna, burned brown and shimmering in the humidity.

I've never been to a remote Amazonian outpost, but if someone asked me to describe one I'd probably come up with something like Karumba—a clutter of galvanized-iron buildings and overgrown yards, a sense of smoldering aggression, a broad and murky river nearby. Karumba is lonelier and smaller than Normanton, sometimes cut off for weeks at a time by the monsoon rains that arrive in summer. Back in the 1930s it was a far-flung refueling stop for the Empire Flying Boats that carried mail between Australia and England. Now it shelters a fleet of prawn and barramundi trawlers whose brawling skippers hang out at the notorious Animal Bar; just up from the old flying-boat slip, it's reputed to be outback Australia's roughest watering hole.

"I was in there last Anzac Day," Paul said as we walked up the street toward the bar. "You should have seen it—these two barra captains were trying to kill each other. Floor was covered with broken glass and these blokes were stomping around in their bare feet, the blood splashing up their legs, too drunk and mad to care, just swinging away at each other's heads."

"Sounds like a good place to meet a nice girl," Thommo quipped.

There was neither broken glass nor blood nor nice girls when we bellied up, just the somnolent buzz of conversation among a few hard-case drinkers—bronzed, bearded, and heavily tattooed, mulling over their beers. The barroom was a concrete arcade, open in front, with the chairs and tables bolted to the floor and a big pool table in the center. It was marginally cooler inside than out. A few faces flashed surprised recognition at Mick, and some of the drinkers came over to congratulate him on his upcoming wedding. We ordered beers. Paul and Thommo started a game of eightball.

Mick drifted over to chat with a couple of well-wishers. Terry and I sat at a table and shot the breeze with a mighty hard-looking ex-con named Andrew; about 6 foot 3 and 17 stone of raw tattooed muscle, honed by working at the stockyards on the edge of town. He told us how he'd picked up a German hitchhiker in Ravenshoe the other day and given him a lift to Karumba. "Fucking guy couldn't speak English so he would sit there for hours, watching the road go by, not saying a fucking word, then blurt out: 'Incredible!' And I'd say: 'What?' And he'd say: 'Nothing.' Then a little while later he'd come out with it again: 'Incredible!' And I'd say 'What?' And he'd say: 'Nothing.' This went on. I was getting really pissed off, wondering what the fuck his problem was and getting ready to slap him on the side of the head if he did it again, when I finally figured it out. He just couldn't believe there was so much nothing out here—mile after mile of nothing. That's what he kept saying: 'Incredible! Nothing!'"

Andrew went off to the men's room. I decided to take a few atmospheric snaps of the Animal Bar—perhaps not the most diplomatic thing to do in a frontier bar full of bail jumpers, drug runners, and wanted felons. Although I was focusing on Paul and Thommo playing pool, and nobody else, a menacing drunk strode toward me snarling: "Unless you got a badge, you better put that fucking thing away. You point it at me and I'm gonna shove it down your throat!"

I was wondering what to say to this when massive Andrew waltzed out of the gents' room, completely unaware of any conversation that had gone on, and asked if I needed another beer. The drunk, stunned almost to sobriety to discover who my drinking partner was, went as white as salt, suddenly remembering he had to be somewhere else. When I told Mick the story later on, he laughed and said that Andrew was arguably the toughest brawler anywhere along the gulf.

We finished our beers and left. On the way back to the trucks, Paul sighed a bit about the bad old days when he was working on building sites up here and the Animal Bar had really been an animal bar. He shook his head sadly as he climbed in his cab. "It's really tame now—not like it used to be."

ASH MADE A FEAST of fish-and-chips that night. Once the dishes had been cleared away, we played a few hands of Five Hundred while he divulged his latest money-making scheme. Like a lot of quick-minded outback Australians, Ash was a shrewd entrepreneur, a wildcatter, with restless eyes always scanning the horizon for opportunity. Besides his fish-and-chips shop, he and his wife Cheryl ran a small motel and had an interest in a barramundi boat, skippered by his son Ronnie, as well as a few other sidelines. He was clever, vigorous, and clearly successful as a businessman around Karumba. But the notion he passed around that evening, as he dealt another hand, struck me as loopy.

He was looking into buying a Mr. Whippy ice-cream van. There was one for sale down on the coast. "I'm going to check it out and see if I can get a good deal on it. A Mr. Whippy van is just what this town needs. I'll make a killing."

I nearly burst out laughing, an image flashing in my mind's eye of a Mr. Whippy van chiming "Greensleeves" as it rumbled across the burning savanna, crocodiles snapping at its tires as it delivered soft-serve cones to this godforsaken outpost. I said: "You're joking, right?"

"Absolutely not." Ash sorted his cards. "Karumba is going to boom—you watch. We're already getting more and more pensioners and tourists coming up here in the winter every year, to get out of the cold down south and do a bit of fishing. In June or July this place is packed. You'd be lucky to get a room in town. But, you see, there isn't much here for them yet except heat and fishing. Even in the winter, temperatures around here can go up into the 90s. Be nice in the hot afternoons to be able to buy an ice-cream cone, don't you think? Nobody else in town is offering anything like that."

Put that way, possibilities began to dawn even in my feeble business brain. And this pleasing thought: In this shrinking world, Australia still offered wide-open frontiers where a regular bloke with a bit of vision stood a chance of making a tidy pile by so simple a means as having the first and only Mr. Whippy van for hundreds of miles.

We called it an early night; we had a big day ahead.

IT WAS A LONG, HOT, DUSTY ramble down remote bush tracks from Karumba to our campsite on the Staaten River. In some places the track was little more than a faint impression in the tall, brown grass that rose above the roofs of the Land Cruisers. There was no break, just mile after mile of tall grass and termite mounds and scrubby boxwood trees shimmering in the white-hot glare. It had been seven months since the last rains fell here. The earth was so dry and parched in places that when we stopped to open gates even the softest footfalls raised clouds of ocher bulldust that drifted into our nostrils. It never settled in that breathless air, but floated like wreaths of smoke. The taste of dust was everywhere. The effect was stifling. The temperature was a temple-pounding 110°F in the shade and the humidity was oppressive ahead of monsoon, which typically began around December but could start anytime.

A sudden rainfall would transform this landscape into a vastness of marsh and mud and shimmering pools dotted with water lilies. Lush tropical grasses would run riot. Spectacular electrical storms would dance across the horizon. It would also leave us stranded for weeks. But for now there was just a flaming sun in an empty sky. The silvery leaves of the boxwoods hung limp. Insects droned.

As we bounced along, Mick passed the time by telling us how he and another officer had once waited out here to catch a murderer. Word had come over the radio that the wanted man was on his way, crossing from Cooktown, more than 250 miles away, in a desperate bid to escape. But his getaway car soon foundered in the rocky, sandy track. At first he tried to plunge ahead on foot, but he never came out at Mick's end of the track; more terrified of the vast, conspiratorial silence of the bush than he was of prison, the fugitive had simply turned himself in.

Although the Gulf Country may not be the easiest place for headlong flight, it earns high marksas a hideout. The ragged and lonely coastline is ideal for smugglers' boats. Marijuana is rumored to grow in remote, viciously guarded clearings. A couple of ne'er-do-well cattlemen, on isolated stations, had recently been busted on drug charges. "Be very careful who you talk to, if we meet anybody out here," Mick explained. "And please—don't mention I'm a copper, okay?"

WE MADE A COMFORTABLE CAMPSITE on the bank of the Staaten River, far more elaborate than the fly-by-night arrangements I had been devising on my own. Thommo set up a solar-powered shower under a convenient tree. We had camp chairs, mosquito netting, hurricane lanterns, and a folding table for card games. We had handlines and nets for catching bait, fishing rods and tackle boxes, and two aluminum dinghies with outboard motors. There were iron skillets, a heavy Dutch oven, and a big steel teakettle. An old pail filled with water was kept hot on the coals for washing up. Implements hung on trees. The fish were filleted, and the dishes done, on the tailgate of one of the Land Cruisers. The big camp fridge in the back of Thommo's truck was filled with slabs of beer and a mountain of chops, snags, and bacon for breakfast fry-ups. We all slept in the open.

Each morning we'd set out in the dinghies, puttering through the murky water, ducking under prehistoric fronds and keeping a weather eye out for crocs. We cast for barramundi—Australia's noblest game fish—in the mangroves, dropping the lures among the tangle of roots and flood-swept debris along the banks, where the cagiest old fellows lurked.

Had Izaak Walton been Australian, he would have waxed eloquent about barramundi: Magnificent fighters, swift and strong, they are famous for leaping dramatically from the water, their silvery sides sparkling in the sun—a spectacle to make an angler drop his rod in sheer wonder. If you're lucky enough to land one, you'll eat some of the sweetest-tasting fish on the planet.

We were lucky—many times over. Our biggest—one of Mick's—ran to 21 pounds.

We lived large, feasting on fresh-caught barras served smoking-hot straight off the skillet. Cold beer or pannikins of strong billy tea washed down the fish as we played cards by the flickering light of hurricane lanterns and talked around the campfire, watching the stars come out and hearing something splash way off down the river.

One evening, coming back late, we couldn't find our camp at all in the dense black shadows along the bank. Thommo found a landing and went ashore. He thrashed his way through the bush until he located our camp, then built up the fire. Guided by the distant flickering light downstream, we got home safe, slipped our dinghies under the overhanging canopy of branches, and tied up for the night.

THE DAYS FELL INTO a rhythm. "Ah—it's hell in the tropics," Terry liked to drawl at the end of an afternoon, too pleasantly sunburned and comfortably sprawled in the dinghy to want to move, and asking whoever was handy to please toss him down a beer. Thommo would be rigging up his shower, figuring to wash away the day's sweat and fish stink, and offering a few ironic observations. Mick generally dressed the fish (this was either fair or unfair depending on how you look at it, since he generally caught them, too). Paul kept the humor flowing, telling outrageous tales of hustling pool in the Animal Bar, or gags he'd pulled on work crews out on Mornington Island, or stealing watermelons as a kid growing up on the wrong side of the tracks in small-town 1950s Queensland.

After we pulled up stakes on the Staaten, we swung back through Karumba for more supplies, then headed out for the Gregory River, about 200 miles west. Mick knew a secret spot there—a miniature paradise, he said, of waterfalls and palm trees and huge barramundi.

He had plenty of time to build up our expectations. Getting there was another long, rough, dusty drive, through the same country that explorers

Robert O'Hara Burke and William John Wills had passed on their final doomed push to the sea in 1861. Totally inexperienced in the ways of the Australian bush—and disregarding all advice—the cocksure pair had bulled their way across the central deserts in midsummer, only to arrive in the Gulf Country during the worst of its wet season. The ground was so marshy that their pack animals bogged down in the mud, forcing the heroic duo to stagger the last few miles on foot. Although Burke and Wills succeeded in their goal to be the first to traverse Australia's unknown interior, they died of exposure, starvation, and exhaustion on the homeward trek, near a lonely water hole called Cooper Creek.

I had never given their sufferings much thought, but my recent long, hot days in the saddle—rationing water and sheltering from the fearful noonday sun—had quickened my interest. Not that the hardships of my bicycle journey remotely approximated theirs, but in extrapolating my own experiences I felt a growing admiration for Australia's early settlers. The seeds of kinship had begun to sprout.

The last few miles to Mick's secret spot were brutal—long, harrowing descents down rocky tracks, punctuated by two burst tires. "Trust me," Mick remarked, as we lurched down a particularly treacherous ravine in the fading light. "This place is worth it. And we'll have it all to ourselves. Nobody in their right mind would ever come down here." We made camp well after dark, throwing down our bedrolls by flashlight and building a small fire for tea.

Dawn revealed a Lost World: Pandanus palms and huge ferns—relics from the age of the dinosaurs—overhung a stream of rushing cataracts and deep, translucent pools the color of freshly cut limes, so clear the tropical fish in them appeared to be flying. It was as though we'd driven back in time. Whereas the Staaten River had exuded a thrilling sort of prehistoric menace—vaguely sinister, with the possibility of saltwater crocodiles lurking in its shallows—the Gregory was completely different. It was a world so fresh and so clean it still had dew on it. These were the last vestiges of the ancient rain forests that had once covered the Top End of Australia, before global warming at the end of the Ice Age dried out the continent. While the rest of the continent's rain forest had withered and died beneath the broiling sun, life went on as usual in these cool, shady, spring-fed gorges.

Mick's hideaway was noisy with birds and teeming with wallabies and lizards and fish and yabbies and crocodiles—although these were the timid freshwater variety, not the man-eating sort, so there were no worries about swimming. In short, life here was idyllic. The water was cool and refreshing, the sun-warmed rocks offered a perfect place to dry off, and the barramundi ran to more than 20 pounds. Yet when you scrambled up the side of the gorge and looked out, there was nothing but hot and blistered dust bowl, an apocalyptic landscape as far as the eye could see—not a hint of the beautiful Lost World that flourished in these crevices. It made you want to crawl back down and pull the lid over you.

Even if this magic gorge could stay fixed in time, human lives move on; the day of Mick's wedding was approaching. We'd become fast friends—mates—over the past couple of weeks in the bush, and I was deeply honored when Mick invited me to attend the wedding. The event was to be held in Mount Isa. We all drove down there together.

CHAPTER 17

A Long Shot Comes Home

MOUNT ISA is a brawling mining town of about 25,000 in Queensland's rugged northwest frontier. We could see the zinc smelter's smokestack shimmering in the glare when we were still miles away. As we cruised up the highway, a city slowly coalesced beneath it—a hot, flat sprawl of heavy industry and corrugated-iron rooftops that owes its existence to a massive silver-zinc ore body about 1,000 feet under the desert. A thin haze of brownish soot hung over the outback city.

We rented cheap cabins at a caravan park near the mine, got haircuts, and headed over to the Irish Club. Mick was a member and he signed us in. We ordered beers and peanuts, picked up a form guide, and settled into an afternoon of investing in horses with such promising names as "Military Assassin." We each kicked in ten dollars for a kitty, took turns placing bets—five dollars maximum—and had one of those hilarious runs of luck you get sometimes when you're having a good time and everything just falls into place. Odds didn't seem to matter: Mick had a long shot gallop home at 52-1 and another wheezing nag somehow romped in at 36-1. We finished the day $150 up, even after allowing for a whole afternoon's drinks, nuts, and chips—and we'd moved on to cashews pretty early in the piece, too, after the first long shots started coming home. We celebrated with a slap-up Chinese meal at a place called the Red Lantern.

We hit town on Thursday. Mick's wedding was Saturday afternoon, a day he was sharing with the Grand Final of Australian Rules Football: North Melbourne versus Sydney. We got dressed at the home of one of Mick's mates, lunching on fried chicken and watching the game. North Melbourne was well ahead when we called time, switched off the TV, straightened our ties, and walked to the church. It was a nice wedding. The reception was at the golf club.

CHAPTER 18

Barkly Tableland

OUR LITTLE BAND broke up the following afternoon. Terry, Paul, and Thommo headed east to their lives back on the coast, while Mick and Kerriann prepared to fly out that evening for their honeymoon in Tasmania. Me, I left Mount Isa in the teeth of a hot and gusty westerly, the temperature in the low 100s and the stink of sulfur in the air.

I camped that night about 30 miles west of Isa on a low, scrubby hilltop in a nest of spinifex—a savage, spiny, needle-sharp grass that can puncture a tire. The full moon was so bright I couldn't sleep. Instead I sat up, listening to my radio. I had 1,000 empty miles to travel before I'd see Darwin, and its distant gaiety was a poor substitute for Paul's hilarious tales, or Thommo's acid wit, or Terry's drawled observations, or Mick's big heart. I remembered an idle afternoon dealing card games in the laundry room behind Ash's motel in Karumba; Mick's good-humored patience when I snarled the line of his second-best reel; our ludicrous run of good luck with the horses at the Irish Club. I missed my mates. I felt as lonely as a pin on a map.

At some point I must have drifted off, because when I opened my eyes the moon was gone and a feeble gray light hinted at dawn. I was achy and tired. There were no stars. The air was already feverishly warm. I rolled up my bivvy, took a long swig of water, then pushed my bicycle through the scrub and back onto the empty highway. A powerful headwind buffeted me. I pedaled off, bound for Darwin, at a creaky and tedious five miles an hour.

Tableland Tales II

FIFTY-ODD YEARS AGO, just after the fall of Singapore, when Australia was under the threat of Japanese invasion, a team of Australian soldiers and American GIs managed to pave a lonely single-lane highway from Mount Isa to Darwin in a frantic 100 days. Nobody seems to have done much with it since, certainly not on the Queensland side of the border. It was as rough as a creek bed. After a few hours of empty jolting highway, searing heat, and blowing dust, I felt like the *Mary Celeste* of cyclists: My loose-fitting shirt flapped in the breeze like a runaway spinnaker, my face was caked with grit, and my tongue tasted like old boot leather.

Nearly 100 windswept miles lay between Mount Isa and the little border post of Camooweal, and the only source of water I knew of between them was a lonely windmill creaking softly a few miles shy of the latter. Although I was now carrying a total of 12 liters of water in my nine bottles and rationing it carefully, I hadn't reckoned on such hot, fierce headwinds—nor had I expected to travel at such a slow pace. Now, as I churned into the wind, I wondered uneasily if my water would last to Camooweal.

An old pickup truck crammed with a family of Aborigines materialized in the shimmering heat. The truck pulled over and the driver—a kind-faced elder named Maurice—asked me if I could use some extra water. I stared as though I'd been addressed by a burning bush, then scrambled to get my water bottles open before this apparition could vanish. They filled all my bottles and gave me a good, long drink.

I remarked on how little water there was along this stretch of highway. Maurice laughed, then proceeded to list half a dozen reliable water pools hidden away in the stony hillsides and crevices from here to Camooweal. "There's plenty of water out here. Pools you can swim in, eh?"

"Nothing like tapping into 50,000 years of local knowledge, is there?"

He smiled. "How far are you going?"

"Darwin, for now."

"Hmmm." He screwed up his face, thought for a minute, and then said without a trace of irony, "I'm sorry. I'm afraid I don't know all the water holes between here and Darwin. You'd better ask other Aboriginal people along the way."

Tableland Tales III

OVER THE WEEKS, as I traveled the outback, I found myself continually redefining previously held notions of "empty" or "lonely" or "bleak." Every day brought a new and heartbreaking vista that transcended anything that had come before. What had seemed supremely godforsaken and isolated on the Capricorn Highway, for example, diminished to merely rural as I pedaled across the dusty immensity of the gulf savanna. By then I thought I'd seen it all and could safely chisel my new definitions in stone.

The highway west of Camooweal, however, took the concepts of empty, lonely, and bleak to a higher and more exquisite plane than my citified imagination could—up to then, anyway—have conceived. Two hundred and fifty miles of sheer sensory deprivation, across a dead-flat spinifex plain, led to the rough old mining town of Tennant Creek. The only relief from the tedium came at the tiny police outpost of Avon Downs, about 30 miles beyond the Northern Territory border, and the Barkly Roadhouse, about halfway to Tennant Creek. Other than that it was just wind, dust, flies, an empty vault of sky, and the aching loneliness of following a highway that seemed to lead nowhere.

The days were eerily quiet. Once an old Bedford truck sputtered past me; when I glanced up several minutes later, I was surprised to find that I could still make it out—a pumpkin-orange dot floating on a watery void somewhere above the road, God knows how many miles away. I pedaled and watched, fascinated, waiting for it to disappear over the horizon. It hung there, motionless, for a long time before suddenly vanishing—*ping!*—like the little dot of white light that lingers and then disappears from an old-fashioned TV screen after you turn off the set. I knew that when I reached that vague horizon, wherever it was, another one just as watery and elusive would stretch out before me. And then another one after that. And on and on and on.

Five hundred and forty million years ago, this was a vast, shallow seabed; now it was an arid limestone plateau dotted with clumps of spinifex—nature's barbed wire. Once I came upon a weather-beaten billboard reading "Wunara Store," with an arrow pointing down a dusty track. No such outpost appeared on my map, but I could just make out a low structure quavering in the heat—or at least a substantial enough mirage to convince me to veer off the highway and imagine myself buying a cold Coke.

The crumbling stone building was real enough, but years had passed since anybody bought a drink in it. Now there was nothing but the creaking of a rusty sign in the hot wind, and the constant humming of flies. I rode away, brushing at the flies in front of my face, amazed and a little horrified at the desolation spreading out around me. I'd always known that outback Australia was frighteningly hostile and barren, but I didn't know how far that could go.

Funny thing was, I still didn't.

Tableland Tales IV

A BIG STORM blew up on my fifth night out of Mount Isa, sweeping the tableland with a spectacular midnight display of thunder, lightning, and screeching wind. It had been leading up to it all day; one of those weather breeders, breathlessly hot and sticky with thunderheads building into the stratosphere and tumbling across the humid, felt-gray sky.

I was into October now. The gathering heat, humidity, and towering clouds were reminders that the dry season was drawing to a close; the monsoons would be coming in the next few weeks, and I had better hustle if I wanted to be south of the tropics before the big rains arrived.

And I did. The monsoons are no joke; torrential rains fall by the foot, sometimes washing out roads and trapping the unwary in seething flash floods that can sweep across the desert overnight. Getting caught in the wrong place at the wrong time could mean—at best—being stranded for weeks in some isolated settlement. At worst, you could suffer the bizarre fate of drowning in the very desert that had tried to kill you with heat and thirst and sunstroke the previous afternoon.

I was bone-weary that evening after 110 sweaty miles in the saddle. I rolled out my camp in the spinifex while the sun dropped in a sullen ball of flame. Not a breath of air stirred. I studied the enormous pink-topped clouds booming across the horizon and talked myself into believing that the storm would track north of me.

I made a nasty dinner out of a tin of bully beef I'd picked up back at the Barkly Roadhouse. While I was devouring that vile meat, I discovered that I'd set up camp in the middle of a colony of tiny, almost invisible ants. They swarmed over my ankles and calves, making my flesh tingle and itch. It was too dark—and I was too peevish—to shift camp, so I brushed off as many as I could and retreated into my bivvy bag, zipping shut the mosquito net with a hard snap of the wrist usually reserved for slamming doors.

Then I lay there.

If it had been hot, sticky, and uncomfortable outside, it was a sauna in that bivvy. I lay on my back, tickled by sweat and a few stubborn ants, staring into the muggy darkness and listening to my radio. A bit of atmospheric trickery brought in 4RO, my old friend from Rockhampton. They were playing Golden Oldies from the 70s. Lying there all alone on that great void, I caught the mood of reminiscence and slid down memory lane, thinking about friends from college, wondering what my life would have been had I stayed in America. I played back the miles since I had cycled out of Sydney: holiday towns on the coast; tea and homemade bread—"morning smoko"—at the shearing shed at Fairfield Station; the glitter of Cairns; the rain forests on the Atherton Tableland; the conspiratorial silence of the savanna. Faces came to me—a mosaic of Australia.

I must have drifted off to sleep, because when I opened my eyes the sky was brilliant with stars. Usually it's cheering to look up and see the Southern Cross, but that night it wasn't. An ominous tension hung in the air. The needle-like sharpness of the stars had the creepiness of surgical steel. The air felt feverishly hot, claustrophobic. I was sticky with sweat. I switched off the radio and tried to get back to sleep, and succeeded in dozing fitfully for an hour or two.

That's when the storm struck.

It rolled across the tableland like a sonic boom, a powerful advance gust jolting me awake. The air was cooler, the sky a sooty void. There was no doubt about what was coming. I could smell it: the wild, bracing, earthy fragrance of a desert rain. I struggled out of my bivvy, entertaining some sleep-dazed notion of wrapping my gear in the tarp. The wind nearly bowled me over, and I had to stamp on my bivvy bag to keep it from blowing away.

Thunder growled. I glanced uneasily around me, grit stinging my cheeks. The landscape was haunting, surreal. A massive blackness, dense with blowing dust, was moving in rapidly from the west, swallowing up the plains, while a blood-orange full moon hung low in the eastern sky, throwing outré shadows across the weirdly twisted scrub and spinifex. It was a landscape drawn by Dr. Seuss, except that now he'd sketched me in too, standing there in my underpants, arms akimbo, the look on my face stolen from the Grinch. It was way too windy to mess with the tarp, so I dived back into my bivvy, weighting it down with my 182 pounds. My bicycle would have to ride its own race.

I wanted to leave the fly open until the rain struck in order to let the cooler air inside, but the blowing dust was too fierce. I lowered the fly and sweltered. The storm grew nearer; the smell of desert rain grew stronger. Lightning hissed and flashed, illuminating the inside of the bivvy in hot white light for an instant before plunging me back into pitch-darkness. Almost immediately would come a crash of thunder that shook the earth and reverberated through my chest. Then another flash and another deafening explosion, again and again.

Finally the rain came—a few drops that spattered noisily on the taut Gore-Tex, then a hard, steady downpour, driven by winds that howled unchecked across the plain.

It was scary, yet there was something fiercely satisfying about riding out such a violent storm, alone in my obscure little camp, miles from the nearest dwelling. I'd felt lonely earlier in the evening, as indeed I had been much of the way across the Barkly Tableland, but the primitive savagery of this storm made me feel self-reliant rather than forsaken, part of the greater wildness out here. I relished my isolation. I fell asleep—soundly this time—to the crash of thunder.

CHAPTER 19

Ants, Sweat, Salt, and Flies

TENNANT CREEK started out as the site of a telegraph station, one of a line of outposts built to service the Overland Telegraph that connected Adelaide to Darwin in 1870. The desert town boomed briefly in the 1930s, when—according to local lore—a blind man and his dog discovered gold in the nearby hills. A bit of gold still comes out of its scrubby hillsides, but these days Tennant Creek is mostly a truckers' relay on the Stuart Highway, and notorious among hitchhikers as a place to be stranded for days. I bought supplies, tanked up on water, and headed north.

The long string of desert highway that runs through town was named after John MacDougall Stuart, a hard-drinking Scotsman who succeeded in crossing the heart of the continent from Adelaide to Darwin in 1862. Although he never achieved the glamour of Burke and Wills (the stuffier elements of Adelaide society wouldn't even let him in their homes), Stuart was the explorer's explorer, a tough professional who kept meticulous notes—and kept his men alive. When the time came to probe the desert, telegraph builders and railroad surveyors turned to Stuart's maps and journal; as a result, his hometown of Adelaide won the coveted—and lucrative—role of being the first Australian city with a telegraph link to London.

Competence and courage, however, play nowhere near as well as Byronic deaths beneath a gnarled Coolabah tree in the South Australian desert. So while Burke and Wills became paragons of heroism, mateship, and noble failure—icons to generations—Stuart got this eponymous truck route. For the next 600 miles, I'd be roughly following his tracks.

The drizzle ceased and the sky cleared. Steam rose from the ribbon of bitumen, which stretched to a point on the horizon. I rode into it, pedals creaking, absently shooing the flies away from my face. I covered 100 miles that day, camping just below Renner Springs, and another 100 or so the day after that, rolling out my bivvy in a copse of eucalypts 20 miles shy of Dunmarra. In those 200 miles the landscape shifted dramatically yet almost imperceptibly, as central Australia's craggy red ranges and spinifex plains slowly gave way to low, flat, lightly wooded scrub.

As I headed north, the air grew hotter and thicker, too. Towering cumulus clouds tumbled through the sticky sky, sometimes thundering ominously but never delivering relief from the oppressive humidity. At least not yet; not here, anyway. The Wet was coming, though. My radio reported that the highway east of Mount Isa had been washed out, presumably from the same storm that had brushed past me the other night. Much farther east, coastal Townsville had copped 16 inches of rain in two days.

The nights were breathlessly hot, with temperatures staying well into the 80s. Every evening I'd lie beneath my mosquito net, wondering if that tickle I felt was sweat running down or ants crawling up. Usually it was both. Some nights I abandoned the idea of sleep altogether and sat up in the bush sipping a water bottle and looking at the stars. Every now and then a road train came booming down the highway, festooned with orange running lights that lit it up like a county fair, high beams scouting for 'roos on the road ahead. Hidden in the scrub, watching these big rigs recede into the hot desert night, I felt a bit like Huck Finn peering at steamboats through rushes on the Mississippi.

By and large, I was making good time. The road was smooth, the winds were light and generally in my favor, and the roadside water tanks maintained by the Northern Territory highway department enabled me to refill my bottles every 40 miles or so. On my third day out of Tennant Creek I had lunch at the Daly Waters pub, a watering hole where early Qantas flights and seat-of-the-pants aviators such as Amy Johnson had called for food and fuel in the 1920s and '30s. I made my own stop quick—just a hamburger and a cold beer—because I was hoping to put in 130 miles that day.

Dusk found me on a lonely stretch of highway well short of that mark, limping along with painful twitches in my knee and thigh. I camped in the tall grass a few miles south of Larrimah and hoped for better on the morrow.

My knee felt okay when I set off in the morning, but by the time I wheeled up to the Larrimah pub, it was throbbing again. I couldn't understand it; these painful twitches had come out of nowhere. It didn't occur to me then that the healthy low-salt intakes I had assiduously followed in my former life might not be so healthy now that I was cycling 100 miles a day through the red center. I was drinking 15 liters of water a day in this heat, but I needed to put back something besides water. That lightning bolt of common sense didn't strike for another couple of days, however. I soldiered on toward Mataranka that afternoon, pedaling a few miles, then walking or resting until the flies drove me on again.

By the time I faltered into Mataranka—a honky-tonk town with rough pubs, seedy video arcades, roadhouses, pool halls, and stray dogs lining the street—I was in a lot of pain. Pride of place in the town's park was occupied by a monumental termite mound—another natural wonder to impress the backpackers who drop down here to visit the local hot springs as an add-on to their bus tours through Kakadu National Park and Katherine Gorge. I thought about taking a dip in the springs myself, but they were four miles out of town and I was in no condition to reach them. All I wanted was a cheap place to flop—somewhere I could rest my aching legs without being driven mad by clouds of flies. It was Friday, a lousy time of the week to come to a place like Mataranka. It was payday if you had a job, pension day if you didn't. Either way there was a lot of cash floating around town and the pubs were literally doing a roaring trade.

I limped along the main street. The bars were noisy and aggressive, jammed with hard-voiced men shouting and swearing and quarreling and laughing. A jukebox somewhere belted out "Sweet Home Alabama." It seemed an oddly appropriate tune, at least if you were sentimental about Alabama in the Jim Crow days. They practice a clumsy sort of segregation in some of these out-back pubs, through a baroque expedient called a dress code—generally along the lines of "shoes" or "no shoes," to avoid legal hassles from do-gooders in the city. I poked my head into one joint, where ragged, barefoot Aborigines drank, played pinball, and shot pool in a dark and grimy concrete arcade, while ragged and dissolute whites—but with dirty rubber thongs dangling from their toes—slurred insults over a more nicely appointed bar in the next room.

I took a site at a caravan park on the north end of town, bought some groceries, and iced my cramped and aching knee with a bag of frozen peas. I hoped that an afternoon off, rest, ice, and a good dinner would see it right; at least to get me as far as Katherine, where I could take a longer break, if necessary, because even on short acquaintance I could see I didn't want to linger here.

Early the next morning—after a long night of drunken shouts, breaking glass, and barking dogs—I rode out of town. I happened to have devoured a large bag of salt-and-vinegar chips with my dinner the previous night. The salt on them bought me about 20 pain-free miles before my knee started to throb again, giving me a clue what the trouble was. Not that it did much good on the road to Katherine. There were no chip shops out here, no Gatorade vendors or salt licks, nor anything else—just an unbroken line of eucalypt scrub on either side of the highway. I was walking the bicycle and limping badly by the time I staggered into Katherine.

I checked into an old auto court that had been converted to a hostel and hunted up a chemist shop, where I bought a packet of salt tablets. I gulped one down and almost hit the wall with it. It was as nauseating as swallowing a bucket of seawater. I managed to keep it down and walked back to the auto court, careful not to bump into anything. I spent the afternoon lying quietly in the cool dimness of my room, ceiling fan twirling softly overhead, watching the classic Saturday-afternoon Elvis movie on TV.

Katherine is a hard-boiled military town with a serious drinking problem on the fringes. Derelicts loiter outside the pubs from early morning onward, snarling at passersby or snoring noisily beneath the trees. The hostel where I stayed called to mind those shabby 1950s-era transient motels you find dotted across the American Southwest in places such as Bisbee or Lake Havasu City, both in Arizona. It was L-shaped and two stories high, with cinder-block walls, numbered doors painted flat gray, threadbare curtains tightly drawn across the windows, and a line of trailer-trash cars—each with a mustard-yellow paint job or racing stripes—parked in front.

The courtyard around the swimming pool reeked of cigarettes and stale beer. Here the residents loitered, chain-smoking, shirtless, and tattooed, sprawled on flimsy plastic pool chairs. They were mostly Australian hard cases—drifters, construction workers at loose ends looking for a job, itinerant fruit pickers. One big strapping bloke, his hair in shoulder-length ringlets, was obviously bad news. His name was Joel, he had a nasty drinking problem, and the word around the campfire was that he was wanted for a string of violent offenses in

Queensland, up to and including attempted murder of a police officer. One day Joel wasn't there anymore. A squad of grim-looking police had raided a house in town looking for him, but he had smashed his way through a rear window just as they arrived, skipping town—and presumably his hostel bill—for the wilds of Western Australia. It was not the last time I would see him, however.

There was also a motley assortment of European backpackers staying there. Most stopped for just a day or so to visit the gorge. A few hung around, hoping for fruit-picking work—mangoes and watermelons were in season—on one of the farms near the river.

Some of the more down-at-the-heels backpackers had swapped drudgery for board, spending their mornings sweeping floors, picking up beer bottles, and dumping overflowing ashtrays. Scraping the grease off the barbecue plate. Pouring chlorine into the pool and plucking waterlogged cigarette butts out of it. An English guy named Gavin had hung on here for a month that way, and a Danish girl named Jacqui was going on for three. I don't know how they did it, or why. There seemed to be a vague notion at work that it elevated them above mere tourists, who came merely to view the gorge and pass on. They affected Aussie slang, smoked roll-your-owns, and were generally more outback than Crocodile Dundee.

I killed three days here, getting my knee and thigh muscles ready to ride again, and the time died mighty hard. I found a bicycle shop and replaced my worn-out rear tire, then spent a day cleaning the bike, sorting my gear, and scrubbing the greenish mold out my water bottles—a by-product of the tropical heat and humidity. On my third day in Katherine, I took a test run out to the gorge, a round trip of 35 miles. It was a fine, hot day. My knees and thighs felt good. Katherine Gorge had a certain stark majesty, but seemed uninspiring after the magical hidden crevices along the Gregory River that Mick had shown me. I ate a picnic lunch in the gorge and rode back to Katherine, eager to shake this town and make the final push to Darwin and its fresh sea breezes.

CHAPTER 20

Buildup to a Downpour

THREE DAYS LATER I pulled up at the corner of Daly Street and the Esplanade, where the Stuart Highway comes to an end. Ahead of me, framed by palms, lay the turquoise waters of the Arafura Sea; above them, a line of mauve thunderheads faded into a hot ocean sky. Indonesia lay 300 miles over the horizon. A light breeze fanned my face. This was Darwin, mid-October, and the tropical seascape that spread out to the north was tangible evidence of the 3,900 miles I'd come since leaving Sydney almost three months earlier.

I was relieved to be here. The ride through the scrub from Katherine had been the ghastliest of the journey—200 miles of breathless heat, punctuated by occasional downpours that only added to the steamy oppression. It had grown even stickier as I neared the coast, the long, hot, thundery, sleepless nights humming with mosquitoes and crawling with ants. By the time I hit Darwin, I looked like a wino who'd slept rough for a year. I was haggard, exhausted, red-eyed, and dirty. My skin was tacky with sweat and three-day-old sunscreen. I smelled.

I checked into a hostel on Mitchell Street, keeping an embarrassed distance from the girl behind the desk, who flashed me a taut smile and presumably held her breath while I signed in. I found my room, slung my saddlebags in the corner, and immediately took a long shower—hot to steam away the grime, then cold to make me feel human again. I shaved and put on a fresh pair of shorts and a T-shirt I'd been saving for the occasion. All I wanted to do at this point was sleep and dream air-conditioned dreams, but first I needed to do a few chores: rinse out my dirty clothes and bring in some groceries. After hanging my cycling rags out to dry—a trifle optimistically, given the humidity—I set off to find a grocery store. My just-showered freshness wilted fast in the glare and humidity. I hadn't gone a block before I was damp with sweat.

I picked up a few things at a supermarket on Knuckey Street and was waiting at the checkout counter when I looked through the plate-glass window and noticed the eerie false twilight that had crept over the city. It was only early afternoon, but the cars prowling the streets had their lights on. Neon signs flickered in front of shops. Pedestrians moved briskly, apprehensive eyes cast skyward. I stepped outside. The air at street level was hot, heavy, and still, ripe with rain, but 1,000 feet overhead purplish-black clouds swirled violently. Looking up at them along the motionless flanks of the buildings made you feel dizzy, as though you might suddenly fall upward and plunge into their clammy, swirling darkness. Thunder growled.

I had gone an anxious block when the first raindrops fell, fat and warm, spattering on the concrete in splotches the size of 20-cent coins. I picked up the pace. So did the rain. I dashed for the cover of an awning, jostling my way into the knot of pedestrians already sheltering there—and just in time, too. A few seconds later the sky burst open in a machine-gun torrent of rain, a roaring sheet of water so dense and gray it created a street-level mist that obscured the buildings on the other side of the road. Within minutes the gutters were overflowing. Buckets of rainwater sluiced noisily off the awning; the few cars still braving the streets sliced hubcap-deep wakes with their tires. Lightning hissed, and thunder cracked sharply immediately overhead. I pictured what it would be like to cycle a lonely highway in such a downpour, with 120 miles between me and a place to dry off. I didn't like the picture, but it was way too early to start worrying about pushing on—I'd only just hit town.

The Greek shopkeeper whose awning it was stepped out and watched the steady downpour for a few minutes, then shrugged and went back inside. As he shut the door he remarked: "You should be here in the Wet—it'll do this for weeks, nonstop." After half an hour or so the rains eased, almost resentfully. A stinging sun burned through the clouds and wands of steam rose from the pavement. I hustled back to my hostel, hopping around the deeper puddles, but with more thunder growling overhead and the shadows fading once again, I said the hell with it and splashed straight across the street, ankle-deep in water. I made it through the door as the next drumroll of thunder began.

I SPENT A WEEK in Darwin. It rained a little every day—sometimes absurd sprinkles that pattered down on only one side of the street, other times the same kind of brief but awesome cloudburst I'd witnessed that first afternoon. Either way the sun would always burn through, more torrid than ever. The steam would rise, and your temples would throb in the searing tropical heat.

Locals call this tease the Buildup—those sultry, evil-tempered weeks ahead of the monsoon when even best mates grab each other by the throat, police blotters fill with drunken assaults, and the steaming sidewalks make New Orleans in summer seem like a sweet wish. The way the heat and humidity fray your nerves can be a little scary. Irrationality rules. You glimpse a stranger in the frozen-food section of a supermarket and suddenly feel an urge to kick his teeth in, simply because you saw him a moment ago browsing in the vegetables and before that in the pasta aisle and now you're sick of seeing his face. Old hands say this is mere waspishness compared with the more probing tests of character that come with the heavy rains.

In a few more weeks, the monsoons will settle over the low-slung city like the long dark of a Norwegian winter. When that happens, tropical depressions dump rain by the foot. Life slows to a crawl. Skeptical bosses ask every would-be employee the same question: Do you think you can make it through the Wet? I met a girl named Phoebe, up from Sydney and looking for a bit of adventure, who had cheerily answered yes to that question and landed a job turning down beds at a seedy motel. That was a fortnight ago. Already she'd had enough heat, humidity, short tempers, and hard-boiled Territorians. "Thank Christ I've still got enough cash left for a bus ticket back to Sydney. They can have this place. I'm out of here in the morning."

I envied her freedom of movement. By coming up to Darwin I'd painted myself into the same sort of corner I had in Longreach. The only way to continue west was to backpedal all the way to Katherine—a hot, sweaty, tedious, thundery, mosquito-infested torment I was not eager to repeat, even with the full weight of the coming monsoon to prod me along. Each morning with soap and a shower, each night of air-conditioned sleep further softened my resolve. Then, too, there was a sense of self-congratulation at having made it here. Darwin was the northernmost point on my journey—nearly 12 degrees south of the Equator—and I wanted time to savor my achievement. Having arrived late in the season, I felt the grudge of a climber who reaches the summit of Everest only to see a bank of ominous clouds on the horizon, and is obliged to turn around after a mere five minutes of enjoying the view he's struggled so hard to reach. And so I lingered, against my better judgment, hoping I might cadge a lift back to Katherine, but knowing I was going to have to get a move on soon regardless.

I was lucky. One of the world's quirkiest rallies, the Solar Challenge Car

Race, was about to set out from Darwin for Adelaide. There were about five dozen entries, ranging from the fabulously well-endowed Honda team—its sleek vehicle said to top 100 miles per hour—to backyard tinkerers who'd be lucky to make it out of Darwin. Northern Sun, a team from Montréal's McGill University, was staying at the youth hostel. They offered me a ride to Katherine in their support van. Because the race didn't start for a few days, I had the luxury to dawdle, relishing my morning showers and air-conditioned sleep.

With a ticket out of town, Darwin can be a nice place to linger—even during the Buildup. The city comes as a curious surprise to anyone who arrives expecting to find a brawling frontier settlement straight out of *Crocodile Dundee.* In truth, Darwin is perhaps the most suburban place in Australia—a cosmopolitan enclave of 80,000 that just happens to perch on a sweltering, far-flung peninsula. Most of its residents are public servants, administrators, and teachers working on two-year rotations. They push pens and work in modern air-conditioned offices, rather than wrestle buffalo or carve sunsets on one another's backs. They live in neat, rent-subsidized, brick-veneer homes—the sort you see in every middle-class suburb in Australia, within easy drive of the usual shopping malls, fast-food outlets, and multiscreen cinema complexes.

But the hot breath of frontier is never far away. The reason the city seems so new is that it is. Virtually blown off the map by tropical cyclone Tracy in 1974, Darwin had to be rebuilt almost from scratch. Again. Throughout its troubled 130-year history, Darwin has been periodically rubbed out and reconstructed half a dozen times; it has been leveled by cyclones, devoured by termites, and bombed by the Japanese during World War II. The Northern Territory's mangrove-fringed coast is as remote and untamed as ever; it just happens to have a crisp new city on it. For now.

While I was poking around Darwin, the solar-car teams spent the week laboring over their vehicles, polishing solar panels to a mirror finish, tinkering with generators, pecking mountains of weather data into laptop computers. All entrants had to pass a safety measure called the "Road Train Test." Because the race would take place on a public highway, the organizers wanted to make certain that the ultra-light, aerodynamic solar vehicles would not flip over in the slipstreams of passing road trains. So they simulated Stuart Highway conditions at a stock-car track just south of the city. Throughout the day the weird assortment of cars would speed, one at a time, toward a road train booming up the straightaway at 70 miles per hour, while officials studied the effects through binoculars and timed the cars with radar guns.

I rode out there midmorning and picked a good viewing spot on a knoll. Thousands had turned out to watch. Vendors made small fortunes selling meat pies, soft drinks, and ice cream. All the cars passed the test. In an unusually thrilling moment, a Japanese driver became confused about which lane he should be in and drove head-on—fearlessly—toward the road train, forcing the flabbergasted trucker to swerve his 100-ton juggernaut out of the way at the last second. Applause all around.

There was something endearing about the whole thing—the quirky vehicles, the friendly yet chauvinistic teams, the panoply of national flags, the picnic-day atmosphere, the bizarre road-train test—that made me feel as though we were living a script for *Those Daring Young Men in Their Jaunty Jalopies*.

SUNDAY WAS RACE DAY. A couple of guys from the McGill team rapped on my door at 3:30 a.m. I had lain awake most of the night, afraid that I would oversleep and miss my ride to Katherine. I splashed cold water on my face and gathered my saddlebags. It was pleasantly cool in the predawn darkness. A few morning stars shimmered. Soft sea breezes ruffled the palm fronds along the Esplanade, already bustling with red-eyed technicians making final preparations. Pole positions had gone to the Honda and Swiss Biel teams, whose multimillion-dollar, secrecy-shrouded vehicles were covered with sheets and cordoned off from prying fingers. Their jump-suited drivers did calisthenics and stretch-

PHOTOGRAPHS BY R. IAN LLOYD except bottom photo by Roff Smith

The remoteness of a Queensland sheep station spells togetherness, not loneliness, for outbackers such as grazier Rob Macintosh and his daughter Emily, seen here trooping back from the milking sheds.

A fly net is a familiar necessity in the outback. Its loose mesh fended off the bush flies that buzzed my head in search of moisture.

By the early light of dawn, Rob Macintosh scouts the olive-drab scrub for sheep before bringing them in for shearing. He runs a herd of 12,000 on his 42,000-acre property 20 miles northeast of Longreach.

This raging brush fire west of Halls Creek in the Kimberley was so intense I thought it would melt my scalp. By dry season's end, all it takes is a stray lightning bolt or cigarette butt to turn the outback into an inferno.

Togged in the latest NBA gear, kids hang out at the Bidyadanga Aboriginal Community in Western Australia. It was disconcerting to find that elements of American pop culture have seeped this far into Australia.

At the remote Sandfire Flat Roadhouse near the Great Sandy Desert, patrons tear off a shirt sleeve and attach it to the ceiling after donating money to the local air-ambulance service.

A fire brightens my bush camp a few hundred yards off the road. Cycling through searing heat by day was the purgatory I endured for the paradise of gazing at the stars by night.

Treading a sandy mirror, tourists on camelback soak up the scenery on Cable Beach near laid-back

Fruit pickers toss watermelons in the 106°F swelter of an irrigated field at Shamrock Station. "This is easier money and a lot more pleasant" than running cattle, says station owner and ex-rancher Jay Simms. "No watermelon ever stomped me into the dust."

Broome. Cameleer Laurie Argyle was leading the rides to earn money for a trip overseas.

Road signs on the Eyre Highway warn of wild critters ahead: camels, wombats, and kangaroos. The main link between Western and South Australia, the route runs 800 miles across the Nullarbor Plain, with only 11 roadhouses along the way.

A chef tends the grill at a winery on the Margaret River, where I joined vintner David Hohnen and some friends for a barbecue amid the grapevines. After too many roadhouse meals of moldy meat pies, I'd almost forgotten there were such things as grilled shellfish, fresh fruit, and Chardonnay—a handy instant marinade for these giant lobsters.

Made in the shade: South of Perth, I found myself rolling through the unthinkable—cool daytime shadows—cast by a forest of towering karri trees. The mottled giants are just one of the 500 species of eucalypts, or gum trees, found in Australia.

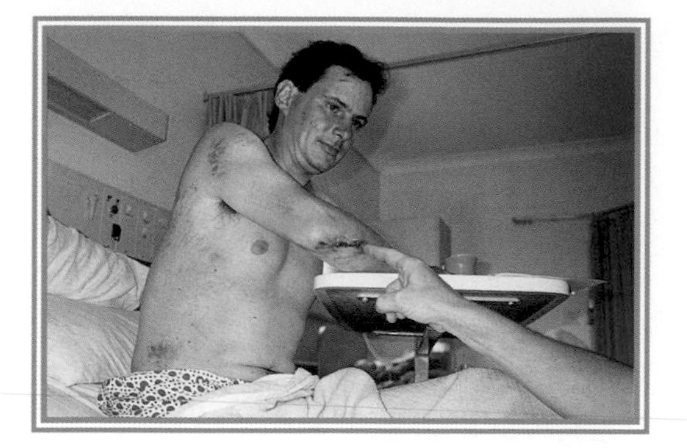

A vicious case of road rash—including this gash on my elbow, which took 12 stitches to close—landed me in the Margaret River District Hospital. I remember coasting downhill at 30 miles per hour, then suddenly realizing that the bloody heap sprawled on the pavement was me.

Ending where I began 10,000 miles before, I revel in some non-saddle time within sight of Sydney's Great Harbour Bridge.

ing exercises or talked world records to TV reporters. Montréal's Northern Sun, my adopted team, had a respectable position in the forward third of the pack.

By dawn, dense crowds thronged the barricades, and helicopters hovered in the thick, expectant air. The starter's gun went off at eight o'clock. Honda and Biel practically peeled out. The rest of the cars hummed and whirred gently to life, then rolled along the palm-fringed seafront, gathering speed, bound for Adelaide more than 2,000 miles away.

We bundled into the chase vehicle and tried to muscle our way through the traffic jam of support cars, press vehicles, race officials, and rubberneckers following the race out of town. We caught up with Northern Sun on the outskirts of Darwin and settled in behind it. There was no time for idle chatter. The team technicians hunched over their laptops, analyzing the car's performance, comparing data, scanning topographic maps of road and cloud conditions, and jabbering excitedly to one another in Québecois French and English. They constantly radioed instructions to the driver, cramped and sweltering under his plexiglass canopy in temperatures of 130°F. I slumped in my corner of the back seat—the heat, humidity, and early start had all taken their toll—and happily watched the highway slipping beneath me at an unaccustomed 35 miles an hour.

We reached Katherine a little before 3 p.m., with Northern Sun in 18th place out of 60 or so vehicles. This was an official checkpoint, so all the cars had to stop. While the team conferred with one another and with the race organizers, I hauled my bike and gear out of the van. Northern Sun made a driver change and whirred out of town in 17th position (a competitor had broken down in front of the newsagent's shop).

I stood on the sidewalk, dazedly watching them go. Then I gathered up my saddlebags, fastened them on the bike, and headed west out of town on the quiet and empty Victoria Highway, glad to be shedding the hoopla.

CHAPTER 21

Lost in the Labyrinth

IT WAS 97°F at eight o'clock in the morning when I pulled into the Victoria River Roadhouse to refill my water bottles. The place was quiet. Flies buzzed lazily in the heat. I stepped inside and treated myself to a cold carton of milk, a purchase that entitled me to a few minutes' air conditioning. I drank slowly, appreciatively, sitting at a table and feeling the heat radiate through the window. The glare outside was blinding.

I'd covered about 130 miles since leaving Katherine, and in that distance the landscape had undergone yet another dynamic change. The flat, tedious acacia scrub had ceded to the distinctive red-rock country of the Kimberley. This is the wildest and most ancient part of the continent: a forbidding labyrinth of billion-year-old mountain ranges, deep gorges, boab trees, and eerie, tiger-striped badlands known as the Bungle Bungles. Cut off from the rest of Australia by its remoteness and by the Great Sandy Desert stretching far to the south, the Kimberley has remained a world unto itself. Even today, in this ancient stony wilderness that is almost as big as Texas, only three settlements—Broome, Derby, and Kununurra—have populations greater than 2,000.

I was heading for Kununurra, a man-made oasis on the eastern fringe of the Kimberley, still a good 200 miles away. The sun was merciless. Daytime highs crept to 115°F, making the broken and blistered ironstone scattered on the hillsides too hot for sitting.

A few weeks from now, when the big rains came, this would all be transformed into a tropical rock garden: Cliff faces would become waterfalls, dusty riverbeds would turn into cataracts, and dense clumps of cane grass would sprout almost overnight from the cracked earth, growing 20 feet a month while the monsoons bucketed down. For now, however, there was nothing but mile after mile of dazzling sun, the ceaseless drone of the flies, and the slithering sound of my bicycle tires on the steamy asphalt.

By now I had traveled more than 4,000 miles since Sydney, the last 1,500 through barren scrub. Until I hit Katherine I had pretty much enjoyed it, finding a fierce and glorious independence in the vast sweep of country that continually spread out before me. There was something magical about breaking camp, then setting out down the highway light and swift and free each morning, that gave me the same jubilant satisfaction I used to feel as a kid when I skipped school to go fishing. But that brutal final push to Darwin had done something to me. The thrill was gone. It was as though the weight of the miles, the steamy heat, the crawling flies, the sleepless nights, and the perpetual motion had all crashed down on me at once.

The rest in Darwin had done me good, but after a few days back in the saddle I was tired and cranky again when I got up in the mornings. I pedaled down this steaming treadmill, as broody as the thermal clouds that tumbled overhead, surviving on warm water that tasted of melting plastic. I counted down the miles to Kununurra.

I crossed the boundary into Western Australia late on a thundery afternoon on my fourth day out of Katherine, stopping to pass the time with the quarantine officer who manned the border outpost. He seemed as lonely and eager to talk as I was.

That night I camped on a stony rise about 20 miles short of Kununurra, beneath a hazy blur of stars. A stray bolt of lightning had started a fire on a hillside a couple of miles east of me. It was Halloween. I sat up watching the evil orange flames lick the darkness.

CHAPTER 22

Watermelon Man

KUNUNURRA WAS DEAD QUIET when I rolled in a little before six o'clock in the morning. I bought a carton of flavored milk at the roadhouse and drank it on the curb while I waited for things to open up.

Forty years ago, this town did not exist. It came into being in 1961 as the product of an ambitious government scheme to tame the Kimberley by damming the 200-mile-long, north-flowing Ord River and using irrigation to turn desert into garden. After a rocky start, Kununurra bloomed into a prosperous community of 6,000. A major stop on the fruit-picking circuit, its caravan parks, campgrounds, and hostels are generally crowded with footloose laborers looking for ten dollars an hour.

I was lucky. Melon season was on the wane, and a lot of pickers had recently pulled up stakes and moved on to Broome or Carnarvon. I managed to land a bunk in the second hostel I tried—a drab, cinder-block barracks of a place set around a derelict school bus that somebody had painted a violent shade of purple. It was your basic doss house: Eight bunks to a room, a noisy, dripping air conditioner that ran only at night, a floor strewn with backpacks, and bunk frames festooned with yesterday's laundry. It was damp, dark, rank—and quiet. Everybody was working in the fields.

I took a shower, bought some groceries, and built myself a lunch of pasta, veggies, and fruit. By midafternoon the pickers were trickling back, drained and dirty. It had been 108°F in the shade that day, and sticky. I recognized a few faces from the seedy crowd at Katherine: a heavily tattooed South Australian named Gary, a German hippie named Christine, and a couple of hoons from New South Wales who had break-and-enter written all over them. And sink my putt if Joel wasn't there too—hard, bright, and cocky about eluding the Territory police. He bounced in with a slab of Victoria Bitter on his shoulder, spotted me, and flashed a cheesy grin of recognition.

I chained my bike in a steel shed and took a stroll around Kununurra's neatly planned streets, lined with frangipani trees and fiberboard houses. The Australian government had given these structures free of charge to anyone willing to move here when the town was founded 40 years ago.

Kununurra spills around the base of a rocky tor called Kelly's Knob. I found the trail leading to the top and made the steep and sweaty late-afternoon climb. Sunlight raked the town's corrugated-iron rooftops below and deepened the greens in the wide moat of sugarcane, melon fields, and mango plantations that surrounded it. Beyond those sharp, well-watered limits, however, lay only the parched desolation of the Kimberley, reddish-mauve, reaching out hundreds of miles in every direction.

Towering thunderheads the dusky color of grapes tumbled in the distance. As the evening gloom gathered, a few lights twinkled on, throwing the town's frightening isolation into even keener relief. Looking out from my rocky crag, I felt like a castaway who had washed up on a far-flung island after many days at sea. The low peals of thunder echoing over the desert reminded me that the wet season loomed—and that I still had many miles to go.

It rained hard several times during the few days I lingered in Kununurra—sudden, thundery cloudbursts that filled the gutters to overflowing and left the streets steaming as soon as the sun burned through again. One day I hiked through Hidden Valley National Park, an ancient labyrinth of blistered tiger-striped formations on the edge of town. I also made a side trip to the old port of Wyndham, on the ragged coast of Cambridge Gulf, about 60 miles to the northwest. Never in my life have I seen a more forbidding place—a cluster of iron shacks and a jetty, blocked off from the rest of the world by the stony shoulders of the Bastion Range and looking out on a vast, steamy sweep of crocodile-infested mangroves and tidal mud flats. The temperature was about 120°F, the noontime glare blinding. The view from the hilltops 1,000 feet above town was haunting, prehistoric: Five primordial rivers—the Ord, Pentecost, Durack, King, and Forrest—slithered through distant deltas before emptying sluggishly into the gulf. It was a scene from the dawn of time.

When I got back to Kununurra—it looked delightfully cosmopolitan after Wyndham—I decided to top up my finances with a little fruit picking. Supposedly the vines had been picked clean, but every morning farm trucks still swung around the hostel, harvesting workers. I got up before dawn the next morning and asked the driver if they could use an extra hand. He shrugged and said to climb aboard. There were about 20 of us, crammed in like refugees. A sticker on the cab's rear window read: "If you drink and drive, you're a bloody idiot. If you make it home alive, you're a legend."

It was about ten miles to the farm. Clear morning sunlight slanted across the fields, painting detail in the sugarcane and casting interesting shadows on the rocky pink mountains out in the desert. It was going to be another hot one—106°F or so, said the local forecast. The truck pulled up at a big corrugated-iron sorting shed, where forklifts were already shunting crates of melons and girls were sorting fruit at long tables. The girls in our truck spilled out to join them. That's the division of labor here: Women worked in the sheds, men in the fields.

A tractor pulled up, an empty wooden bin on its forked front loader. The driver—a chain-smoking hard case with a Mohawk haircut and wraparound mirror shades—yelled at us to climb aboard. We scrambled in; the tractor hoisted us up. We lurched and bounced into the melon patch, where the sun was starting to bite and the taste of dust hung in the air.

Ask anyone who's ever done it—picking melons under a summer sun is the sweatiest, dirtiest, most backbreaking work yet devised. On the other hand, compared with cycling through the Top End in the thundery heat of the Buildup, it was a doddle: A big plastic water cooler stood handy with a chunk of ice melting in it, a shower awaited me at the end of the day, and I was getting paid. I couldn't get the smile off my face.

We worked quickly and steadily, filling our buckets with not-yet-ripe melons, trotting behind the tractor that constantly prowled the rows of vines, and dumping the fruit—gently! gently!—in its big wooden bin. Once that was filled, the tractor lumbered off to the sorting shed and we rested on our overturned buckets until it returned.

Hours dragged by; the sun grew mighty. By ten o'clock I had settled into a dogged sort of rhythm, mentally spending the ten bucks an hour I was earning, when I came to the end of my row. I glanced up to see where I should pick next, and saw the older hands trudging toward the shed, empty buckets swinging from their fists. That was it—the last of the melons. We were now unemployed. The tractor driver loaded us into his melon bin like unwanted toy soldiers and carted us back to the shed. I hitched a ride back to town.

The next day was the Melbourne Cup—the horse race that stops a nation. For three minutes starting at 3:20 p.m. on the first Tuesday of every

November, Australia holds its breath while the nation's best stayers gallop two miles around the track at Flemington. Australians—inveterate gamblers and racehorse lovers—desert their city streets, fill every pub in the nation to bursting, or wait expectantly for airline pilots to announce the placings.

Having overlooked the two-hour time difference between Kununurra and Melbourne, I nearly missed post time and had to run to the pub. Inside it was crowded, noisy, and smoky—ideal conditions for watching the cup. A couple of drunks were getting the bum's rush when I arrived. I muscled my way through the mob, managed to place my bets, and ordered a beer. I was just in time; they were off. The cheering and shouting were deafening throughout but reached a crescendo on the final straightaway. My pick lumbered valiantly down the straight, a good 20 lengths separating it from second place and widening all the time—and about 25 lengths separating it from first. My record remained unblemished: 14 consecutive losing horses. I tore up my stubs on the way back to the hostel, my day's wages blown. Not disposed to wait around in Kununurra for the mangoes to ripen, I set out for Broome the next day.

CHAPTER 23

Life's a Beach

THE OLD PEARLING PORT of Broome, with its fresh sea breezes and its raffish tropical charm, was the first really attractive place I had come to since some of the pretty seaside villages on the Queensland coast. It sits on a stubby peninsula, looking onto the peacock-blue waters of the Timor Sea, its back turned resolutely to the searing desert that stretches out behind it. It was 90°F in Broome the day I arrived, but it felt pleasant after the insane temperatures in the desert, and the sunset breeze that sprang up off the ocean made the air feel almost brisk.

I sat that evening on a bluff overlooking Cable Beach—a stunning, 15-mile-long crescent of pure white sand along the coast north of town. It was nearly deserted, just a few beachcombers staring quietly out to sea, marveling as the sky shifted through a suite of pinks and mauves, eager to catch the green flash that occurs at the instant the sun disappears into the water. This atmospheric phenomenon—the briefest flicker of pure green light, usually observed from a ship at sea under perfect conditions—is so subtle and elusive you can't be sure you saw it. So you come back the next night, drawn by curiosity and the larger wonder of sitting on a silent beach at the edge of the world and watching a day slip into eternity. Maybe you'll glimpse the green flash, maybe you won't. During the ten days I stayed in Broome, I caught it four times.

Lingering was pressing my luck; sooner or later, I knew, the heavy rains would catch up to me. My radio had reported that it was bucketing down back in Kununurra, and parts of the Great Northern Highway—a ribbon of road stretching from Kununurra to Port Hedland—had flooded. It was only a matter of time before it started here. The afternoons were thundery and oppressive, with storm clouds boiling 40,000 feet above the sea and sheet lightning pulsing in the night. Locals spent their weekends clearing their yards of potential flying debris and nailing down loose bits of corrugated iron on their roofs. At a stall in front of the supermarket, emergency services personnel passed out what-to-do-in-a-cyclone pamphlets and blank maps, so people could plot the approach of any tropical cyclones and be aware of what was happening. It was coming.

But Broome was my ultimate prize, the most exotic, remote, and romantic of Australia's sunset ports. Getting here on a bicycle from Sydney was an accomplishment I wanted to savor. It wasn't just the 5,000 miles; coming here is like reaching another world. This is a steamy, ceiling-fan sort of place that belongs in a Joseph Conrad novel, more Asian than Australian, with its legacy of Japanese pearl divers, Malay seamen, Arab and Indian gem merchants, Chinese traders, Afghan camel drivers, and the seagoing riffraff from every seedy port in the Orient—almost anyone chasing fast money. Back in the 1920s a fleet of more than 400 pearling luggers operated in these waters, street signs had to be written in Chinese, Japanese, Arabic, and English, and the only regular contact with the rest of Australia was the steamer that puttered up the coast every six weeks.

The luggers are long gone, done in by the advent of the humble plastic button after World War II. Broome slid into a genteel decline until the 1980s, when paved roads and an airport capable of handling jets made it possible to holiday here, if you had the time and money. Even now getting here is no simple matter. It's easier and cheaper to fly to Hawaii. But where in modern Hawaii are you going to find an empty strand of fine white sand 15 miles long, let alone one with the unbuttoned easiness of the Australian outback? This is a town where you can buy a $200,000 string of perfectly matched pearls in the showroom at Paspaley Pearls on Carnarvon Street, or walk around the corner and grab a beer at the Roebuck Hotel—a rough-as-guts pub straight out of *Crocodile Dundee*, where a notice tacked by the door forbids fighting, throwing furniture, begging for liquor, or "urinating outside the toilets provided."

For me the town felt homey, too. I couldn't walk down Carnarvon Street without seeing a familiar face, members of the community of drifters who were sliding down the coast. As they said about Rick's seedy Café Americaine in Casablanca, everybody comes to Broome. There was Gary, a mechanic I'd met up in Kununurra, and Bernadette, a pastry chef from Perth who was looking for work as a cook on one of the outlying cattle stations. Ian and Jennifer, a couple I'd met on the road several times since Katherine, were also in town. One evening I looked up to see Joel checking into the hostel, still on the dodge, a slab of Emu Bitter on his shoulder. He flashed me another conspiratorial grin. It was like running into my neighbors.

There were others there too, people who had come to rest in Broome and—like me—hesitated to move on. There was a pleasant, middle-aged Swedish woman named Li, no fixed address, who graciously parried any questions about her past. And Tony, a lean and leathery 50-something with a shock of gray hair and heavily callused feet, who spent his days drinking coffee and smoking endless roll-your-owns ("Keeps me young and handsome!"), eyes peeled for his next job. There was Tanami, a girl from Perth, who worked as a cook on a pearling boat, and Jela and Helen, two girls from inner-city Melbourne who were figuring out their next move, and a high-spirited Dutchman named Perry.

Life was pleasant. Money was no problem. There were plenty of casual odd jobs floating around. Gary and I teamed up to unload trucks by the depot. Once we delivered a load of hay for Allison, a cameleer who ran sunset camel rides for tourists along Cable Beach. The object was to earn just enough to cover costs. The rest of the day was spent lounging around: reading in the shade, taking long walks on the beach, going for afternoon swims in water as warm as a bath. This was low season on the tourist calendar, and at times the beach was deserted. On the busiest day, I counted 34 people and half a dozen striped umbrellas.

Some nights a group of us would go into town to the Sun Picture Gardens, the world's oldest outdoor movie theater, built by pearling master Ted Hunter in 1916. It hasn't changed much since the days the first talkies were shown. You still sit on canvas slings, eating popcorn and watching the film on a screen framed by palm fronds, ignoring the croaking frogs and the occasional fruit bat that flutters in front of the picture. On Saturday night a group of us watched Mae West and W. C. Fields in *My Little Chickadee*, then walked the three miles back to the hostel. We followed the beach, listening to the hollow boom of the rollers. The night was warm and clear, the tide was up, and the moon cast razor-sharp shadows. Take it from me: Broome was a good place to be.

MAKING IT LOOK PARTICULARLY GOOD was the fact that south of here the road ran through the Great Sandy Desert—more than 400 waterless miles to Port Hedland. It looked bad enough on my road map: a thin line through a white void, with nothing along it but the Sandfire Flat Roadhouse until you reached Port Hedland, a hard-fisted iron-ore port sweltering on the Indian Ocean. Locals assured me the desert was much worse than it looked. We were coming into high summer now, when desert temperatures could easily top 140°F in the direct sun. There was little shade to be found anywhere, and no water—just burning sand and scrub and spinifex for hundreds of miles. People urged me not to risk it; to put my bike on the daily bus that ran to Port Hedland.

I had no intention of doing that, and explained that I was well used to desert travel—as indeed I was—but inside I felt a lot of misgivings. The crossing to Port Hedland was by far the most godforsaken stretch of highway I would see on my whole journey, and I was approaching it at the most dangerous time of year.

I left Broome on a hot and thundery afternoon, the sky a jumble of gray, black, and mauve thunderheads, the air dead and sticky, the light flat. I had inspected my bike carefully, stashed five days' worth of food in my panniers, and tanked up with water. Having just bought an insulated six-liter container in Broome, I was now carrying 22 liters. The bike was so heavy—80 pounds, all told—that the tires looked flat even before I saddled up.

My plan was to get as far as I could that afternoon, riding into the relative cool of the evening, then get up early and ride as hard as I could the next morning, gaining as many miles as possible before the heat grew too intense. I thought I might be lucky. Although people in Broome continually insisted "there's nothing out there, mate," I had come across a large-scale pastoral map in town that showed a couple of cattle stations in the desert—Nita Downs and Shamrock—both seemingly fairly close to the highway. Nita Downs, I soon learned, had burned to the ground a couple of summers ago, when a dry-season lightning strike sparked a blaze that torched more than 200,000 acres of tinder-dry scrub. But there was an answer when I dialed the number for Shamrock, where a man named Jay Simms said I could stop by for water. Shamrock was 100 miles away.

I made good time, cruising out of Broome at a steady 16 miles an hour despite the heavy freight on my bicycle. Just past the Roebuck Roadhouse the highway forks, one branch heading back east across the Kimberley, the other dropping down through the lonely expanse of the Great Sandy Desert. I turned right and began the long grind toward Port Hedland.

Twenty-five miles later, with the sun setting in a ball of flame and shadows creeping across the desert, my shifter cable began to jump, then the chain slid down onto the rear cogset's smallest gear. Glancing down, I saw the cable dangling loose. The anchor bolt—the same one that had broken back in Ravenshoe—had snapped again. I was stuck in the hardest gear, with Port Hedland more than 350 miles away. After a few moments' slow burn, I turned around and began a sullen plod back to Broome, doubly irritated because, having built myself up to make the desert crossing, I was anxious to get on with it.

Darkness soon overtook me and, with apologies to Edward Bulwer-Lytton, it was indeed a dark and stormy night. Lightning hissed and crackled, shooting across the sky from horizon to horizon. Thunder boomed. I could feel the reverberations in my rib cage, and the constant flashes of lightning painted the clouds a dingy yellow, like the smoke from so many cannon. No rain fell, but the atmosphere was absurdly theatrical, matching the overblown drama I'd concocted about this desert crossing and the "tragedy" of my broken anchor bolt. I felt a bit like God was sending me up, casting me as a comic hero in a spoof of a Wagnerian opera. I lacked only horns for my helmet. It was so over the top that after a few miles I found myself laughing out loud.

There was no way I was going to make it back to Broome that night, so I pulled over and made a quick bivouac in the scrub. But the fates weren't done with me. I fell asleep to the sound of thunder but woke several hours later, hearing voices in the bush—very close by. I sat up cautiously, peering over the top of the grass, and saw a family of Aborigines making camp by the light of the headlights in their four-wheel-drive. They must have come in from one of the remote communities, gotten tired of driving, and pulled over here. They were only a few feet away, but in the darkness they couldn't see me. I lay still so as not to startle them. After a few minutes they switched off their lights. We all settled down. Then, a few minutes later, the old man started snoring. Loud. I began to laugh. I could hardly contain myself: the absurd dramatics of the storm and now, with a couple of hundred thousand square miles of silent West Australian desert all around me, I wind up beside a guy who snores like a grampus.

I rolled back into Broome around seven o'clock the next morning, stiff and damp and glum. The Kimberley Bakery was just opening. I ordered a meat pie and a doughnut, to which the cheerful woman behind the counter added a sweet roll, a bag of fruit slices, and a steaming mug of coffee—then refused to take any money. This unexpected act of kindness, coupled with the fresh-baked goodies and hot coffee, cheered me. The world seemed a better place, and Broome already suited me anyway. I sat at a plastic chair and table on the sidewalk, eating my breakfast and watching the town wake up.

When the businesses opened around nine o'clock, I hunted up a bicycle shop and ordered a replacement bolt. It would have to be flown up from Perth—three days, the man said. I rode back to the hostel and reclaimed my old room, grumbling a bit about broken bits and delays, but quite content that evening to sit on my knoll overlooking the beach, a sea breeze fanning my face, and watch another sunset.

CHAPTER 24

Father Matt of Bidyadanga

IT WAS TEN O'CLOCK in the morning and already the battered thermometer hanging in the shade of one of the trees at Shamrock Station read 102°F. I had left Broome on my newly repaired bicycle the previous afternoon, camped 40 miles south of town, then ridden hard since before dawn to get to the old cattle station before the sun really started to bite. The bike was shifting smoothly and traveling well. It was a relief to be confronting this feared desolation at last.

And odd, too. When I broke camp that morning, it had seemed like any other prosaic length of highway—something that came as a mild surprise to me, having inflated this Broome-to-Port Hedland leg into a trail of bleached bones. Of course, when you view the world from a bicycle saddle, your horizon is only a couple of miles away. The fact that you're on a waterless crossing of 400 miles recedes to an abstraction. It's better that way.

But as tedious hours passed and the heat-warped horizon stayed as elusive as ever, it was hard not to project it forward several long, thirsty days. The sun climbed higher into a brassy sky, the temperatures soared, and I felt like I was riding through a furnace. I rode almost ten miles on my first liter of water, six miles on my second, and was gulping down a liter every three miles by the time I reached the turnoff for Shamrock Station, almost 60 miles down the road from my camp. A minute later I was thirsty again, as if I hadn't touched a drop all week. My face was flushed, my temples throbbed, and my throat felt as dry and cracked as an outback riverbed.

The track that led to the homestead was deep in soft, hot sand. There was no riding through that. I had to get off and push. The bike kept sliding out from under me, the front wheel lurching in the mushy sand. That quarter-mile trudge to the shed was some of the hardest, hottest work I did all morning. By the time I stepped into the dusty clearing, my legs were wobbly and my calves felt like rubber. A few station hands, smoking in the shade of a corrugated-iron shed, looked up and stared. A big, gruff man in worn and sweaty khaki came over and introduced himself as Jay Simms, owner of Shamrock and the man I'd spoken with on the phone. His accent had surprised me then, so I asked him about it now: He was a New Mexico cattleman who had come out here in 1968 "because it was the farthest and loneliest place I could think of where they still spoke English."

He invited me into the shed, cool and dim after the glare outside, and pointed out a huge plastic water cooler on the table. "Help yourself, there's plenty." I unhooked my pannikin from my saddlebag and scooped up great mouthfuls of water, so icy cold and delicious I could have cried. It stung my throat. I drank some more, then wetted my bandanna to try to cool my head. I slumped onto the rough wooden bench and looked outside into the dazzling glare, humming with flies.

Jay returned a moment later, sat down at a rough-hewn table, and resumed making calculations in a well-thumbed ledger. Although he came from a long line of cattlemen dating back to the 1880s range wars and Billy the Kid, here in the Great Sandy Desert he was counting watermelons, not cattle. Jay had discovered water beneath the sands on his property; with a bit of outback ingenuity and initiative, he had decided to try his hand at horticulture in the desert, plowing furrows and rolling out cheap plastic irrigation hose. It worked. "It's like hydroponic farming," he explained. "The sand just supports the roots, while we pour on the fertilizer and water."

Every day a road train pulls up to this shed to haul a load of watermelons or sweet potatoes to Perth. "We're the loneliest market gardeners in the world," Jay boasted. "Our watermelons come on ahead of everybody else's, and for a few weeks around Christmas we pretty well have the Perth market to ourselves. I still run cattle, but this is easier money and a lot more pleasant—no watermelon ever stomped me into the dust."

Jay's partner in the horticulture business was a Roman Catholic lay missionary named Danny Fyffe, who had come up from Melbourne a few years earlier to help out at the Bidyadanga Aboriginal Community about 40 miles away. "It's an interesting place," Fyffe told me. "I know the missionary there. If you like, I'll call up Father Matt and see if he can put you up for a few days."

Father Matt and the community elders were agreeable. Father Matt told me to meet him at the Bidyadanga turnoff, about 12 miles farther down the road, around sundown.

FATHER MATT—Japulu, or "spiritual leader" to the Karrajarri people—was a sandy-haired, athletic-looking man in his early 30s who originally came from New South Wales. It was dark when we pulled into the mission compound, the warm tropical air thick with insects. "Want to know how remote we are out here?" Father Matt laughed as he led me into his study. He pointed to a framed photo of a younger self meeting Pope John

Paul II during a papal visit to Sydney. "Some of the guys here saw that and wanted to know who was the bloke talking to Japulu."

We had dinner of pasta and tea. Greg, an old high-school mate of Father Matt's, was there. He'd come up to visit for a few weeks after quitting a job in the gold mines down in Kalgoorlie. He and Matt had been preparing the compound for the coming cyclone season, nailing down loose iron roofs, boarding up windows, picking up any debris that might become lethal missiles in 150-mile-an-hour gusts.

A line of transportable workers' shacks stood on the opposite side of the mission compound. Greg and I had one each—a bunk, a dresser, and a noisy but efficient air conditioner. The three of us sat up until midnight, talking about everything from cycling to cyclones to Greg's stories from the goldfields to the days when farmers and graziers were the wealthiest members of Australian society. When it was time to go, Matt handed me a flashlight. "Shine it everywhere you go. There are a lot of death adders in the dust around here. I've even had a couple on my veranda. It wouldn't do to step on one."

"Excuse me Father, but before I go, am I in a state of grace?"

He laughed. "You're in the state of Western Australia."

I walked gingerly, as though traversing a minefield—not a bad analogy as far as death adders are concerned. Shy and small, they nestle in the sand, wiggling the tips of their tails to mimic worms and fatally attract birds. You can step right beside a death adder and it won't move a muscle, but tread on one and it'll spring up like an antipersonnel mine. A cattleman once told me that a typical death-adder bite isn't on the ankle, as you might expect, but well up on the thigh. I got to my shack without seeing anything more vicious than a venomous centipede—nasty enough—and flicked on the air conditioner, grateful for the turn of fortune that had brought me here instead of to some sweltering camp in the bush.

MATT TOOK ME AROUND to meet the community leaders the next morning after breakfast. We sat on the veranda of John Hopiga's house. He was a wiry and active man who looked to be in his 40s—an age that, sadly enough, qualifies him as an elder among Aboriginal people. John had alert eyes, a hospitable manner, and a quick sense of humor. He spelled out the sacred places around the community—usually trees or rocks—where I was not permitted to wander (some of which even he, as a man, could not visit) and told me just to ask someone if ever I was in doubt.

I liked the Aborigines. It was nice to be among people who understood intuitively what I was trying to accomplish in my slow journey around Australia. No Aborigine ever said it was harebrained to tackle the outback alone and on a bicycle, or delivered long-winded lectures about how vast the distances were, how hot the heat could be, or how big and aggressive the road trains were. They thought it was a fine thing for a man to spend a few months wandering the countryside. On foot, on a bicycle—it didn't matter. Sympathy for the land was what counted. How different from white Australia, where passersby often felt it their bounden duty to point out my pigheaded foolery in traveling through the outback on nothing better than a bicycle. Inevitably the phrase "It's a big country" would pop up, delivered in a wise and lofty tone, as though I had yet to figure out that Australia was big despite four months of cycling around it. None of these doomsayers ever asked what preparations I had made or how much water I carried—nor would they have recognized sensible answers to those questions.

For that matter, no Aborigine ever demanded money for water, as would occur to me at a few roadhouses along the way. If a vehicle full of Aborigines happened down the road, they invariably stopped for a chat and asked if I'd like my water bottles topped up. It was a social occasion, usually with a slew of kids playing in the scrub, joyful at briefly escaping the confines of back seat or flatbed. Their parents would tell me about the country I was riding through,

I'd tell them about some of the places I'd seen, we'd have a bit of a laugh. Nobody was in any hurry to get anywhere or do anything.

As I traveled slowly through their ancient land, sleeping each night under an eternity of stars, I grew to appreciate the Aborigines' relaxed approach to time. It is probably the sharpest division that exists between our cultures. Most of us spend our lives marching in quiet desperation to the ticking of clocks, marking appointments and deadlines in calendars, and rushing to be on time for them. We spend fortunes on Palm Pilots and Filofaxes, develop ever-faster computer chips, and devote countless billions to correct Y2K problems that impishly fail to materialize.

Aborigines long ago adopted, in everyday life, Albert Einstein's simplest yet most profound theorem: All time is now. The unassailable philosophical common sense of this can be infuriating to those who live by the clock—and, of course, it's not terribly practical when it comes to running a business. But the more I traveled the outback, setting my days by the sun and the stars, the more I found myself living each moment as it came.

AS FAR AS MY PRESENCE in Bidyadanga went, the locals regarded me with a mixture of curiosity and good-natured tolerance. Japulu's friend—he must be okay. The town itself was a scattering of concrete houses and corrugated-iron sheds in the dusty glare near La Grange Bay, where the Great Sandy Desert abruptly meets the waters of the Indian Ocean. About 600 people from several different tribes live here. Despite the mix of clans, it is a relaxed and gregarious place, noisy with barking dogs, rough-running cars, laughter and quarrels. Life is lived in the open, in the shade of mango trees or in dusty front yards. Doors are left wide open. Everyone drags their beds and chairs and tables outside. Television screens glow in the twilight as families and friends gather to watch a movie or football match by satellite.

At Sunday Mass I was privileged to share a hymnal with a distinguished gentleman named John Dodo, at 86 the oldest person in the community and one of the last repositories of Karrajarri culture. He was a distinguished-looking man, with a wise face and a flowing, cottony beard. He spoke several Aboriginal languages, as well as English and Latin, which he'd learned from missionaries long ago. Mass was sung that day in his native Karrajarri, a soft, musical tongue that sounds vaguely Italian. A good crowd turned up. Ceiling fans swirled the heavy air, a few dogs wandered in to sleep on the cool concrete floor, toddlers played on their mothers' laps. The altar was elaborately decorated in mother-of-pearl. I thought of John Hopiga's stories of how, in the old days, Aborigines regarded pearls merely as curios—pretty baubles given up by the sea for the amusement of children.

After the service John Dodo and I stood talking in the churchyard. He was happy to discuss events of the day, or a few generalities about Aboriginal politics, but if we strayed into the deeper waters of the Karrajarris' relationship with the land, he graciously but firmly steered the conversation back to the shallow end. John Dodo had a subtle sense of humor. When I commented that everyone had been warning me about the death adders around the place, but that I hadn't seen any yet, his face crinkled in a gentle smile: "That's just it. You never do."

Standing beside me, deep in worried conversation with Matt, was another elder named Joe Roe. A few weeks earlier, some unscrupulous fossil collectors had stolen a beautifully preserved *Stegosaurus* footprint near Broome, sawing it out of the bedrock one night and spiriting it away—probably to Japan or North America, where it would be worth a fortune. Joe was worried sick about its loss. The particular patch of land from which the footprint had been stolen was his family's Dreamtime responsibility. To Joe this was no vulgar theft or irritating inconvenience, as the unauthorized taking of someone's Toyota would have been. The disfigurement of the rock and the loss of the footprint were sacrilege, carrying the prospect of cosmic retribution for contravening the ancient laws. Joe Roe was a worried man, unswayed by Father Matt's reassurance that it wasn't his fault. (I hoped that whoever now had the footprint was enjoying all the luck of the Hope Diamond.)

There are not many elders like John Dodo or Joe Roe left. The kids at Bidyadanga seem to drift in a sea of borrowed American pop culture. As an expatriate, it was unsettling to see Aborigine teenagers, some bearing the scars of ancient initiation rites, hanging out at the basketball court, decked out in NBA gear, Nike runners, and baseball caps. (For some reason the girls all favor the Charlotte Hornets, whereas the guys invariably go for the Chicago Bulls.) When they heard I was an American, the questions came thick and fast: "Hey, man, do you know Michael Jordan? What about Shaquille O'Neal? Ever been to Hollywood?" And my favorite: "Ever gone out with Pamela Anderson?" ("Of course," I joked, "but we broke up: She wanted me only for my body.")

This was the first time I had stayed in an Aboriginal community. It's one thing to read about the poverty and the killing diet of cigarettes and alcohol that takes its toll on Australia's indigenous people. It's quite another to walk through a weedy graveyard in this far corner of the outback, as I did one afternoon, reading birth dates such as 1969, 1972, or 1977 on forgotten concrete crosses already crumbling in the tropical heat.

CHAPTER 25

I Love a Sunburnt Station

I SPENT FOUR DAYS at Bidyadanga, setting off on the fifth morning with a lunch of cheese-and-mustard sandwiches and a few liters of fresh cold water. I wasn't going very far—just to Shelamar Station, about 40 miles away. Shelamar wasn't on my map. I hadn't even heard of it until a couple of nights earlier, when Father Matt had Jack and Jean Elezovich over to dinner. (Out here, a 40-mile drive through the scrub makes you next-door neighbors.) Over a dinner of desert-raised beef and sweet potatoes, the Elezovichs invited me to stop by their place on my way south.

I was glad I didn't have far to go. The highway was deathly still, heat dancing on the shimmering horizon. Low, flat, dusty scrub stretched off for untold miles along either side of the road. Nothing moved, not even birds. Once a car went by, a battered two-tone Holden crammed with Aborigines from Bidyadanga on their way to visit families near Port Hedland. They tooted and waved—I shook my head to indicate I didn't need water—and they swept by.

The hum of their tires on hot asphalt faded in the distance. After that the only sound was the rhythmic creak of my bicycle chain, now much in need of lubrication. When I stopped to drink, about ten miles farther down the track, I noticed my water bottles were already heating up. A roasting headwind kicked up early in the afternoon and slowed me to a crawl.

I got a glimpse of the homestead, shimmering in the heat, from the top of a rise. It looked tantalizingly close. I lost sight of it on the flat, then pedaled on for a couple of long, dreary miles until I decided I must have ridden past the turnoff. Then I spied a tiny black dot up ahead, most likely a mail drum. I wondered if my computer-strained eyes of a few months ago could have picked it out in the glare. It was indeed a mail drum, with a sign beside it reading "Shelamar."

FROM THE TURNOFF to the homestead was more than a mile, and once again I had to walk the bike through deep, hot sand. I met a road train coming out, a boiling cloud of red dust in its wake. The Elezovichs—the first to discover underground water in the Great Sandy Desert—now shipped daily loads of desert-grown sweet potatoes and watermelons to Perth.

Jack and Jean had used some of their aquifer to pretty up the homestead. They had a small, neat lawn trimmed with beds of Madagascar periwinkles; an in-ground swimming pool shimmered in the backyard. It was weird to stand beside the pool, or walk along the edge of the shimmering green watermelon patch, and look out on the thorny scrub, spinifex, and reddish desert sand that started just a few feet away and stretched to the horizon.

I spent several days at Shelamar, helping out in the shed, sorting sweet potatoes and boxing them on pallets for the morning road-train pickups. There were five of us: Jack and Jean, their two station hands, Greg and Mark, and myself. The days started a little after five with a breakfast of stew, hash browns, coffee, and bread, and they finished after sundown with a few cold beers. Although Jack had spent much of his 50-odd years working cattle in the Kimberley, he had grown up on a farm in the Swan Valley, not far from Perth. Farming was in his blood, so when he found water on his property he was delighted to start working its sandy soil.

Jack's family had come to Australia by ship in 1921, emigrating from a little island off the Dalmatian Coast on the Adriatic Sea. He liked to tell the story of how his father had gone back to visit the old country a few years ago; like many of those who had moved away, Jack's father took the opportunity to crow a bit about how well his children had done. A little exaggeration in this regard was expected, even tolerated. But when the old man said his son in Australia owned a cattle ranch of more than half a million acres—larger than their entire island—the little family gathering grew restive. Finally an uncle shook his head and broke the silence: We never thought you would lie to us.

Now that he was getting on in years, Jack was ready to quit. Shelamar was up for sale. He fancied buying a caravan and gypsying around Australia, living simply and earning a bit of extra money by picking fruit. "My dream is to find someplace I can pick cherries. I would love that: to pick cherries all day and eat as many as I like. That would be enough for me."

One evening John Stoate stopped by for dinner. He was the manager and part owner of the secluded million-acre Anna Plains cattle station, a little farther south in the desert. A soft-spoken cattleman in his 50s, Stoate was an old-school grazier who exuded a dignified reserve that put folks on their best manners—but pleasantly so. He invited me to drop in on Anna Plains: "Tell me what time you'll be coming by the gate and I'll have someone meet you."

A couple of days later I set off, fortified with a lunch Jean had prepared for me: salt beef, pickles, and homemade bread. Twenty miles down the highway, I reached the Anna Plains gate. Geoffrey Klunder, the station's windmill man, was there. He was a sunburned, laconic man in his 50s—high, hard cheekbones, strong handshake—who used to run logistics for oil-exploration teams in the desert. He took me up to the homestead, a prosperous place set in a landscaped compound of maintenance sheds and workers' shacks and flaming poinciana trees. I slung my gear in one of the guest cottages and went out with Geoff on his bore run.

The windmill man is a key figure on a big outback spread. There were 20,000 Brahman cattle scattered across Anna Plains' 1,600 square miles of pindan, Buffell grass, spinifex, and dunes, and all of them needed reliable water to survive. The series of bores, tanks, pumps, and troughs had to be continuously checked and maintained, not to mention the 600 miles of fencing that needed regular patrolling. Being the windmill man out here meant making a lurching, lonely, 300-mile circuit, mostly on deep, sandy tracks and in low-range four-wheel-drive. Geoff had to do it every other day, stopping to make repairs and casting an eye over the herds. Dozens of bores dotted the property; to keep them straight they had been given names, such as Top Tank, Curly, Bluey, and McPhee. "In the early days this was all done on horseback," Geoff explained. "The bore riders lived in lonely camps and often went weeks without seeing anybody."

It must have been like living on the floor of hell. The heat and desolation out here were beyond belief, even to someone who had cycled all the way from Sydney. I can't imagine what the temperature reached on the hotter, flatter parts of that station. Sometimes I'd look out toward a distant horizon, watery with mirage, and see what I thought was a small town: a strange-looking row of tall, narrow buildings in various shades of black, white, and brown. As we rumbled over the hardscrabble terrain, these "shacks" would float and waver in and out of focus until at last I decided they must be something else—a line of dish antennas for some far-flung Telecom outpost, perhaps. Then, as we drew nearer still, the shimmering objects would suddenly resolve into their true shape and scale: gaunt cattle, all ribs and shoulder blades, gathered in the dust around a lonely Southern Cross windmill creaking rhythmically in the desert heat. After the dust settled, we'd climb out of the truck, into the sickening heat, and inspect the windmill, the pump, and the water level in the trough. Then back into the truck for the long, grinding drive to the next water hole.

On the way back to the homestead late that afternoon, Geoff took a detour to show me the ruins of Telgarno. The British government had built this top-secret tracking station in 1959, during the chilliest days of the Cold War, as part of the hush-hush testing for its *Bluestreak* ICBM. The idea was to launch the new missile from the sensitive Woomera Rocket base in South Australia, then track it 2,200 miles across the loneliest deserts in Australia to a splashdown in the Indian Ocean, just off the West Australian coast.

But the project had been abandoned, and the well-hidden tracking station was never used. Some of Telgarno's buildings were torn down; others were left to rot under the tropical sun and monsoon rains. Today they look like something out of an *X-Files* nightmare: creepy, overgrown, concrete structures, with heavy iron security doors and rusted strands of barbed wire. They were damp inside, their dark recesses havens for scores of large green frogs waiting patiently for the coming wet season.

AT THE END OF THE DAY, the half-dozen or so ringers who worked on Anna Plains usually gathered at the Leisure Bar, a jumble of old yard furniture scattered around a tree near the transportable shacks that served as quarters. We sipped cans of Emu Bitters and talked until dinner. The ringers were smallish, tough, and lean, hard-living country-bred guys in their 20s who had started working for a living when they were about 12 or 14 and got away with it because they were hard for their age. They worked long, dangerous, lonely hours; every six weeks they got a three-day weekend in town.

The outback is a surprisingly small and constantly shifting world. As we talked, I realized that we knew, or had met, a fair few people in common: graziers, ringers, publicans, or shearers on stations or in small towns scattered across the country. One of the guys, Conrad, had done some shearing once for the MacIntoshes back at Fairfield. A couple of us grumbled about the ill-tempered publican at Currabubula. Another fellow knew Sherry Vincent, the mural artist I'd met on the Atherton Tableland; he hadn't seen her in many years and wondered how she was getting on. I passed along the news.

The cook was a touchy New Zealander named Peter, who didn't like to be disturbed until he clanged us to time with his iron triangle. The mess was a couple of long wooden benches beneath the corrugated-iron roof of a lean-to, with a television high on a wooden shelf. Meals were long on meat—steaks, roast beef, sausages, chicken. Afterward some of the guys watched an old war movie on TV. Conrad and Yuppie drifted over to the corral, where they fooled around with breaking in a skittish new colt named Mustang. I sat on the top rail and watched. Dusk fell. Cattle lowed in the distance and the crickets began to chirp.

I spent three days at Anna Plains, mostly making bore runs, which meant I got to see a lot of the property—and, since I was riding shotgun, to open a lot of fiddly gates. We'd start off at dawn, after a hot, meaty breakfast in the mess, filling up the water jugs and packing any tools or parts Geoff was likely to need for repairs. There was no coming back to the homestead—some of the bores were 80 miles away. The days were filled with intense heat, dust, and those apocalyptic mirages of the cattle gathered around the windmills. Sometimes we saw wild camels trotting through the scrub.

Anna Plains' western boundary was the Indian Ocean, and once we drove down onto the beach, the longest and loneliest strand I have ever seen: 90 miles of clean white sand with nary a footprint on it, other than those of the sea turtles who breed there. Another time we drove up a rocky promontory called Mount Phire, a steep and tortuous drive, and looked out upon the frightening immensity of red dunes and spinifex of the Great Sandy

Desert. We spotted a tiny smudge on the distant horizon: almost certainly Conrad and Yuppie driving out to repair a line of fence.

MY LAST NIGHT at Anna Plains, John Stoate and I shared a bottle of good red wine, some port, coffee, and chocolate up at his quarters. Stoate's quiet dignity, straight-from-the-shoulder manner, and stern, paternal competence reminded me of Ben Cartwright on *Bonanza.* He created a sense of being in command of every square inch of Anna Plains' million acres. He had been a cattleman all his life, and what he didn't know about beef wasn't worth knowing. But like a lot of Australia's old-school graziers, beef was not all he knew. Stoate was a widower now, but earlier he and his wife had traveled the world. His conversation flitted between fine wine, observations Plato had made about life, and his admiration for the architecture of a cathedral in the Dalmatian coastal city of Split.

When we got to music—swing-era jazz, specifically—Stoate really hit his stride. The albums came out in plenty: "Oh, you've got to hear this one!" Benny Goodman and Glenn Miller, the March of the Bob Cats, Big Noise from Winnetka. We sat up late listening to records and drinking port. When I stepped outside and walked across the compound beneath a sky sparkling with stars, I laughed to myself to think how much I had dreaded crossing the Great Sandy Desert.

That was my last laugh for a while. I set out the next morning for Port Hedland, 200 miles across the desert. Yuppie did the bore run that morning. He dropped me off at the Sandfire Flat Roadhouse, beside the property's southern gate.

I LEFT SANDFIRE FLAT a little after eight, tooling down the empty highway, whistling Big Noise from Winnetka, having already forgotten how quickly the sun can rear up and bite when you're pedaling a bicycle out here.

I'd left Broome almost two weeks ago. Until I departed Anna Plains, the biggest threat I'd faced so far in the Great Sandy Desert was high cholesterol from too much good living. In what must have been a cycling first, I had joked to John the previous night, I was crossing one of Australia's most forbidding deserts in high summer and gaining weight in the process.

As the miles passed and the sun crept higher, the joke faded. I wasn't thinking of Big Noise from Winnetka any more; now it was the Anvil Chorus—and not the bouncing Glenn Miller arrangement that John had played for me, but the slow hammer-and-tongs Verdi had in mind when he wrote the piece. A hot, nagging wind had kicked up out of the southwest, slowing me down. I shifted into a lower gear and pedaled on. My legs were jelly. My throat burned.

The heat was insane. I was gulping down a liter of water every three miles—a rate that would leave me high and deathly dry long before I reached Pardoo Roadhouse, 85 miles distant. I crested a low, scrubby rise and looked ahead: The straightaway before me fluttered in the shimmering heat like a series of vague black pennants. It was as though five or six phantom highways had been piled one on top of another. I was on the highway to hell.

I pulled over and found a tiny patch of shade near a clump of spinifex. There was a nest of beef ants there, but it was so hot and miserable that even they were taking the afternoon off. I fell asleep, waking up hours later when the daily bus from Broome to Port Hedland whizzed by. I rubbed my eyes and looked around. The light was much softer now; the heat had broken. The highway looked almost solid enough to ride on. I opened another bottle of water and broke out the brace of sandwiches that Peter had cut for me that morning. I set off half an hour later, riding into the shank of the afternoon, feeling fit again, and whistling Big Noise from Winnetka.

CHAPTER 26

Death March to DeGrey River

I MADE THE PARDOO ROADHOUSE just before six in the morning, having camped in the scrub a few miles east of it the night before. The place was dead quiet. Huge old mining trucks from the abandoned Goldsworthy Iron Mine rusted in the sun and weeds. A sign on a gate—"Protected by Guard Dogs"—warned off potential trespassers, but the fence was broken. Maybe the dogs had run away. I wished them luck.

The roadhouse opened at six. I bought a meat pie and some coffee and lingered inside, grateful to escape the flies. I hadn't planned to go far that morning. I'd heard back at Anna Plains that there was water in the DeGrey River—about 40 miles farther down the track—and figured I'd hole up there during the worst of the day's heat. There would be trees for shade and water to drink. So I dawdled at the roadhouse until 8:30.

Big mistake. The 40 miles to the DeGrey River were a nightmare.

It was 106°F in the shade when I left Pardoo, and the sun hadn't even grabbed hold yet. The wind sprang up, holding me to little more than walking pace. In the rare moments when it slacked off, the heat radiating from the bitumen took my breath away. I was frustrated—angry at the wind and at myself for setting off so late. There was no relief anywhere—just miles of silent desert scrub and a fiery sun.

I should have called it a day and sought shelter in the scrub, but a maddening desire to push on to the DeGrey and help myself to its water locked me in its grip. The last few miles I was babbling to myself, fighting the searing winds in a struggle to keep going. When the river finally hove into view, my bleary eyes nearly wept with relief.

There are few genuine rivers in the outback—at least not what a North American would call a river—and the DeGrey proved no exception. It was a chain of muddy water holes stretched along a dry, cracked, and sandy riverbed, the dregs of last year's wet season that hadn't yet evaporated. I didn't care. I dropped my bike on its side, kicked off my shoes, and stumbled madly toward the largest of the pools.

Another big mistake. Those sands were hot as a griddle, and my bare feet hissed as I hopscotched into the water, yelping and cursing.

But then—ahhh. The water was knee-deep, smelly, and as tepid as a boarding-house bath—in other words, delicious. I dropped gratefully onto my knees, then sprawled on my back, staring like a dying fish into the faultless blue sky, occasionally splashing water over my face and temples. I loitered by the river the rest of the day, dozing and reading Ernestine Hill's *Great Australian Loneliness* in the shade of the eucalypts that grew along the banks, and periodically—armed with thongs this time—throwing myself back into the muddy pool, working my water purifier to refill my bottles.

When the sun dipped below a certain branch, I set out once more. I made camp another 13 miles down the road and was on the road again the next morning well before sunrise.

Caked with dust and mad as a cut snake, I hit the outskirts of Port Hedland a little after eight o'clock. My much-anticipated cold drink was delayed by a mile-long freight train coming in from the desert, hauling tens of thousands of tons of iron ore from the giant Mount Whaleback mine. I straddled my bicycle as the train rumbled by, looking out over Port Hedland's charmless landscape of blistered rock, high-tension lines, and glaring industrial sprawl. It may not have been pretty, but having just crossed the Great Sandy Desert I found it a beautiful sight.

CHAPTER 27

Shagsie and the Python

PORT HEDLAND ISN'T PRETTY. When English buccaneer and explorer William Dampier sailed along this coast in 1688, he remarked in his journal that not even the excitement of discovery could make him like the place, the "most barren on the globe." Ditto the Dutch merchantmen who scoured the West Australian coast in the 17th century, looking in vain for anything worth trading.

None of them could have guessed that these ancient rocks hold riches beyond belief: treasures of iron, gold, and copper, while beneath the pearl-rich beds of the Timor Sea lie billions of cubic feet of natural gas. They knew only what they saw. This coast is apocalyptic in its bleakness; barren hill-sides tumbling up to the Indian Ocean, sweltering in humidity. Add Port Hedland's sprawling loading docks, its heavy machinery, rail yards, iron-ore stockpiles, and blinding-white mountains of salt waiting for export in the morning sun, and you get a *Mad Max* sort of flavor.

There's only one reason anybody comes up here, and that's money: hopefully land an 80-grand-a-year job with company-subsidized housing at one of the big iron mines in the interior or with the huge offshore Northwest Shelf Gas Project. If not that, at least some well-paying work with one of the scores of contractors in Port Hedland or Karratha. Stay for a couple of years at most and get out—generally with enough money to buy a house or start a business back home.

It is a young man's game, a unionized gold rush, with rumors of big hirings constantly flitting around the pubs. "Hedland's off the boil now, mate, it's all in Karratha." Then somebody else will say just the opposite. The latest whisper the morning I hit town was that "they" were looking for 200 "sparkies"—electricians—for the new hot-briquetted iron plant being built just east of Karratha.

I took a shower at the Ampol Roadhouse, ordered a hamburger with the lot and half a gallon of chilled orange juice, and settled in with the local newspaper to escape the heat and the flies. A Perth girl calling herself "Shagsie" had placed an ad in the personals to let "all you bikers and Harley Riders" know what dates she was coming through Port Hedland and to "Meet me at Gecko's!" So few women, so many lonely $80,000-a-year pay packets.

Late in the afternoon I pushed out of Port Hedland, westbound for Karratha, a couple of days' ride away. I covered 35 miles in the relative cool of the evening, cruising at the comparatively speedy pace of 13 miles per hour now that the winds had died away. The billion-year-old landscapes here were more interesting than the tedious scrub of the Great Sandy Desert: handsome purplish-red ranges, with golden sunlight raking the spinifex plains to give them depth and texture. I made camp near (bone-dry) Poverty Creek and hit the road again before dawn, aiming to reach the Whim Creek Pub before the heat grew too savage.

When I arrived around 11 a.m., it was already 110°F in the shade. Whim Creek competes with the equally down-at-the-heels Marble Bar, a couple of hundred miles to the east, for the dubious distinction of hottest place in Australia. (Marble Bar rates a mention in the *Guinness Book of World Records* for its 163 consecutive days of 100-plus temperatures, set in 1923.) The pub is a rambling two-story prefab, painted a musky pink, that was shipped here from England around the turn of the century, when Whim Creek was a rollicking copper-mining town. Now the old pub is all that's left.

I parked my bike on the veranda and went inside. It was a large, high-ceilinged room, with old newspaper clippings, beer memorabilia, and black-and-white photos on the walls. Ceiling fans slowly circulated the air. It felt cool after the glare outside, but the thermometer beside the bar read 96°F. The crack of billiard balls came from the other end of the room, where a couple of ringers were having an early-morning game. I ordered a beer and a meat pie. While I was eating, I noticed a faded Polaroid of a nightmarishly large desert python crawling along the bar. The caption read: "If seen around the bar, please do not harm. She's a pet."

Lowering my drink, I glanced apprehensively around the room. I'm not particularly scared of snakes, but if one's in the bar where I'm drinking, I like to know where it is. The beast in the photo looked like a case of the DTs: about 14 feet long and as thick as my calf. I sidled over to the bar, cleared my throat, and in a hushed voice asked the barkeep if she would mind pointing out where the snake was.

The woman sadly shook her head. "The Health Department heard about her and said she had to go. Said we couldn't keep animals in here. So we drove her out to the desert and turned her loose. Seemed pretty unfair. Everybody liked her."

"Maybe they were afraid the drinking would corrupt her."

She thought about that for a moment, shook her head again, and said: "No, as far as I know, the snake never drank. We used to have a camel who'd come in here. Now *he* drank! But the snake just crawled along the bar."

"Camel had to go too, I suppose?"

"Yup, poor fellow. He certainly loved his beer."

We toasted absent friends.

CHAPTER 28

Roadhouse Blues

AT KARRATHA the road turns sharply south, setting off across hundreds more miles of nameless scrub to the old coastal town of Carnarvon. There is nothing between the towns except wind, sand, and stars, an archipelago of lonely roadhouses, and a couple of riverbeds which, at that time of year, may or may not have water in them. From Carnarvon the highway treks south through another few hundred miles of arid desolation to the town of Geraldton. And from there, still more scrub, another 300 miles to Perth.

In that T. S. Eliot poem, J. Alfred Prufrock regrets a life measured out with coffee spoons. He should have tried doling out life in forkfuls of roadhouse food. These petrol stations with diners appended were the high points of my desert existence—cornucopias brimming with human voices, public toilets, tap water, and meals of greasy, microwaved, extortionately priced food. I had studied my map so many times, I knew the line of succession by heart:

Fortescue River, Nanutarra, Minilya, Wooramel, Overlander, and Billabong.

I had a good incentive to make time: Tropical Cyclone Nicholas. I heard about it on a weather bulletin in Karratha. It was a Category 1 storm—a mere baby, but deepening nicely out on the Indian Ocean. It was several hundred miles away and heading for the Australian coast. Broome or Derby were considered its likeliest targets: They were on red alert, with Derby residents in particular warned to gather food, blankets, and medicine and get ready to dash for the emergency shelters. But cyclones are fickle; there was still a chance that Nicholas could veer, so Karratha had been put on yellow alert.

There were no quick miles to be had in these headwinds, however. Pedaling into them was like riding up a one-in-three grade that stretched all the way to the sun. I churned in low gear throughout the afternoon, my head down, watching out of the corner of my eye as the scrub crawled by. When I finally pulled off the road to camp in the spinifex near (bone-dry) Devils Creek, I found that my hours of toil, frustration, and sweat had bought me just 20 lousy miles—and at the cost of half my water supply. Fortescue River Roadhouse, my next chance to refill, was another 40 miles away.

It was a glum evening, despite the glorious blaze of stars that stretched across the sky above me. I sat up nibbling dried apples and watching the occasional road train barrel though the night. I felt a pang when I saw one heading south: lucky bastards. Tomorrow at this time they'd be in Perth, a city whose lights I wouldn't see for weeks. And I'd be—well, I'd be in another dry and dusty camp just like this one, a few miles farther down the track, after another long, sweaty day in the saddle, bucking heat and headwinds and flies. The next day would be the same, as would the next, and the next, and the next. Unless, of course, Tropical Cyclone Nicholas showed up to add his unwelcome variety. So I tuned in ABC National—the only station you can pick up out here—for an update.

It was approaching one o'clock in the morning, and the Perth-based station was taking requests. The callers seemed to come from another, brighter and cheerier, world; a world of city lights and restaurants and nights out at the movies, a world of dinner parties and friends. Then a lonely man's voice came on the line, long distance from the Overlander Roadhouse. His name was Wayne. The DJ asked him what it was like out there. "Man, it's boring; nobody here, just me and the flies. I wonder if you could cheer me up with 'Roadhouse Blues' by the Doors?" It made me laugh; it was so perfectly in tune with the moment. I turned up my radio, and for a few rollicking minutes the old Doors song—"Keep your eyes on the road, your hands upon the wheel"—chased away the melancholy, a brief sparkle in the dark and silent scrub.

Two sparkles, perhaps: I felt a note of kinship with the bored bloke in that roadhouse, 400 miles across the void. I resolved to shake his hand when I passed through—in about a week's time, if I was lucky—and thank him for the tune.

I HIT THE ROAD around four o'clock the next morning, judging by the tilt of the Southern Cross, and made Fortescue River Roadhouse a little before nine. While I was filling up my containers, I overheard the radio say that Tropical Cyclone Nicholas had fizzled into a tropical depression, but it was nevertheless dumping rain by the foot over Derby and Broome.

So much for the good news.

The same report announced that a new tropical cyclone, Ophelia, had formed over the Cocos Islands and was rushing headlong for Karratha, packing winds of 110 miles per hour. The weather bureau expected Ophelia to come ashore in about 48 hours.

Wasting no time, I pushed off into the dancing heat for the Nanutarra Roadhouse, a little more than 100 miles across the desert. It was weird to be worrying about floods. Rain and thunder seemed as remote as Times Square; the sky was brassy and cloudless, the sun approximately three times larger than it should be. The headwinds came from a giant blow-dryer set on scorch. I creaked and wobbled over the scabby outback at a miserable five miles an hour. The horizon never drew any nearer.

I WISH I COULD CLAIM that I filled these long, empty hours with ennobling introspection, but the outback had long since beaten that out of me. I passed the time trying to remember the lyrics to songs—anything from Cole Porter to heavy metal. ("I Get No Kick from Champagne," though grotesquely out of place, appealed to my growing sense of irony.) I recalled dialogue from old movies, ad-libbed some new lines myself (and terribly witty repartee it seemed, out there in the sun), made lists of U.S. presidents or state capitals, and recited the starting infield of the 1969 Chicago Cubs: Ferguson Jenkins (P), Randy Hundley (C), Ernie Banks (1B), Glenn Beckert (2B), Don Kessinger (SS), and Ron Santo (3B). Another game that took my mind off the miles was assembling six people—anybody past, present, or fictional—that I would invite to my dream lunch. One of my favorite groupings included Mark Twain, Sir Richard Burton, Lola Mantez, Captain Smith of the *Titanic,* Wild Bill Hickok, and Clancy of the Overflow. It was all to escape the here and now, the awfulness of nagging thirst, furnace heat, monotony, aching loneliness, and millions of humming flies, circling my head in maddening clouds, seeking out the moisture in my eyes, nose, the corners of my mouth, the sticky film of sweat on the back of my neck.

As nightmarish as these miles were, a part of me also enjoyed dueling with the desert. Those fleeting moments mostly came at night, when the battle was over and won for the day, when the sun had retreated and a magnificent swath of stars stretched across the sky. For the next few hours I cherished being absolute master of my fate.

But then a new day would start; a broiling sun would loom over the eastern horizon, the flies would start to buzz, and a few miles down the road the water in my bottles would be too hot to refresh me. Even in the midst of battle, though, there could be moments of satisfaction. From the insulated six-liter water container lashed to my rear racks, I carefully refilled the smaller and more accessible bottles on my bike frame throughout the day. I enjoyed this task: tucking the empty between my feet to keep it from blowing over in the hot gusts, pouring cautiously so as not to lose a precious drop. This was life, and I had it in my hands.

I bought distance with that water, sometimes as little as one mile per cup. By ten or eleven o'clock in the morning the heat was usually so intense that it was poor economics to continue, no matter how ghastly the flies were or how desperately I wanted to be somewhere else. Like every other desert creature, I'd find whatever scraggly patch of shade I could, lie still in the hot dust, and wait.

CHAPTER 29

"Sure Hope You're Heading South!"

I MADE NANUTARRA ROADHOUSE around noon, having covered 70 miles that morning in direct-sun temperatures that must have been crowding 140°. The last of my water supply ran out three miles from the roadhouse, and I stumbled in half-crazed with thirst. I slumped sweatily in a chair, set up $24 of cold bottled water and sports drinks, and returned the stare of the road-train driver at the next table. He was short and bristly, with opinionated blue eyes. He smiled and spoke with that smugness some guys exude when they have the privilege of delivering bad news: "Mate, you know there's a cyclone coming?"

I said I'd heard something about it.

"Tropical Cyclone Ophelia," he continued, cutting the corner off his steak. "A Cat-3 storm. Coming in fast. Expected to hit Karratha sometime tomorrow. Sure hope you're heading south! Me, I gotta drop a load off in Hedland tonight, but then I'm turning around as fast as I can and hauling ass out of here. A storm can cut the highway for weeks. Christmas is coming and I want to be with my family. Know what I mean?"

He finished shoveling his steak, paid and tipped, and set out on his dash to Hedland. I watched him go, strutting through the blinding glare to where his triple was parked. I could feel the heat radiating through the diners' windows. I left a little while later, carrying my full 22 liters of water, and thinking what madness it was to pedal away from the air-conditioned sanctity of this lonely diner only to dissolve in shimmering waves of heat. The Minilya Roadhouse was 140 miles away.

SOME TIME THAT NIGHT a high, thin veil of cloud crept over the sky, as stealthy as a cat on a mantelpiece. I rolled up my camp before daybreak, not troubling myself with breakfast, just wanting to make quick time while the temperatures were relatively sane. I suspected this cloud was the forward edge of Ophelia. If it scared me a little, it was also a blessing in disguise. The powerful southerlies that had been reining me in had stopped. The air was still, and for once I made good time. The thin cloud layer also kept the temperature from climbing above a muggy 95°. I barely cast a shadow.

I grabbed this bit of luck with both hands, riding as hard as I dared. Hours passed. The clouds thickened into an opalescent swirl. The sun became fuzzy and indistinct. The feeble light made the olive-and-rust landscape even more drab and tedious than it normally was, but I didn't care: I was hauling. I covered 100 miles by noon and kept right on pedaling.

Feeling woozy as I worked my way up a long grade, I suddenly remembered I'd had nothing to eat since last night. I stopped, broke out a packet of dried apples, and after swallowing a few decided things might go better if I sat down. Rather, my legs gave way and I followed, making excuses. After a minute or so of this, a lie-down struck me as an even better idea. I sprawled on the hot gravel in the middle of the road, looking up into the mauve-gray sky, feebly gumming the apples and trying to summon the energy to chew. By and by the packet slipped from my nerveless fingers.

Although I don't remember falling asleep or know how long I slept there—20 minutes, perhaps—I can state with confidence that no road trains barreled through my power nap. What woke me was a deep boom of thunder, followed almost instantly by a cloudburst—as though somebody had sluiced me down with a bucket of cold water. I sat up gasping and sputtering, looking around in a daze. The temperature had plunged. The sky was dark. It was raining pitchforks.

I gathered my sodden apples, finished the packet, and slowly saddled up, drenched to the skin but oddly refreshed. I hit Minilya Roadhouse about an hour later, cold and wet enough to break out my fleece. I bought a hamburger and learned on the radio that Ophelia had foundered before she hit the coast; still, she had packed enough of a wallop to send a line of thundersqualls booming into the interior.

I TOOLED INTO CARNARVON the next morning a little after eleven, haggard and beat and badly in need of a shower after racing Ophelia across the desert. I found a hostel on the waterfront, replete with ornamental palms and fresh sea breezes. I told the guy at the desk it was nice to be somewhere cool. He stared at me like I was crazy. "We're having a heat wave. It's 102°."

I sat up that night at the Café Paradiso, a cheap eatery beside the hostel. There was only one other guy there, a weather-beaten old horse-breaker and prospector named Ernie, and we fell to talking. He was just killing time, waiting for the 10:30 bus to Port Hedland—the start of a long journey that would take him to Brisbane and a visit with his daughter. "I got lung cancer," said Ernie, plucking yet another cigarette from the pack of Horizon 50s at his elbow. He lit it with the butt of his last, then chuckled at the look on my face. "Smoking don't hardly make a difference any more. Doctors say it's hopeless."

Ernie told me about his life, a quiet summing-up of 56 years; starting out as a rouseabout traveling with a band of shearers working along the Gascoyne River, then a spell breaking horses at Minilya station, then volunteering for Vietnam. He spoke in a retrospective voice, as though already regarding himself in the past tense. After the war he worked in a factory for a while, served some time in prison, then got out and drove road trains around the outback, grateful to have so much wide-open space around him again. The last few years he had spent prospecting, living off the land, shooting rabbits and kangaroos, in little camps well away from civilization.

Ernie had been on paying dirt down Meekatharra way when he got the hard news from the doctors. He cashed in $3,700 worth of grit and nuggets, sold his old car and traps, and bought his bus ticket. This was going to be his last big trip, over the top to Darwin, seeing some old stomping grounds along the way, maybe getting a look at Cairns, and eventually coming to rest in a Brisbane suburb. For Ernie, the bus couldn't come soon enough.

CHAPTER 30

"We *Sell* Water Here!"

THE FIRST 24 HOURS out of Carnarvon showed me the best and the worst of the outback.

It started at the Wooramel Roadhouse. I rolled up around noon. The place seemed eerily deserted, baking in the breathless 113° heat. I circled the building, wondering if it was open. There were no visible cars, or people, just the hum of a diesel generator. I tested the door. It slid open and I walked into the dim coolness of the diner.

A woman stood behind the counter, arms crossed, glaring at me with a face as hard as a coin. I ordered a meat pie and a Coke and asked where I could fill my water bottles.

"We *sell* water here," the woman snapped. "Four dollars a bottle."

It was about 50 miles to the next roadhouse, so I sat down to estimate how cheaply I could get there in this heat. The woman glared at me some more. A lean, sour-faced man stepped out of the kitchen and helped her glare.

While the two of them were busy glaring, a woman with two small kids rolled up in a steaming Holden. She looked haggard and overwrought. "Can you help me?" she asked. "My car's overheated and I need—"

They both cut her short. "We *sell* water here."

It was a cute act. The motorist tried to explain that it wasn't even drinking water she required, that she was desperate, but it was just chin music to these two. The woman behind the counter told her to get a better car; the man told her to get out if she wasn't buying anything. Mother and kids went outside, sheltering from the sun in a scraggly bit of shade offered by a tree. Ten minutes later another car drew up. I could see her talking to the driver.

A couple of hard-bitten pickup trucks pulled in, jackaroos off one of the stations stopping for lunch. The woman scribbled down their orders.

The proprietor cast a surly glance in my direction.

"What are you looking at?" he snapped.

"I'm not looking, I'm staring."

His eyes narrowed and he walked around the counter toward me. Suddenly I felt far from friends. He leaned over my table. "Yeah? Guess what? I don't want you around. Get out."

"What's up? This is the most inhospitable place I've ever seen."

"Well, now, isn't that just too bad. I suppose you think we ought to go around smiling at you all the time?"

"You could try. Wouldn't cost you a dime."

"People would think we was weird."

"What do they think now?"

"Get out."

"I'm eating my lunch."

"Not any more. Eat it outside. I want you off the property."

I took another bite of my pie.

"That your bike out front?"

"Sure is."

"I'm going to go smash it."

"Touch it and I'll break your arm."

He marched out the door. I followed hard behind him. He brushed past the bike without molesting it, then ducked into a little door that looked like it led to his private office. He smirked at me over his shoulder.

I didn't like that smirk. He might have been going in there to sulk or shadowbox or do his bookkeeping. On the other hand, he might have been the kind of guy who keeps a rusty .22 and a box of shells among the office litter.

This was a lonely place. I slid. I didn't leave a tip.

I HADN'T GONE TWO MILES when I heard a four-wheel-drive slow beside me. For an instant I thought the headcase at the roadhouse had come after me. Instead it was Dave Steadman, owner of the 400,000-acre Wooramel sheep station. "I'm awfully sorry about that back there," he said when we both pulled over. "I wouldn't want you to get the wrong impression of us out here just because of him. I'd like it if you'd stop by and spend the night with us. What do you say?"

I said thanks.

He told me they'd all be down at the shearing shed. The turnoff was about ten miles down the road. He gave me directions. It would be easy to find: Just head for the smudge of dust a few miles off on the western horizon.

Quite a few people were there when I arrived. Dave had ridden off on his dirt bike to fetch a mob of sheep, but he had told them to be on the lookout for me. Kimberley Elliott—a tall, rangy, deeply tanned and black-bearded man who was the head stockman—said hello and chuckled. "Heard you almost got into a fight down at the roadhouse. I wouldn't worry about it. Last time I was there I almost got in a fight with the guy myself."

It turned out that Dave and his wife, Margot, had come to the rescue of explorers before: Robyn Davidson, the author of *Tracks: A Woman's Solo Trek Across 1,700 Miles of Australian Outback,* had come to their property in 1977 when one of her camels took sick. They had just finished the shearing and were now busily shifting their 15,000 sheep around the station by road train. It was easier on the animals than trying to push them on foot through the scrub in this killing heat.

There was a rush to get things done. Christmas was coming in a couple of days. Kimberley was off that night to visit his brother in a mining town about 400 miles away. Margot was off the next morning to do some shopping in Carnarvon. And Neil Smith, a red-headed gentle-giant of a farmer who moonlit as a road-train driver, was eager to get back to his wheat property near New Norcia for Christmas and the harvest.

DAVE PUT THROUGH A CALL to his mate David Stone—AKA "Boulder," the publican at the Billabong Hotel—the next morning to let him know I'd be passing through. "He's my representative in that part of the world," Dave explained to me over breakfast. "He'll look after you."

It was already hot and windy when I set off from Wooramel, a full load of fresh water in my containers. My first port of call was the Overlander Roadhouse. I didn't really need anything, but I hoped to meet the guy who had cheered my lonely evening on Devils Creek with his radio request for "Roadhouse Blues." The only man there was a blond sourpuss who was snarling racial abuse at a couple of terrified Japanese girls in the parking lot. They scuttled back onto their waiting Greyhound, peering out the window at him, clearly anxious for the bus driver to finish his pie and cigarette and get moving. I didn't think I was going to care much for this place, but I went up to him anyway and asked if he knew the guy who had requested "Roadhouse Blues" on the radio a week or so back.

"You mean Wayne? I fired him."

"Why?"

"Because of shit like that. Calling up a radio station when he was supposed to be working. I pay for work."

"But it was one o'clock in the morning."

"What's it to you?"

He had a point there. "Oh, nothing. He just sounded like a nice guy."

"Bah." He regarded me with cool disdain. "You're stupid."

"Yeah? Why's that?"

"Riding a pushbike around the country."

"I wanted to see Australia. Meet all the nice people."

He glowered at me. "We used to have a nice country. Until they started letting you goddamned foreigners in."

Sometimes you just can't help yourself. I pasted on my broadest Bermuda-shorts American accent and exclaimed: "Golly! Are you a real Aborigine?"

I COVERED THE 30 MILES to the Billabong Hotel in record time, the blond guy's rage a hot wind at my back. That was the second roadhouse in a row I'd been chucked out of. The routine was getting stale. Pretty soon I would have to develop a whole new set of manners; the old ones had apparently worn out.

I needn't have worried about my reception at Billabong. Boulder—an encouraging bloke whose advice on road conditions turned out to be rock solid—was leaning against the door of the pub, looking out into the glare, when I rode up. "It's 110° out there," he called out. "There's a pool out back—jump in and cool off, then come on in for some sandwiches and a cold beer!"

CHAPTER 31

Christmas in Geraldton

BY THE TIME I was approaching Geraldton I had grown to hate the happy-voiced weatherman on the ABC radio. Every morning as I rolled up my camp, his chirpy voice told me to expect another day of strong headwinds, 25 knots along the coast, with gusts to 45. "Fresh sea breezes" he called these withering 108° blasts, making them sound like gentle puffs spiced with sea salt and scented with coconut oil; what he presented as delightful kite-flying weather struck me as a sentence of hard labor.

These same insistent winds wrecked the early Dutch explorers 300 years ago, driving them unexpectedly onto a mysterious landmass they called *Terra Australis*—"Southern Land"—as they sped across the southern Indian Ocean on their way to Java. The most gruesome tale was the wreck of the *Batavia,* on the shoals off Geraldton in 1629, after which the survivors mutinied in an orgy of killing and torture that was trumped only by the savage punishments meted out by the rescue party. Two of the youngest mutineers were spared, abandoned as castaways near the mouth of the Murchison River. They were never heard from again.

That ancient river was murky and still, shaded by limp gum trees and wrapped in conspiratorial silence, the afternoon I nosed my bicycle through the scrub and down its rocky banks, seeking water and shelter from the scourging winds. I had thought I might sit out the worst of the heat here, but I hadn't reckoned on the zillions of flies filling the hot, still air. I ate a hasty lunch and clambered back up the bank and onto the road. The winds were as fierce as ever, buffeting me into the weeds along the highway like a discarded paper cup. Sometimes a sudden gust would simply stop me in my tracks.

And not just me, either. A couple of miles south of the Murchison River I came upon a car stranded by the side of the road, out of petrol, its driver having misjudged distances and the drag the powerful winds were exerting on his car's mileage. He was trudging along the desolate highway toward the petrol station at Binnu, fingers hooked around the handle of an empty jerrican. Intending to do him a favor, I pulled into the station when I got there to see if someone would go out and meet him. But my own plodding pace had been scarcely any faster than his: I could still see him, a speck in the distance behind me, walking grimly through the blowing dust.

That day was the toughest cycling I have ever experienced, before or since. By sundown I had covered 95 miles, but it felt like 200. My legs were wobbly, my shoulders ached from wrestling the handlebars, and the skin on my face was chapped by the ceaseless hot, dry winds.

I wheeled into Northampton just on dusk, down a pleasant turn-of-the-century main street of false-front stone and brick. It was an old-fashioned farm town, the sort I hadn't seen since way back east, and it came hard on the heels of the first grain crops, tractors, and silos I had seen in months. I made camp in a darkened grove of eucalypts a couple of miles south of town, picking my way over a barbed-wire fence to get there. It was a niggling reminder that I had come in from the wide-open freedom of the desert, where you simply trudged through the spinifex until you found a likely spot.

That night it was cool—the winds were indeed fresh now—and I broke out my sleeping bag, another first in many months. I listened to the wind moan through the branches. The lights of several farmhouses twinkled in the distance. Although they were still a couple of miles away, it felt strange and a little claustrophobic to be camping so close to people, with a kind of regular purr of traffic on the highway. While I was thinking about all these changes, I remembered it was Christmas Eve. Unbidden, a quintessentially ironic Australian version of "Jingle Bells" replayed itself in my head:

Jingle Bells

Driving through the bush
In a rusty Holden ute;
Kicking up the dust—
Esky in the boot!

Kelpie by my side,
Singing Christmas songs—
I'm off to draft a mob of sheep
In my singlet, shorts, and thongs!

Oh! Jingle bells, jingle bells,
Jingle all the way;
Christmas in Australia
On a scorching summer's day—hey!

Jingle bells, jingle bells,
Christmastime's a beaut!
Oh what fun it is to drive
In a rusty Holden ute!

THIS WASN'T THE FIRST TIME that Christmas had sneaked up on me. After 15 years in Australia, I still can't accept the notion of Christmas falling in midsummer. I can accept January as a month of searing heat and bushfires, and I can come to terms with skiing in July, but Christmas occupies its own special frosty season. It is a time of sleds and hot chocolate and mantles of snow over steepled villages—not a barbecue on a sweltering afternoon, drinking beer and playing beach cricket with zinc cream on your face to protect against UV readings beyond extreme. No matter how many years I spend here, doing my Christmas shopping in sweltering heat as a department store's crackly gramophone plays "I'm Dreaming of a White Christmas" will always seem surreal.

Not that the highway was decked with boughs of holly. So far the only Yuletide signs I had seen were a few wilted strands of tinsel in some of the roadhouse diners and a handful of refrigerated trucks zooming down from the trawler docks in Carnarvon with fresh lobsters for family lunches in Perth. Now, suddenly, the big day was here. I spent it lying exhausted on a park bench in Geraldton, too worn out after yesterday's ride to know or care. The town—at 25,000 the biggest I'd seen since leaving Darwin in October—was dead quiet. I had hoped that some pizza place or other might have stayed open, providing me a big, cheap feed. But the only restaurants open were out of my price range, with fancy set-course dinners, party crackers, and a lot more gaiety than I could muster.

Growing bored, I walked my bicycle through town, along quiet, sunny sidewalks, and back out to the highway. I stopped at a BP Roadhouse on the outskirts to refill some water bottles. Ever since those hospitality hiccups at Wooramel and Overlander, I had been leery of West Australian roadhouse managers, so when a middle-aged woman stepped purposefully from behind the counter, came outside, and approached the taps where I was filling my bottles, I was quickly on guard.

"It's Christmas Day!" she exclaimed.

"Yes?"

"Are you on your own?"

"Yes."

"Have you had your Christmas dinner? You wouldn't have, would you?"

"Well, no, not exactly."

"Well, come on inside. We have plenty."

Jan and Des had just reopened their roadhouse, having shut down for an hour to enjoy their Christmas lunch. While Des improvised a table—an ice-cream advertising placard placed on top of a freezer—Jan brought the food from out the back. The next thing I knew, a Christmas-size feast of meats and salads and bread rolls had been set out in front of me. My favorite tipple over the past months had become fresh cold water, and there was plenty of that as well, followed by rich, homemade trifle for dessert. Jan insisted that I have at least two very large helpings of her trifle—and it was no trouble at all to accommodate her. When I eased back from the makeshift table, it was the first time I had felt really full since leaving Anna Plains, more than 1,000 miles back.

But there was more than hospitality and good food involved here. The scenes of nastiness at the Wooramel and Overlander roadhouses had rankled me far beyond their worth. Desert heat can warp mental horizons as readily as physical ones, and weeks of grime and toil and my maddeningly plodding pace into the wind had frayed my nerves and eroded my self-confidence. Small things start to matter. The hospitality of the Steadmans, and Boulder's easy manner back at the Billabong Hotel, had gone a long way toward correcting my perspective; Jan and Des's Christmas lunch completed it, exorcising the ghosts of roadhouses passed. The day *felt* like Christmas—if not the Currier & Ives version of my New England childhood, then certainly a good old-fashioned Australian one.

CHAPTER 32

Down to Perth

I CAMPED THAT NIGHT on a lovely little hilltop near a place marked Walkaway on my map. I found it quite by accident. The winds had picked up savagely in the afternoon and I had veered inland, desperate to escape them. I was still struggling into the wind at dusk when a grating sensation beneath my feet told me that I could add a worn-out pedal bearing to my list of woes. I stopped to appraise the damage, debating whether to head back to Geraldton and wait for the shops to open after Boxing Day or risk pushing on to Perth.

I had just decided to continue south when I looked up and saw a gate opened invitingly into a field. I felt oddly drawn to it. A softly lit panorama of wheat fields spread out before me. Lights glowed with an odd mix of hominess and exclusion in a farmhouse a couple of miles away. My field had been freshly plowed, the warm earth making an invitingly soft mattress after weeks of pitching camp on hardscrabble soil in the desert. The place seemed magical—a Christmas gift from the fates, and unexpected recompense for weeks of hot gales, flies, thirst, and loneliness. I slept for 11 blissful hours.

In the morning, the winds had obligingly abated. I set off toward the coastal highway, congratulating myself on my luck and figuring that today, at least, I could put some serious miles under my wheels. A couple more tranquil days like this would be all I'd need to get myself to Perth and a badly needed rest.

But that calm soon wore off. By midmorning the hot gusts were back and I was churning into them at a toilsome five miles an hour, as worn and ragged as I'd ever been in my life. The temperature climbed into the low 100s. I ground my way over a series of coastal hills that seemed to stretch on forever.

My frustration was compounded by the knowledge that if I'd passed through here a few weeks earlier, I would have been treated to the kaleidoscopic spectacle of Western Australia's springtime wildflower display. More than 7,000 named species in all—and thousands more unnamed ones—in every color, shape, and size, most of them found nowhere else on earth. But spring had long since faded into the harsh glare and searing heat of summer. The flowers were gone. Now there was only dense, drab scrub.

My eyes had been feeling raw and stinging for a few days now, and by the time I hit Dongara my right eye felt like it held a bucket of sand. I dabbed at it with a moistened corner of my bandanna, trying to flush out the wind-driven grit, but to no avail. I pushed on, grinding out another 50 miles—to the sand-mining town of Eneabba—with my right eye squeezed shut.

I reached Eneabba, flushed and badly beat, early in the afternoon. After downing a liter of cold milk at the roadhouse—and failing again to clean the dust from my red-rimmed eye—I sought out the Royal District Nurse's office, praying that somebody would be on hand on Boxing Day.

I was in luck. "You don't have any grit in your eye," a nurse named Enid told me. "You've got a raging case of conjunctivitis." This sort of eye infection, brought on by long exposure to heat and dust, glare and flies, had plagued Australia's early explorers. Enid peeled back my eyelid and squirted in a dab of antibiotic ointment. I felt my eye glue shut. She gave me the rest of the tube. "Put that in your eye twice a day. When you get to Perth, stay off the bike for a while."

I creaked toward the door, feeling twice my 38 years. "It'll be a pleasure."

Outside the hot winds were blowing, the little mining town baked in the glare, and in the distance loomed the line of rolling sand hills I'd have to cross to reach Perth.

THAT FINAL PUSH TO PERTH was a slow-motion nightmare, the sort where you try to run but your legs are made of clay, or you look down to discover you're wading through quicksand. However hard you try, you get absolutely nowhere. This was the bad dream's extended-play version—three days and nights of hot, fierce gales and a Sisyphean roller coaster of hills. Of all the miserably lonely stretches of outback I had ridden, this had to be the cruelest. I spent an hour inching my way up a single thigh-burning grade, battling not only the wind but my own gathering and impotent rage.

The rage stemmed from knowledge—knowledge that there would be no reward at the top of each rise for all this low-gear torment, no easy glide down the far side. Nagging though the headwinds were going uphill, they were far stronger on the southern flanks—so powerful, sometimes, that when I crested a hill they brought me to a standstill and forced me to walk the bike down the other side.

That night, about 70 miles out of Perth, I crumpled onto the sand in the scrub, too exhausted to roll out my bivvy. The next morning, my chest and arms felt so heavy I could hardly move. I sat bleary-eyed on the sand, head on my knees, for a long, quiet while, trying to summon the gumption to mount up and ride.

Eventually I set off, wobbling down the highway, concentrating on cranking those pedals, counting down each roadside milepost as it crept into view and then creakily dropped behind me. I felt as weak as a kitten, but the speedometer on my handlebars said I was making almost ten miles an hour. The winds had died down, and I seemed to have shed the nightmarish hills.

By midmorning, more traffic appeared on the road; panel vans and boxy sedans whizzed past my elbow. The distances between gas stations and roadhouses grew shorter. Houses and horsey properties and hobby farms—the outermost planets in a big city's orbit—materialized in the landscape.

Sometime in the early afternoon my rheumy eyes beheld Perth's glass-and-steel skyline shimmering in the distance, as smooth and polished and aloof as the Emerald City. It was a vision of the Promised Land—the first real city I'd seen since Brisbane, by now so many miles and events removed that it felt like a childhood memory.

Perth—Australia's answer to Dallas—looked brash and bright. Its sudden wealth had been built on iron ore from the Pilbara, gold from Kalgoorlie, natural gas from the Northwest Shelf, and diamonds from the Kimberley. Back in the high-rolling 1980s, the town was home to Western Australia's most notorious corporate buccaneers; their slick deals and political cronyism came to be known as WA Inc. The storylines coming out of here—rigged horse races, insider trading, grand-scale art fraud, and billions of dollars of taxpayer money vanishing in the snap of bejeweled fingers—would have beggared anything dreamed up for J. R. Ewing and *Dallas.* By the early 1990s it had all ended in tears, with a string of bankruptcies, Royal Commissions, and indictments that fascinated, amused, and outraged the rest of Australia. The goings-on confirmed Western Australia's already colorful reputation as a world apart, a rollicking frontier where anything could happen—and often did.

I was too weary to ride farther by the time I reached the bridge over the Swan River. At any rate, I felt so woozy that I didn't trust myself in traffic. I trudged the last mile over the bridge and up Adelaide Terrace, shuffling one foot in front of the other in an exhausted trance, stopping now and then to ask directions to the youth hostel on Williams Street.

The hostel was nearly full, but the girl at the desk found me a room on the top floor. I struggled to get there, climbing the stairs slowly, my thighs stinging, pausing on each landing and regarding the next flight as though it was the final pitch on Mount Everest. I found my room, collapsed in front of the fan, and slept—sprawled across the bed in my grimy clothes—for 18 hours solid. When I opened my eyes the next morning, saw a roof over my head, and gradually came to understand that I had arrived in Perth—that today I would have to face neither wind nor heat nor hills—I nearly cried with relief.

PERTH IS THE LONELIEST city in the world, they say. A glance at the map bears out that verdict: Perth's nearest city-sized neighbor, Adelaide, sits more than 1,000 miles to the east across a waterless, wind-scoured void known as the Nullarbor Plain. (The region got its Aboriginal-sounding name in 1865 from South Australian surveyor Edmund Delisser, who bastardized the Latin for "no trees"—*nullus arbor*—into Nullarbor.) To the west there is nothing but empty Indian Ocean until you hit the South African coast. Antarctica lies to the south. And to the north—well, I knew all about that: more than 2,000 hideous miles of burning sand and spinifex all the way to Darwin. Even then, of course, Darwin is a town of only 80,000 souls; to find a truly urban northern neighbor for Perth, you'd have to push on to Jakarta.

I could feel this isolation and the breath of the bush even in the heart of downtown—in the flocks of parrots that screeched down the streets, in the wildflowers and wallabies in King's Park, and in the brass plaques of the mining companies on all the grandest buildings in town, names that evoked huge mineral projects in the remotest corners of the outback. My relief at arriving in Perth mingled with an uneasy sense that the deserts I'd come through—with their wind and sand and flies—were not all that far away: I was in a walled city under siege.

I had made it through the gates, all right, but it had been a photo finish. A stranger's face peered from the shaving mirror—older, gaunt, windburned, and haggard, with a shaggy mop of brown hair and raw, red eyes. I guessed that I had lost 20 pounds since rolling out of Darwin nine weeks earlier; in fact, I would discover during an unplanned hospital stay a few miles down the road, I had lost 35.

I was utterly famished. All I'd been able to rustle up for breakfast that morning was a cup of coffee and the last of some stale gingersnaps that had been in my panniers since Carnarvon. I walked hungrily down the bustling, sunny sidewalks, looking and feeling shabby and shy. Just before 11 o'clock a pizza joint near one of the cinemas opened up, a card in the window spruiking its lunchtime special of all-you-can-eat pizza, pasta, and salad bar.

I went inside, parked myself at a corner table, and went to work. The pan pizza was nice—oily, meaty, and crammed with calories—but what I couldn't get enough of was the salad bar. A couple of months had elapsed since I'd seen fresh vegetables, and now my body simply couldn't shovel them in fast enough. Carrots, green peppers, sprouts, onions, and lettuce. Cucumbers, tomatoes, raw broccoli and cauliflower—anything and everything. I piled my plate as high as I could, tomatoes tumbling off the top, then ravenously wolfed it all down. I went back again and again and again. People stared. When the waitress came to see what I wanted to drink, I ordered a tall glass of ice water—not because I was being cheap, but because the luxury of drinking as much chilled water as I liked was a fantasy that had dominated my thoughts for weeks. I chugged it and immediately asked for another. Four glasses later, the waitress caught on and decided to save us both some bother by bringing pitchers instead. I had several of those—probably a couple of gallons of ice water in all.

I lingered in that pizza parlor, contentedly grazing and drinking, keeping myself company with a battered paperback of P. J. O'Rourke's *Holidays in Hell,* until the waitresses cleared away the buffet around 3 p.m. A few subsequent visits hastened my convalescence in Perth.

Having carried me—plus another 80 pounds of food, water, and gear—over thousands of miles of rough outback roads, my bicycle was as worn out as I was. Both tires were shot, the chain was stretched, and the bearings on the pedals had been grinding noisily for the past 300 miles. The torn tape on the handlebars fluttered annoyingly in the breeze. All cables were frayed; the brakes were soft and squishy. Most serious of all, a crack had developed in the rim of my rear wheel—the penalty for carrying so much weight. I was lucky to have made it to Perth. That wheel could not roll much farther without pretzling. I found a bicycle shop in Fremantle and came out $200 lighter.

Once the raw edges of malnutrition had been dulled and my relief at reaching Perth had worn off—it took but a few days, surprisingly—I began to grow restless. City walls seemed too confining, the nights too noisy, my legs too underutilized. I had no hankering to head out into the desert again—none whatsoever—but a gentle ride away from the city along the well-watered southwest coast seemed like a good idea.

CHAPTER 33

Road Rash

BY THE END OF THE FIRST WEEK in January I had made my way down Australia's west coast as far as Margaret River, an offbeat little community nestled in the lush vineyards and towering karri forests 100-odd miles south of Perth. It was cool there and green, with a pretty coast that reminded me a little of Maine and big, glassy rollers that drew surfers from all over the world. The town itself was a mix of aging hippies, farmers, feral greenies, urban refugees who had escaped the rat race to become potters or winemakers or open a B&B, and a smattering of wealthy professionals who'd bought and restored farmhouses as elegant weekenders. A few communes were still scattered through the forest, holdovers from the 1960s, whose residents—now respectable musicians or artists or organic farmers—referred to their properties as "multi-occupancy dwellings" and grumbled about wealthy newcomers forcing up tax rates.

Surfing is the religion and the great class leveler here; everyone surfs, and on the water everyone—tourist or local, rich or poor—speaks the same language and looks identical in shiny wetsuits. Chairman Mao couldn't have worked it any neater. It's nothing unusual to go to a beach parking lot early in the morning and see an impossibly battered 1969 jeep or a clapped-out kombi van parked beside a gleaming Mercedes owned by an affluent surgeon down from Perth for the weekend—and everybody having a good time together in the green waves.

There are two denominations: surfers and windsurfers. Surfers rule the mornings; windsurfers take over in the afternoon, when the sea breezes pick up. Life's priorities are clearly understood and cleverly accommodated. Employers ask prospective employees whether they surf or windsurf, then roster surfers to work the afternoons and windsurfers the mornings. A charming, quixotic little community—and an absolute dream after months of gritty tank towns, hardscrabble desert, and searing heat.

My outback shell shock was wearing off nicely. I had put on a little weight, the infection in my eye had largely cleared up, and I was pedaling comfortably again. Everything seemed perfect. The afternoon I left Margaret River was bright, sunny, and cool, and I figured to make it as far as Cape Leeuwin by sundown.

If paradise always has its serpents, this one had maggots. I stopped off at a main-street diner where I was served a hamburger crawling with them. By the time I spotted the maggots, I had eaten half the sandwich. A cleansing Coke didn't help much. I rolled out of town full of grubs and misgivings.

Even those began to fade as I coasted along Rosa Glen Road, a leafy and narrow country lane freckled with afternoon sunlight. There were no cars, the air felt fresh and cool, the fields and forests a lively, summery green. Three thousand miles or so—and a crossing of the Nullarbor Plain—still separated me from Sydney and the end of my journey. For now I planned to stick to this cool, green pocket of forest, hugging the shady, fertile southwest coast as far as the old whaling town of Albany before heading back into the wind and glare. It would add a little distance, but it might save my sanity; hell, this was a holiday.

I remember cresting a hill about ten miles out of Margaret River, then coasting down a steep grade toward a sharp curve obscured in shade. What happened next is a bit of a blur. There was a flash of premonition that something very bad was about to happen, a horrifying glimpse of potholes and broken bitumen, and then my bike was bucking like a rodeo bull out of a gate. When the world finally righted itself, I was sprawled beneath it, my T-shirt drenched in blood, my right arm hanging limp. My ribs felt as if the entire Australian cricket team had just had a go at them with two bats each. I didn't move. A sickening feeling of "You've really done it now!" crept over me like a dark shadow.

If the gods had been shirking a few moments earlier, they gave me their fullest attention now. Less than a minute after I'd splattered onto the broken pavement—my wheels were still spinning uselessly in the air—a dark green Range Rover crested the rise, driven by a local woman named Andrea Lindsay. She stopped and ran over to me. Catching a glimpse of my right arm, she winced and looked away. "I think you've broken your arm."

I nodded. I didn't care to look myself.

Her little boy did, though, wide-eyed with wonder: "Wow!"

Andrea helped me get up and limp to the Range Rover. By then another four wheel-drive had appeared, this one driven by a Canadian woman who gathered up my bike and panniers, loaded them in her vehicle, and followed us back to town. Fifteen minutes after I'd flown off the saddle I was stretched out on a table in the emergency room of the Margaret River Hospital, looking at the clock and marveling that not much more than an hour ago I'd been contentedly chewing a maggot-burger. When I asked the nurse for some water, she held off, cheerfully pointing out that I might be undergoing surgery in a short while. I said "Oh, shit!" and lay there watching the second hand tick around the clockface, waiting for the arrival of a Dr. Clarke. He stepped through the door about 40 minutes later, as drily ironic as a M*A*S*H medic. The surf had been huge that morning, crashing breakers 15 feet high, and his day had been one long cavalcade of broken bones, dislocated shoulders, and deep lacerations.

My arm wasn't broken, it turned out; the bone that Andrea had glimpsed under all that blood and torn tissue was still in one piece. The doctor trimmed the gash with a scalpel and closed it with a dozen stitches. I also had a few broken ribs, a yanked or torn tendon in my right shoulder that meant I couldn't raise my arm at all, and a lovely constellation of bruises and contusions—cyclists call it "road rash"—down my right side. (A few days later, the physiotherapist in town ventured that I had probably fractured my shoulder blade as well.) Bad as I felt, the gouges on my helmet told me things could have been much, much worse. The hospital kept me overnight for observation. I shared a room with a stoical farmer who'd been thrown by his horse.

The hospital dinner was plain—lamb, veggies, bread and butter, a banana—but it was an elaborate improvement over my larval lunch. Andrea came by that evening to check on me. She brought along a chocolate bar, a newspaper, two cans of Sprite, and a pink lady apple. "Sorry if the look on my face scared you," she laughed, "but the sight of that arm made me feel faint." Andrea paused, then added: "I don't know whether I should tell you this, but my little boy says a lot of crows are pecking the pavement where you fell."

MY BRUISES HAD STIFFENED UP wonderfully by the next morning, leaving me feeling like I'd been run through a mangler. There was no way I was cycling anywhere today, tomorrow, or anytime soon. I checked out of the hospital and into Surf Point Lodge, a chic youth hostel by Prevelly Beach, now a sort of sanatorium for yesterday's surfing casualties. I hobbled into the TV room and took my place with the other wounded, lounging in casts and bandages, water bottles and painkillers within easy reach. I stayed there for the next three weeks.

When I look back on 10,000 miles of outback travel and think of all the places I could have been laid up—Halls Creek, Tennant Creek, and Whim Creek loom large as ghastly possibilities—I can hardly believe my good fortune that my tumble occurred in Margaret River. The weather was sunny and bright and pleasant, the seaside hostel was brand-new (clean white stucco, high ceilings, rattan matting on the floor), and there were plenty of trendy wineries nearby to try out. A glass of decent Shiraz of an evening, along with a plate of local cheeses, soon took the place of hospital-issue painkillers. I got ultrasound treatments on my supraspinitis tendon (my new word for the week) from a physiotherapist in town, who also tipped me off to a pretty fair bookshop. Although I couldn't ride, I never felt grounded. Hitchhiking was a doddle in this funky corner of the world: Just stick out your thumb and go—generally as quick and easy as if you owned a car yourself. Take it all around, I lived pretty well.

Perhaps a little too well. This was the first long break I'd had since leaving Sydney—and I liked it. I enjoyed slipping into routine; daily showers, shopping for groceries in town, faces that grew familiar, the certainty of where I would sleep each night. It was nice to be at rest. Life on the road had well and truly lost its appeal.

Three weeks passed. My stitches came out, the ribs healed, and by and by I regained the use of my right arm. Physically I was ready to ride, and sooner or later I was going to have to pull up my stakes—it was expensive to linger here—but with the Nullarbor waiting to be crossed I tarried anyway. Twice I resolved to leave and went so far as to eat a final breakfast, only to postpone my departure on some flimsy pretext. Finally, on the first of February, I moved on.

CHAPTER 34

Robo-Biker Rebounds

I GAVE THE ILL-STARRED Rosa Glen Road a wide berth on my way out of Margaret River. Instead, I followed the old Caves Road to Cape Leeuwin. It was a scenic route that wound 40 miles through towering karri forests to the lonely sentinel of rock at the extreme southwestern tip of the continent, which Matthew Flinders had used as the starting point for his circumnavigation of Australia in 1802.

The road was quiet and hilly, shady and cool. I rode cautiously, a new hesitancy nibbling at the back of my mind. Over the months of mishap-free hard riding between Sydney and Margaret River, I had somehow reached the understanding that I was invulnerable. This wasn't exactly cockiness—I came well prepared with tools, spares, and plenty of water on the long desert crossings, and I had learned much over thousands of miles. Rather, my sense of security was based on the fact that in all that time nothing really bad had ever happened. It was hard even to imagine. A few seconds on Rosa

Glen Road had changed all that. Now I could picture it well—and, that first morning back in the saddle, often did: I relived the adrenaline-burning instant of pitching headlong over the handlebars, the sickening violence of flesh and smacking pavement, the scary tangle of feet and legs and bicycle frame. It was all too vivid. I eased the bike down the hills, gently riding the brakes.

For the next three days I followed a zigzag route through the southwest, from Margaret River to Augusta to Nannup to Pemberton, staying in hostels rather than camping because my ribs were too sore for hard ground. I hit Pemberton midafternoon, just as the whistle at the lumber mill hooted the end of a shift. Although the day had started out hot and humid, a cool, thundery rain front had since moved in.

Pemberton is a logging town deep in the karri forest. The hills around it were bathed in mist, and cold drizzle sifted out of the sky. I was feeling more at ease on the road by now—I'd been getting plenty of practice riding hills—and I slithered confidently down the long, wet, curvy grade into town. I was enjoying once more the sense of arriving in a strange town, rolling up the main street knowing that I'd be on the move again by the time the shift whistle blew the next morning.

The following evening found me in Walpole, after a slow and rainy ride through the Valley of the Giants—an ancient forest of monstrous, 2,000-year-old eucalypts. I shared a room at a boarding house there with a traveling teddy-bear salesman, a portly, middle-aged South Australian who roved the country peddling stuffed toys out of the back of his 20-year-old Volvo. His gray innocuousness and lonely wanderings around the continent created an instant Norman Rockwell tableau of a traveling salesman playing solitaire on his sample case in a squalid hotel room. After snoring like a walrus all night long, the teddy-bear tout nearly ran me over the next morning, tooting a cheery greeting as he sped past within a gnat's whisker of my wheels.

More faces and towns came and went over the next few days: Albany,

Jerramungup, Ravensthorpe, Esperance. The tall forests slipped away. The land opened up and became windier and more arid. At Esperance I turned north, heading for the goldfields—and for the Eyre Highway across the forbidding Nullarbor Plain.

CHAPTER 35

The Southernmost Norseman You Can Find

A CENTURY AGO, Norseman was a wide-open gold-rush town of thousands of hopeful prospectors and boisterous two-story pubs, one of half a dozen boomtowns that sprang up overnight on the nugget-strewn fringes of the Nullarbor Plain. Like Kalgoorlie and Coolgardie, Norseman's dusty streets—wide enough to accommodate the turning radius of a camel train—were busy with bicycle traffic in those days. Because the water needed to keep a horse alive was nowhere to be found on these hardscrabble plains, many of the prospectors who raced to Western Australia's goldfields in the 1890s did so on bicycles. Look at old photos of the pubs and you'll see scores of bicycles lined up in front of them; almost anywhere else, horses would be tethered there instead.

There were no other bicycles—and not much of any traffic at all—on the scorching morning when I rolled into town. It was already well over 100°F, with not a patch of shade to be seen. The glary streets of Norseman—

a last-chance water hole for anyone heading east across the Nullarbor—were dozing in the heat.

I had camped the previous night just north of a place called Salmon Gums, only about 50 miles away, but I decided to make it a short day and rest up in Norseman before heading out across the Nullarbor. I took a room at a cheap motel, stocked up on groceries, then idled away the long, hot afternoon listening to the hum of my dripping air conditioner and watching a puddle of water spread across the floor beneath it. Time dies hard in a place like Norseman, and as the hours dragged by in a blur of afternoon TV, I often wished I had just pushed on. Dinner was chips and a greasy chiko roll, bought at a roadhouse. If I hadn't been so hungry, I would have used it to lube my bike chain. It tasted like someone already had.

I set out the next morning before sunup, headed for the scrubby immensity of the Nullarbor Plain. At the edge of town, a sobering red sign warned me of my folly: "Scant Water Ahead, Next 800 Kilometres."

CHAPTER 36

"Refusal Often Offends"

THERE HE SAT, fat as a butterball, high in the cab of his crimson-and-chrome Kenworth, hands clasped behind his head, steering his 90-ton rig with his bare feet as he highballed down the highway at 80 miles per hour. Eyes wide in disbelief, I skittered off the bitumen into the weeds and watched him rocket past. He was grinning hugely, toes wiggling on the steering wheel. A cloud of grit spattered my cheek—a stinging rebuke for my impudence in mixing it up with the big boys out here, trying to cross "the paddock" (as long-haul truckers fondly call the Nullarbor). The whine of his tires receded in the distance. Shaking my head, I set off again.

Two days out of Norseman, I was wondering what kind of outback circus I had ridden into. The Eyre Highway has a reputation as Australia's lawless road, an eerily lonely strand of bitumen across nearly 500 miles of almost uninhabited desert, where the redneck justice of the truck-driving man is held in check by a single police outpost at the old telegraph-relay station of Eucla. This is the getaway route of choice for felons on the dodge from authorities back east. I'd heard the horror stories: robberies, assaults, murders, psychopathic hitchhikers. I'd been warned to keep my campsites well hidden, to keep my eyes peeled, and to be wary of anyone loitering around the lonely rest areas and water tanks.

By day the silence and bright emptiness of the road make an uneasy counterpoint to the litter strewn in the bush. Sunlight sparkles on broken glass, refracts through discarded Coke bottles, and shimmers on the strands of cassette tape festooning the saltbush. Crumpled cans of Emu Bitter are everywhere. Signs are peppered with bullet holes—not piddling .22-caliber punctures, but great gashes torn through the metal by .303s and 12-gauge slugs and impressive spreads of double-ought buckshot. A sticker on one bullet-riddled sign read: "Register Poofters, Not Guns! Before They Kill Us All!"

When does all this stuff go on? I often felt I was riding through the morning-after of a particularly nasty party—a mess the goblins had left.

Every so often another speck appeared on the gray-blue eastern horizon, then grew into a road train. Here comes "Stray Dog," "The Bitch," and "Pist-'n'-Broke," their handles emblazoned on the plastic trim above their bull bars. They stopped for nothing. A month earlier, just out of Norseman, one late-night cannonballer took out a herd of 16 wild camels that had been warming themselves on the still-hot bitumen. The police came out and finished off seven cripples; when the trucker pulled up in Perth, bloody clumps of hair were still strewn over his grill.

IT WAS 112° IN THE SHADE the morning I rolled into Caiguna. The low-slung roadhouse shimmered in the glare, the first sign of life after a mind-numbing 90-mile straightaway. A sign greeted thirsty folk: "Please don't ask for water, as refusal often offends." Inside the diner, a rough take-it-or-leave-it aggression hung in the air like the odor of stale cooking grease.

A couple of road-train drivers—each about 225 pounds of hard, red flesh—tucked into plates of steak and chips at the truckers-only table (the only one benefiting from the joint's wheezing air conditioner). They were gruff, morose men, in blue singlets and King Gee shorts, with faded tattoos on their forearms. A haze of cigarette smoke circled their heads. They grumbled about the heat; their engines were running hot.

The truckers gave me a baleful stare. I took a seat by the window. Heat radiated from the glass. For motorists—or cyclists—who hadn't got the message yet, a T-shirt tacked to a bulletin board spelled out the pecking order: "On the first day, the Lord maketh Caiguna. On the second day, He maketh the first truck. On the third day, He maketh the first truckie. And for the rest he didn't give a $%#&!"

Eventually the waitress got around to me. I ordered a hamburger and bought $14 of water to refill my bottles. As I opened my wallet to pay for it, I fought an urge to tell them the story of Wall Drug Store in Wall, South Dakota. Back in 1931, a struggling pharmacist named Ted Hustead had made his fortune by a simple ruse: He offered free ice water to lure passersby into his shop, speculating that they would probably buy an ice-cream cone or chocolate bar as well. Hustead's business boomed immediately. Seventy-odd years and ten million glasses of ice water later, Wall Drug Store is a national icon worth millions of dollars.

There was no point in telling that parable here, of course. If they believed me at all, they would only have shaken their heads at what a mug the guy must have been to give away so much free water. Peevish, I stepped outside, into the breathless heat, and carefully began to pour my precious water—which cost more than twice as much as the roadhouse's outrageously priced gasoline—into my bottles.

A sunburned man squatted in the thin slice of shade beneath the overhanging roof and watched me. He had been sitting there since I rolled up, and I had assumed he was a stranded hitchhiker. He wasn't. The phone lines were down all along the highway, thanks to a dust storm the previous day, and as a result it was impossible to do any credit-card transactions. He had limped in here low on fuel, lacking the cash to buy enough petrol to reach Balladonia, another 120 miles farther down the line. And so he waited. He had used up the last of his cash reserves buying cool drinks, and for the last four hours nobody at the roadhouse had offered him so much as a cup of coffee or a drink of water. I gave him some of mine. He took a long swig and passed the bottle back.

"Thanks," he gasped. "You know, I've got a nasty feeling that if you didn't have the readies out here, they'd really let you die."

CHAPTER 37

Nullarbor = Much Ardor

THE NOONTIME MIGHT OF THE SUN had broken by the time I left Caiguna. I rode toward Cocklebiddy under a gathering pall of opalescent cloud. A southerly had blown in off the Great Australian Bight, prodding me along and making me feel uneasily like a fast-food wrapper skittering down a cold and cracked alleyway. I made good time. The air felt unnaturally cool, and the heavy blue cast over the saltbush gave the landscape a surreal effect.

As the light faded, scores of kangaroos gathered on the roadside, drawn by the warmth radiating from the bitumen. The animals were almost invisible in the twilight. After a couple of heart-pounding near-collisions—kangaroos blend in superbly with the brush along the road—I decided to call it a day. I would have had to stop anyway: By now the wind had risen to a blustery gale, and thunder rolled across the plains. A storm was coming.

I made camp on a scabby piece of earth a few hundred yards off the highway, wrestling my bivvy bag to the ground as the wind moaned through the saltbush and raindrops stung my face. Lightning flashed, casting outré shadows in the scrub. I hunkered down inside my bivvy, munching a muesli bar and a few dried peaches before drifting off to sleep.

I woke twice in the night, once to a noisy patter of rain and the second time to the eerie yapping of dingoes. They were nearby. I lay there listening carefully and was just dozing off again when I heard a snarl, very close this time—no more than an arm's length away. I lay awake for a long time after that, reassuring myself that no wild dingo had ever been known to attack an adult human—yet.

I must have drifted off to sleep. The next thing I knew, a feeble light was filtering into my Gore-Tex cocoon. Another day was dawning on the Nullarbor.

WITH A GENTLE TAILWIND giving me a welcome push down the road, I covered 100 miles that day. The morning drizzle slowly burned off. Bright sun filtered through the thinning cloud and warmed the air into the balmy 90s. By midafternoon I was coasting down Madura Pass, the halfway point between Perth and Adelaide, where the highway makes a long, winding descent onto the low tablelands at the edge of the Great Australian Bight.

The view was as stunning as it was unexpected. Until that moment, I had thought of the Nullarbor as a dead-flat chunk of real estate from one end to the other. But from the top of Madura Pass I could look down onto a sea of mallee scrub hundreds of feet below, hazy with dust and glowing in the afternoon sunlight, vanishing into the eastern horizon. The slant of the sun, the play of light and shadow on the clumps of mallee gave the plains texture and depth. I cruised down the long grade, pedaling comfortably at a brisk 20 miles an hour.

The pleasantness of the afternoon and the fact that I was likely to crack a century that day—my first such ride since the accident—gave me a sense of well-being. After weeks of headwinds and heat, I was finally getting somewhere. As the fluid miles passed beneath my wheels, I began to project ahead: Another day like this and I'd be well into South Australia. Two more—maybe three—and I'd be all the way across, the Nullarbor safely behind me. I camped that night in a copse of eucalypt scrub, convinced that the Nullarbor wasn't such a bad place.

It still seemed okay the next morning, if noticeably warmer and stuffier. I hit the road before dawn, eager to take advantage of the reasonable conditions and make the South Australian border that afternoon. I covered 30 quick miles before stopping for a drink and a muesli bar. By then, I reckoned, I was about 13 miles from the Mundrabilla Roadhouse—easily on course to notch another century.

I knew I had been riding hard. Even so, the amount of sweat that sprinkled onto the road when I took off my helmet surprised me. It was too early to be this hot. And the flies! As soon as I halted they swarmed all over me in nightmarish millions, humming in the hot, still air like some apocalyptic lost chord. Never in thousands of miles of outback riding—not even on the Barkly Tableland—had I run into so many of the teeming bastards. They crawled over my face and into my ears; they went for the moisture in my eyes and in the corners of my mouth. A dozen or so drowned in my water bottle as I opened it to drink. I had to strain their loathsome little bodies with my teeth.

Puzzling over the feverish heat and the insane plague of flies, I heard a hollow boom in the distance. It sounded so much like the rumble of an empty road train that I glanced around to see if one of the big trucks was coming my way. The highway was empty and lifeless as far as the eye could see.

I stood perplexed, suddenly not liking where I was and wishing I was far away. A moment later a savage gust of heat, tumbling down from the rocky hills to the north, rocked me back on my heels. My bike clattered onto the pavement. I blinked in disbelief, eyes burning and watering in the hot desert wind. The temperature soared 20° in the space of a few minutes, as though someone was blasting the landscape with a giant acetylene torch. Never had I felt heat like this. I stood a moment, bracing myself against the searing winds, wondering what was going on. Then, with an alienated sense of amazement, I realized that if I didn't get out of this quickly, I could die.

It took me more than two hours to reach Mundrabilla, wobbling along against those powerful gusts, pausing every couple of miles to slurp down a liter of water, frightened by the blasts of heat and wind. My temples throbbed, my breath came in rasps, my throat burned. My legs grew weak and rubbery.

I thought about a news item I had heard on the radio a few weeks earlier: A seemingly healthy motorcyclist had dropped dead in 113° heat in the Simpson Desert. At the time I had thought it a quirky story, but not one that spoke to me. After all, I had ridden a bicycle (not just straddled a motorcycle) in temperatures that hot—and hotter—before. But this withering wind made my flesh crawl, then turned it as dry as ancient parchment.

No quantity of water could slake the thirst you get by standing still in such a wind, let alone by pedaling into its teeth down a scorching desert highway. I could easily imagine dropping dead in these circumstances, whether cycling or sitting in a chaise longue. I thought now of the fit and cocky trapper in the Jack London classic *To Build a Fire,* who ventures into the wild believing he can handle anything nature throws at him—only to learn, to his horror, the diabolical reach of nature's torments.

Out here, that reach is far indeed. Edward John Eyre, the explorer who barely survived the Nullarbor's savage heat and wind when he crossed the plain in 1841, described it as "the sort of place one gets into in bad dreams."

He was exactly right. The wind gusts dug under my emotional enamel, probing the stuff of character and finding the rot spots with exquisite skill. Tormented by heat, I grew angry, then irrational, then boiled over with helpless rage. It was all so goddamn unfair! Nothing, but nothing, was going right. Or could go right. Or would ever go right again. A lifetime of smoldering insecurities bubbled to the surface. My face flushed still redder. I was being mocked by some leering fate, my puny efforts disparaged. My resentment grew. This was a stupid country, and it was full of stupid people. I began recasting my entire journey in this grotesque crucible, recalling and magnifying every real or imagined slight, every perceived injustice or rip-off, every jerk motorist who had cut me off over the past 7,500 miles. A couple of drivers whizzed by, tooting and waving encouragement; they were smug, air-conditioned bastards who delighted in my torment. I hated them all, every single one. But most of all I hated me—for putting myself in the clutches of this hideous desert.

Finally I glimpsed a Caltex sign flickering in the heat haze maybe two miles away. I had to stop three times to slug down water in that distance. The last of those water breaks took place only a couple of hundred yards from the door of the roadhouse; by then I was no longer riding my bike but staggering with it through the white-hot glare and a swirl of wind-driven dust.

THE ROADHOUSE MANAGER watched me approach through the window of the diner. His eyes were wide. "God, you must be glad to get here," he exclaimed as I stumbled through the door. "This blew up out of nowhere. It'll go 120° today, easy." I nodded and slumped in a chair, cradling my face in my elbow. After a few minutes, the throbbing in my temples eased; so did the anger. When I found my voice, I rasped out an order for a couple of liters of flavored milk, some orange juice, and a bottle of chilled water.

According to the battered old thermometer in the roadhouse veranda, the shade temperature reached 124° that day. What it was in the direct sun, who knows? "The heat's bad enough," grumbled one road-train driver, who said his rig's thermometer was recording an air temperature of 133°, "but Jesus, that wind! I was making good time this morning and then—wham! Knocked off 20 kilometers an hour." Now nobody was making good time. Most of the trucks pulled over to avoid straining their engines or bursting their tires in the heat. The bitumen on the road was hot licorice.

I sheltered at Mundrabilla until dusk, when the thermometer read only 98°, then set off for Eucla, another 30-odd miles down the road. With the forecast calling for several more days of this heat, I figured that Eucla—its roadhouse reputedly the nicest along the Nullarbor—was the place to get heat-bound.

Flies notwithstanding, it was a surprisingly pleasant ride. A thunderstorm had loomed in from the west. I could see it behind me, a swollen mass of purplish clouds against the liquid orange of the sunset, draping a black, gauze-like veil of rain over the desert. A moderate tailwind boosted me up the long, winding grade toward 180-foot-high Eucla Pass. Cooler temperatures meant the road trains were on the move again, and a string of them boomed past me in the deepening twilight, hurrying to regain lost time.

It was dark by the time I reached the top of the pass. Eucla's famed neon traveler's cross—something out of Stephen King—shimmered across the desert like a lighthouse beacon, guiding me in.

I rolled out my bivvy in the scrub a couple of hundred yards from the roadhouse. The earth was still hot. It was like sleeping on an electric blanket.

WITH THE MERCURY CREEPING toward 100° and the air acrawl with millions of flies, I walked my bike over to the roadhouse early the next morning and checked into one of their motel rooms. The temperature that day reached 117°F, reported Eucla's official weather station. I spent the day in my room, curtains drawn, the air conditioner rattling valiantly. I re-upped for a second night. It would have been insanity to think of pushing on that evening. Although another roadhouse beckoned only ten miles farther east at the South Australian border, beyond that lay 120 empty miles to the Nullarbor Roadhouse. The memory of my 13-mile death march into Mundrabilla persuaded me not to tackle the waterless stretch to Nullarbor if there was even a chance of getting caught in similar conditions.

As it turned out, the next day's high soared to 119°, and the winds continued to blast down from the Great Victorian Desert for hours. Life on the highway came to a virtual standstill. The roadhouses stopped pumping petrol because it was vaporizing in the heat. Birds dropped dead from the air.

Not just the Nullarbor was suffering this heat. All of southern Australia was in the grip of the worst heat wave in decades. Adelaide broiled through its most stifling heat since 1939, while Melbourne and Sydney—suffering their hottest February in a century—recorded hundreds of heatstroke victims and several deaths.

But at least I was comfortable in Eucla. For more than a century—since the first transcontinental telegraph line was laid in 1873—Eucla has been a welcome way station for intrepid travelers crossing the Nullarbor. The ruins of that original telegraph station are now almost buried in the shifting dunes along the coast. The modern roadhouse is on rocky ground, a few hundred feet higher up. It is the last of the old family-owned and -operated roadhouses on the Nullarbor, a friendly joint built 30 years ago by Gedeminas and Pajauta Patupis, who emigrated from Lithuania after World War II. In almost 8,000 miles it was the only roadhouse I had come across that served such niceties as fresh salad and homemade lasagna. Even so, there's not much to do in a truck-stop motel room except watch TV, play solitaire, and read. In the three days I was laid up there I worked my way through Agatha Christie's *Murder on the Orient Express,* 700 pages of James Clavell's *Tai-Pan,* and started in on the Gideon Bible. One morning at breakfast I jokingly remarked to Rasa Patupis, who manages the roadhouse her parents built, that I was really getting into the begats. She laughed and brought me a handful of Ross Thomas paperbacks to keep me going. Rasa also showed me the latest satellite weather map, faxed from Perth, which indicated that the heat was finally breaking up. On my fourth morning in Eucla I set out again. I was at the South Australian border an hour later.

CHAPTER 38

Of Headwinds and Headcases

THE BILLBOARD beside the caravan park at Border Village reads: "Beware UFOs Next 111 Kilometres. We Border on the Unbelievable."

Indeed, there does seem to be some weird *X-Files* affinity between the terrestrial void of the Nullarbor Plain and the vastness of outer space. Just east of Eucla the highway doglegs around a meteorite crater some 600 feet in diameter, and the desert floor is littered with gravel-sized blackened metallic meteorites known as tektites. In 1979 NASA's ill-fated space station, Skylab, slammed to earth in a rain of fiery debris on the Nullarbor. Travelers out here often report seeing strange lights in the sky at night. In 1988, a family driving along this lonely highway claimed that a flying saucer had picked up their car in its tractor beam, carried it a distance, then tossed it into a ditch.

I would have welcomed the assistance of friendly aliens that morning. The cool southerly buster that had dissolved the heat wave was also kicking up fierce headwinds. As grateful as I was for the chilly temperatures and the drizzle, I was starting to feel trapped in a zero-sum game as I churned into the wind at five miles an hour.

The Eyre Highway through here skirts the edge of what must be the most forbidding line of cliffs on the planet. Australia comes to an end with frightening abruptness, the sheared-off edge of the continent dropping hundreds of feet to the booming surf of the Southern Ocean. Occasional side roads lead to the brink—and to achingly desolate views of banded limestone cliffs stretching into the salt haze for miles in either direction.

I straddled my bike atop this precipice one afternoon, a cold wind in my face, looking out on a heaving gray sea that reached to Antarctica. Behind me the dead-flat scrub of the Nullarbor Plain stretched into infinity. Nothing brought home Australia's isolation more than standing at the edge of these lonely cliffs, listening to the hollow boom of the breakers far below. There was no other sound. I was the first—or the last—man on earth.

Those few days on either side of Eucla were a seminar in the dangerous fickleness of the Australian climate. Whereas it had been more than 120° when the blistering winds first roared down from the north, now that the weather was blowing in off the Southern Ocean I was shivering with cold. The air was damp and raw. A bitter rain stung my face. The winds were too strong to wrestle, so I spent the afternoon hunkered down on that desolate cliff top, wearing every stitch of clothing I had and using my bike as a windbreak.

The next day was only a little better. It took me three lonely days to ride 120 miles along the cliff tops to the Nullarbor Roadhouse. I was out of food and low on water when I finally rolled in, hungry for breakfast, early in the morning.

A SHIFT IN THE WEATHER brought clear, warm skies. I rode 110 miles that day and camped in a handsome stand of eucalypts near the Yalata Aboriginal reservation. Another two days' hard riding through lonely, arid scrub and scraggly wheat country brought me to the outskirts of Ceduna—the desolate South Australian fishing port and farm town generally regarded as the eastern terminus of a Nullarbor crossing. I could see Ceduna's skyline of white grain elevators shimmering on the horizon a few miles before the town itself came into view. I pulled up at the quarantine station, declared that I was carrying no fresh fruit from Western Australia, and rolled down the gentle grade into the first real town I'd seen since pedaling out of Norseman almost two weeks earlier.

I checked into a caravan park and took a long, steamy shower. Although my legs were at the point of mutiny, I made them trudge to the supermarket to buy the makings of a slap-up dinner. I celebrated my successful crossing of the Nullarbor with a pound of spicy sausages, a half-pound packet of rice, a heaping plate of steamed vegetables, a cantaloupe, a quart of cherry yogurt, half a gallon of fruit juice, and two packets of gingersnaps.

The TV was on—something forgettable—and I drifted off to sleep. It was still on 14 hours later when I groggily looked around the caravan, wondering where I was and piecing together the last 1,000 miles. After breakfast—an entire box of muesli, another quart of cherry yogurt, half a gallon of orange juice, another cantaloupe, three cups of coffee, and a toothpick—I slung my saddlebags onto my rear rack and rode out of town.

CHAPTER 39

Answering Einstein's Question

ALTHOUGH THE NULLARBOR is generally reckoned to end at Ceduna, the 300 miles across the Eyre Peninsula to Port Augusta aren't much different. It is hot and dusty and lonely, and even if the farm towns are a little closer together than roadhouses on the Nullarbor, they are still widely scattered enough to maintain the Nullarbor's sense of windswept desolation. This is hardscrabble wheat country, some of the poorest and bleakest in Australia. The struggling grain-elevator settlements out here exude a laconic despair reminiscent of Dust Bowl Oklahoma.

The road through the country was open and hot. I covered 270 miles in two days. Late in the afternoon on the second day, my legs wobbling with exhaustion, I passed a billboard spruiking a motel up ahead in Iron Knob. I resolved to press on and reward myself with a soft bed.

Iron Knob is an old iron-mining town in the saltbush country on the eastern side of the peninsula. I got there at dusk. By then a heavy blue cast had settled over the landscape, giving the low-slung town a sullen feel. A storm was brewing. I could smell rain in the darkness, and the restless gusts held a chill that had been absent half an hour earlier. I walked my bike up a gloomy main street of fiberboard shacks, rusty trailers, corrugated-iron sheds, derelict steam shovels, and weedy lots, all nestled at the foot of the gouged-out crag where they used to mine iron ore.

The Shell Roadhouse was dark. Equally deserted was the motel whose billboard I had seen some miles back. Although cars were parked in front of the houses, not a glimmer of light showed through the shades, no Saturday-night laughter drifted from any doorway—only the low, menacing growls of unseen dogs. It was creepy. I considered riding back to the highway and pushing on, but it was full dark now and the storm was getting closer. I wished I had never come to this place, regretted that my foolish whim to sleep in a bed had enticed me to pedal the extra miles. Had I pulled over at my usual time, I would have been in a nice, snug camp right now.

I was just about to risk camping on the edge of town when I glimpsed a faded electric sign advertising West End Beer. My heart lifted—a pub! Australian pubs generally have rooms for travelers.

I leaned my bike against a fence and stepped inside a cramped room, cluttered with brewery memorabilia, where a dozen patrons on the downhill side of middle age lounged against chest-high tables. They were watching a TV show called *Heartbeat,* a series set in 1960s Yorkshire, on the television above the bar. A veil of cigarette smoke hung in the air. The buzz of conversation ceased abruptly. Nobody turned to look at me, but I got the idea that anybody in the room could have, if asked, described me down to the hole in the toe of my left shoe. I made my way to the bar, where a lynx-eyed matron stood with her arms folded across her chest. She said: "Yeah?"

"Do you have accommodation?"

She regarded me without speaking for about 30 seconds. I was about to repeat the question when I noticed her eyes flick past my left shoulder to field a signal from somebody behind me. She said: "Yeah."

"What's the rate?"

There was another flick of the eyes, another signal. "Twenty-five dollars." She threw out the words as though she was laying down a challenge. It was a steep price for a room in such a poky, out-of-the-way pub, but I was in no position to dicker. I placed three tens on the counter. "Done. Is there anyplace I can park my bike?"

The woman eyed the money, then pushed the bills back at me. "I think you'd be better off at the motel. Why don't you go there?"

"Because it's closed."

"Folks that own it live just across the street. I'm sure they'd open up and give you a room. Why don't you do that?"

A heavyset, putty-faced man sidled up to me, very close, pointedly trespassing on the bubble of personal space we all like around us. He leaned even closer, his face an inch or two from mine, and said: "I think that would be your best bet. Go to the motel."

A few seconds passed on tiptoe. Then I gathered up my money. "Sure. Why not?"

I eased out of the joint and back into the night. I'd come across the odd bit of hostility on the road, but Iron Knob's display of xenophobia was really creepy. I pushed my bike up the darkened street, with its sullen shacks, weedy lots, and those unseen snarling dogs. I found the motel owner's house. It was a beige transportable with a rusty chain-link fence around its scrubby yard. I knocked. A dog growled on the other side of the door. There were no lights on, although I could hear a radio playing. There were no live voices. I was tired and lonely, and more than a little worried by this time, wondering where to sleep on a windy night in the world's meanest town.

I walked along the street some more, hoping for inspiration. Then, out of the corner of my eye, I spotted a blue light I hadn't noticed before—the police station. Just a house, really, where the sergeant outposted to Iron Knob lived. His name was Trevor and he was just setting out to visit friends in Whyalla when I knocked on the door and told him my troubles. He was sympathetic. "No worries," he replied, telling me the police department had just set up a children's camp on the edge of town; clean beds, showers, a stove to cook on, a television to watch. He led me around to the place. "Oh, don't worry about paying," he scoffed. "Get a good night's sleep and lock up when you go."

An hour later I was sinking into a deep sofa, a mug of Lapsang Souchong tea warming my hands, listening to the wind rattle the branches. The TV was on—some old movie or other. As I listened to the rain lash the windows, I thought back over the miles and months on the road; how every time things looked bleak, or the turkeys seemed to be getting the upper hand, something or someone invariably came along to make things right. Maybe one of the more important lessons this journey was teaching me was the answer to Einstein's great philosophical question: Is it a friendly universe?

CHAPTER 40

Back to the Barossa

SIX MONTHS of hard outback travel came to an end at a wall of purplish mountains rising from the saltbush plains east of Port Augusta. I rode eagerly toward them. The empty highway stretched ahead of me, a thin, gray thread that appeared to hit a dead end at the foot of the cliffs but actually wound through them over a hidden pass. On the other side of that range, I knew, lay the gentled farm country of South Australia's "Mid-North," bronzed in the late-summer sun, with old grain-silo towns such as Wilmington, Melrose, and Gladstone dotting the highway every ten miles or so. For the rest of the journey, from here to Sydney, there would be no more 100-mile desolations, no more pushing on through long, weary hours on miserly sips of water, no more brushing aside the flies and surviving to the next roadhouse. On the other hand, Port Augusta marked the end of picaresque outback freedoms: rolling out my bivvy bag anywhere I pleased, that glorious sense of self-reliance, or the exhilaration of riding down a barren desert highway without seeing another soul for hours on end.

Near the top of Horrock's Pass, I stopped and looked back at the flat drabness of miles of silver-gray saltbush dissolving into the western haze. I took a long look, replaying in my mind's eye a cavalcade of fading images and memories. As I rolled down the other side of the pass, I felt a vague sense of loss.

An hour later I was coasting past rippling wheat fields and shady gum trees, marveling that I had never appreciated the beauty of Australia's drowsy farmlands. I had driven through this kind of countryside scores of times over the years, and if I thought of it at all I regarded it as a meridional version of North Dakota, the gnarled shapes of its gums interesting only for their eerie resemblance to an illustration from one of my college geology textbooks: This is how the Pleistocene looked—just add buffalo.

It used to puzzle me the way Australians could rhapsodize about a dusty stand of gum trees along a roadside, a reedy pool of water in an otherwise dry creek bed, and wide-open fields of wheat. My eyes saw only a parched, tawny blandness. But then I had never battled heat and thirst and flies and loneliness for months on end in the outback, nor did I have the collective memories of a born Australian buried in my subconscious. None of my ancestors had fought bushfires or drought; I had no nostalgic memories of visiting aunts or grandparents who lived on the land; I had never memorized "I Love a Sunburnt Country" at school.

But thousands of miles and much experience had deepened my perceptions. Now, as I rolled through the open, sun-burnished countryside, my eyes saw things differently. I noticed the subtle shades of color in the trunks of the stately gum trees along the road, the astonishing clarity of the South Australian light, the long, lazy caws of the crows. A new and satisfying appreciation came over me; whatever pioneering myths underlay this settled farmland seemed to be a part of me now as well.

My route took me through the grazing and wheat-farming country of the Mid-North, the old copper-mining town of Kapunda, and farther south into the broad vineyards of the Barossa Valley. It was late summer and the grapes were ripe for harvest. I rode into the valley through the hamlet of Seppeltsfield, following an avenue of Canary Island date palms with sweeping views of acres of Shiraz and Chardonnay vines. In the distance, air guns boomed to scare the parrots away from the fruit. The vineyard roadsides were lined with the cars of grape pickers. Old, slow farm trucks, their beds piled high with grapes, lumbered down the road before me.

The Barossa Valley is Australia's premier wine-growing region, a pocket of the Old World dotted with the steeples of Lutheran churches built of local stone by Prussian and Silesian settlers more than 150 years ago. The phone books overflow with German surnames: Heuzenroeder, Lehman, Linke, Graetz—fourth-generation descendants of the early pioneers. The little German villages still have their own brass bands, and some of the older folk continue to speak an Australianized form of German known as Barossa-Deutsche. Barossa Valley Bakeries sell German breads and pastries; butcher-shop windows are crammed with smoked meats and sausages made from old family recipes. I stopped in at Linke's butcher shop on Murray Street in Nuriootpa and treated myself to one of their pungent garlic mettwursts—the best in the valley.

I knew where to go for mettwurst because I knew the Barossa quite well. I had once lived less than 25 miles away—in the outer-Adelaide suburb of Gawler—and had spent a lot of time in and around this valley. These steepled villages and broad vineyards were the first bits of truly familiar terrain I had encountered since leaving Sydney the previous July. Yet the valley seemed strangely different: deeper, more complex and intriguing. Riding through it now, after so many months on the road, was like going back and rereading, as an adult, a worthy novel that I had scanned and cast lightly aside as a high-school sophomore. With a twinge of embarrassment, I wondered why I hadn't noticed its richness before. It had been there all the time.

CHAPTER 41

White-Line Fever

FOR EIGHT MONTHS NOW, ever since I pedaled out of Sydney, I had enjoyed a rude good health, traveling thousands of miles through all winds and weathers with nary a sniffle. I had come to regard my body as a sort of reliable engine— something that required regular input of food and water, and sensibly had to be kept from overheating, but required little other consideration. So I was stunned one morning when I woke with a thumping headache, dripping sinuses, and a sore throat that made me feel like a sword-swallower with whooping cough. I felt betrayed.

I saw a doctor in Angaston, a dour old man who cocked his head back and peered down my throat through a pair of half-moon spectacles and diagnosed the same wicked little virus that he had been seeing so much of lately. He recommended rest and a brand of cold tablets. So I lounged around the valley for a few more days, eating well and lying low. I still had a nagging chesty cough when I set out again; a bit of fresh air and exercise, I figured, would clean the fusty dampness from my lungs.

I took the back way out of the valley, over the Barossa Ranges and down the long, winding grade toward Sedan—and, in the hazy distance beyond that, the wide, dusty plains along the Murray River. (Still awash in the snug civility of the Barossa Valley, I had decided not to brave the hassle and bustle of Adelaide.) Only 40 miles or so separate Angaston from the old river port of Mannum, but I was bone-weary by the time I got there, coughing, sputtering, and uneasily aware that this virus hadn't finished with me yet.

I lunched on aspirin, water, and dried fruit. Midway through a hot and drowsy Sunday afternoon, the shady park along the riverbank was bright with picnicking families and fathers teaching their sons how to fish. A century ago, Mannum had been a bustling steamboat hub, a southern-hemisphere Vicksburg, its wharf piled high with bales of wool; now it is a sleepy holiday town of fishing shacks and houseboats. I dozed, nursing my groggy head in the sunshine, vaguely psyching myself up to push on.

The rest helped. I caught the ferry across the river, then pedaled another 20 miles downstream to Murray Bridge. I barely made it. Hitting town just at dusk, feverish and exhausted, I walked my bike across the century-old iron bridge toward an old-fashioned neon sign that shimmered "H-O-T-E-L" in glowing red letters against a backdrop of palms and a pale orange sunset.

Everything ached, deep in my muscles and joints. I took a room at a pub and sat up late watching a gangster movie on TV, shivering under my blanket, coughing and sipping endless cups of tea. I listened to the night train from Adelaide rumble through town on its way to Melbourne and imagined myself aboard it, covering the next 500 miles in a comfortable railway carriage. Instead of pedaling for days down a thankless highway on weary legs, I would arrive in Melbourne—refreshed, shaved, and breakfasted—early tomorrow morning. In short, I would be free of this ride, which by now felt like a sentence.

A FEVERISH BLUR was the next few days. I saw another doctor, in Tailem Bend this time, who told me I was running a low-grade fever but reckoned I could carry on—providing I took it easy, that is, eating hearty, sensible meals and sleeping in warm beds rather than camping on cold ground. I pressed on, spending the night at a tatty caravan park in a wide spot on the highway called Tintinara. Following doctor's orders, I ate a heaping plate of rice and vegetables, feeling utterly miserable and lonely beneath the bare 60-watt bulb that dangled over the table.

The next day—a gray and blustery one—I covered nearly 100 miles and wound up in Naracoorte, exhausted and shaking with chills. I spent another fitful night in a caravan, followed by a bleary wakening with a throbbing headache and sore throat. Common sense should have told me to quit for a few days, but a delirious stubbornness had seized me. Perhaps it was a side effect of following the road for so many thousands of miles; somewhere at the savage core of my being, life itself had become intertwined with the linear progression of miles, leaving me no option but to press on.

Massaging my pounding temples that morning, I sagely decided to ride only as far as Penola. After downing a Demazin tablet, a couple of aspirins, and three cups of caffeine-rich black coffee, however, I felt stronger. The fresh air helped too. Penola came and went. I chewed a few dried peaches in the shade of a chapel dedicated to Mother Mary MacKillop, a Penola teacher who founded a religious order in the early 1900s— and who, having been beatified by Pope John Paul II in 1995, needs to chalk up only one more miracle cure to become Australia's first saint. I sensed that my case would not be the one to push her over the top.

Feeling wrapped in gauze, I followed a back road heading east. It's very likely that I passed through pretty farm country, but I don't remember it. On the far side of the Victoria border, I eventually arrived in a town called Coleraine about 6:30 in the evening. I was mighty sick by the time I got there, running a fever and shaking. I paused in front of the Commercial Hotel, a nice-looking place, and was about to stop when, for no logical reason—particularly since I could barely stand—I decided to walk a little farther down the street.

Fate was singing a siren song. I found myself at the door of the National Hotel, another two-story pub on Coleraine's old-fashioned, false-front main street. Something about the banks of flowers in the window boxes told me this was the place. I went inside. The hotel was nice enough—the bed warm and comfortable, the shower gratifyingly hot and steamy—but what will always set it apart in my memory is the blokes from the Apex Club who were meeting there that night. They treated me to a hot lasagna dinner and some (strictly medicinal) rum-and-cokes. Then one of them—a guy named Simon—got on his cell phone, called his brother-in-law down near Warrnambool, and passed the phone to me. I found myself talking to a pleasant-voiced mandolin-maker named Steve Gilchrist, who offered me a place to stay the next night. I gladly accepted.

Grateful as I was, I had no idea then how wonderful—nor, indeed, how potentially lifesaving—Steve's offer would turn out to be.

A bit more than 80 miles separated the National Hotel from the old whaling port of Warrnambool. I barely made it up the big hill on the outskirts of Coleraine, but once on top the Demazin, Panodol, and caffeine kicked in, and I pressed on. The day was cool, gusty, and bleak, with damp gray clouds scudding across the sky. The hills were brassy and open; this was some of Victoria's finest sheep-grazing country. I was heading for the coast. Beyond that I don't remember much of the morning, other than a vague recall of passersby in Hamilton staring at me as a hacking cough doubled me over on a street corner.

Afternoon found me at a little roadhouse diner in a place called Hawkesdale. I had stopped there, shivering and coughing, for a cup of coffee and a rest; my head was buzzing, and the Gilchrists' house was still 25 miles down the road. I sat at a table by the big roadside window. The highway was empty. A gloomy pall had settled over the countryside.

As I sipped my coffee, I noticed a dense wall of purplish-black clouds creeping in off the Southern Ocean. It was damp and dark and full of rain, and it was low enough to dissolve the distant landscape with its sooty tendrils.

My heart sank. I paid for my coffee and stepped outside, digging an extra fleece and rain parka out of my pannier. I thought—foolishly, but then I wasn't firing on all cylinders—that if I pedaled quickly enough I could outrun it.

I was wrong. The swirling black clouds overtook me a few miles down the track.

It was the dirtiest of weather—exactly the kind of raw, blustery southwester the old whalers feared, the kind that gave this rocky, storm-lashed edge of the continent its reputation as the Shipwreck Coast. Freezing rain fell in torrents, a wall of cold water driven into my face by the powerful southerlies. My pace slowed to a crawl. Thunder boomed. I was in open country with no place to run for shelter, and nothing to do but put my head down and ride. The wind drove the cold rain into the little gaps around my collar and up the sleeves of my parka. I could feel the icy water trickling down my clammy skin. My nose ran. Mud and water splashed up from the road, drenching my shoes. My feet grew chilled; my bare legs felt like cold, wet pasta.

For three hours I rode into the teeth of this deluge, hacking deep, hollow coughs, battling hypothermia, and—toward the end—talking to myself to stay alert (or at least conscious). Like the little engine that could, I repeated "I think I can, I think I can, I think I can!" For motivation I conjured up victories, such as the one at Mundrabilla when that heat storm had come out of nowhere and I had still made it to the roadhouse, or the hellish struggle to reach the DeGrey River way back in the Great Sandy Desert. If I had made it through then, I tried to convince myself, I could beat this too. In short, I was scared.

Finally too wobbly to keep my balance, I trudged the last mile on numb feet, my shoes squelching water ever step of the way. I was flushed, feverish, and unable to stop shivering.

I remember that Steve Gilchrist was just coming out of his workshop when I arrived; that he and his wife, Christine, got me straight into a hot shower; that a pot of hot black coffee was waiting for me when I got out. I don't remember much else. The next morning, Christine flatly forbade me to leave; I didn't argue. I spent a bleary day by the wood stove while the cold rain continued to dash against the windows.

That night—it was Good Friday—we had pizza, and I passed out at the dinner table. Steve bundled me off to the emergency room at Warrnambool Base Hospital. The nurse told me I was running a fever of 104°F. The doctor was worried about my being alone; because I was a stranger traveling through town, he decided to admit me to the hospital. Steve wouldn't hear of it. He stepped up and said they'd look after me.

CHAPTER 42

Making Mandolins

STEVE, CHRISTINE, and their four kids treated me like family. I'll never forget waking up on Easter morning to find that the Easter Bilby had left chocolates outside my door, a kindness that warmed me as no fire could and healed me more than any antibiotic.

I spent days in Steve's workshop, poring over books on vintage mandolins while he enthusiastically explained the finer points of his craft. It was lovely to sit there, a steaming mug of coffee in my hand, savoring the fragrance of raw maple and spruce, listening to bluegrass music and the loving rush of sandpaper on wood as Steve put the final touches on another exquisite mandolin. The rain rattled the windows in a pleasing counterpoint to the well-lit warmth and the crisp curls of wood in the workshop.

Steve had been building fine musical instruments—mandolins and arch-top guitars—for more than 20 years, and now his French-polished masterpieces fetched thousands of dollars apiece. Top bluegrass and rock musicians from around the world eagerly added their names to the 18-month waiting list. One former owner of a Gilchrist guitar: Jerry Garcia.

Browsing through some coffee-table books, I found Steve described as "one of the finest living makers of mandolins." When I mentioned the passage, he gave me an embarrassed smile, in that understated manner Australians often have when confronted with evidence of their own achievements. "Well," Steve shrugged, "mandolin-making isn't exactly a crowded field."

One day when I was feeling better and the sun was poking through the clouds, Steve took the afternoon off to show me around. Victoria's southwest coast from Warrnambool to Geelong is the most spectacular in Australia; a mixture of windswept cliff tops, mountains cloaked in rain forest, and—most famously—the dramatic stone spires that early mariners dubbed the Twelve Apostles. The storms that brew up from the Roaring Forties, coupled with the treacherous offshore currents and rocky shoals, made this a graveyard for ships; more than 200 wrecks are strewn along the coast.

The most tragic of these was the *Loch Ard,* an immigrant ship that foundered off Mutton Bird Island on a foggy night in 1878. Of the 54 people on board, only two—Eva Carmichael, a well-bred Irish girl of 18 who had lost her entire family, and Tom Pearce, the ship's cabin boy of the same age—survived the sinking. Half drowned, they were washed into an inlet, since known as Loch Ard Gorge. Pearce managed to climb out of the ravine the next morning and summon help. Sentimentalists hoped the two young survivors might marry, but the social gap between them proved wider than Loch Ard Gorge. Eva returned to Ireland, while Tom went back to sea—where, in a long career, he survived two more shipwrecks.

Steve told me all this as we walked the cliff top. "I think of this as the site of my parallel existence," he said, peering down into the seething gorge. "You see, my family was meant to sail on the *Loch Ard,* but their train was delayed and they missed her by two hours. They came out on the next ship."

CHAPTER 43

Black-Stone Roadway by the Sea

THE GREAT OCEAN ROAD is Australia's most dramatic drive: a narrow, twisting, 200-mile-long road that hugs Victoria's spectacular Shipwreck Coast. Cliffs, flowers, and sparkling ocean views line one side of the road; the lush green rain forests of the Otway Ranges, some of them in Otway National Park, line the other. The road was built as a memorial to the soldiers who fought in World War I. When finished in 1932, it linked a number of pretty but hard-to-reach seaside resort towns with Melbourne.

Cyclists love the Great Ocean Road, and I had looked forward to its curvy dramatics for months. Now that I was finally on it, though, my mind was as much on my brittle health—could I complete my circumnavigation?—as it was on the breathtaking scenery around me. The virus had faded, but it left me feeling as fragile as blown glass. I made short runs, bedding down early each day in a youth hostel or motel, keeping a weather eye on the blustery squalls that rolled in off the sea. The last thing I needed was to get caught in another icy downpour, suffer another bout of hypothermia, and relapse. For the most part, I was lucky: I stayed fairly dry.

East of Port Campbell and the Twelve Apostles, the road wound inland through the cool dampness of the Otway Ranges, dense with huge tree ferns and remnants of the ancient temperate rain forests that once covered Australia. Then it was back down to the coast and a line of dazzling seascapes: the fashionable, century-old resort towns of Apollo Bay and Lorne, followed by the surfing mecca of Torquay.

Early one afternoon, three days after I left the Gilchrists, I rode into Queenscliff, a historic lighthouse town overlooking Port Phillip Bay. The old fort here was built in the nervous post-Crimea days to protect the seaward entrance to Melbourne from a much-feared—if ludicrously unlikely—Russian invasion.

From here I had a choice. I could ride up to Geelong and dodge traffic along the Princes Freeway, passing the sewage-treatment facility to enter Melbourne through its rough west side, or I could take the ferry across the mouth of the bay to the old seaside resort town of Sorrento, then approach the city from its prosperous and leafy southeast. It was a no-brainer.

It had been a cool, gray day, and a light rain was starting to fall when I drew up to the ferry landing. I caught the three o'clock sailing and landed in Sorrento about 45 minutes later.

The general idea was to ride into Melbourne and catch the ferry across Bass Strait to the island of Tasmania. By now I was worn, jaded, and tired of life on the road, but I clung to my my original plan—to cycle through each state in Australia—with the unthinking stubbornness of a monkey with his fist stuck in a cookie jar. I over-nighted in Sorrento, then rode 60 miles up the Mornington Peninsula, along a line of beachside suburbs, to reach Port Melbourne. The *Spirit of Tasmania* was in port, preparing to sail to Devonport, Tasmania, on the evening tide.

CHAPTER 44

A Tasmanian Devil

I WENT ABOARD AT THREE O'CLOCK, took a shower, and stretched out on my bunk for a nap (after the drizzly ride up from Sorrento, I was feeling the raw edges of that virus again). I had a two-berth cabin down in steerage, and after a couple of hours during which nobody entered to claim the other bunk, despite all the commotion and bumping baggage in the corridor, I began to entertain hopes that I might have the cabin to myself.

Suddenly the door burst open and a guy staggered in, so loud and clownish—a caricature of the seatmate from hell—that I thought he must be a shipboard comedian. He was the halo before the migraine, with no front teeth and a three-day stubble of iron-gray beard. He wore bright pink reflective wraparound sunglasses and a shiny blue nylon pin-striped sport coat over a badly stained red T-shirt. His baggy green work pants looked like they would drop to his ankles at any moment. Dirty green thongs were on his feet. He reeked of body odor, nicotine, and cheap cask wine.

He yelled: "G'day!"

I blinked and stared, sincerely believing for those few seconds that this was some kind of joke—a drunk-o-gram delivered to the wrong cabin, perhaps? But the redolence of nasty Moselle was bringing home the truth pretty quick. The grimy gym bag he tossed onto the opposite bunk sealed it.

"Just you and me, eh? Off to Tasmania! You don't have to worry about me, mate—I ain't a poofter and I ain't violent. No sir, we're going to have a big night in the pub tonight—you and me, eh? Music, grog, and dancing—that's what I'm all about!"

As he lurched around the cabin, he was delighted to discover that our bathroom was equipped with a real flush toilet. He worked it three times, amazed. Equally astonished, I took a couple of aspirin. When he went up on deck to light his smoke—promising to come back real soon to collect me so we could start our big night at the pub—I slipped out and climbed to a quiet corner of the B-deck to start my big night of hide-and-seek.

IT WAS CHILLY ON DECK, a cool wind blowing off the bay, kicking up whitecaps in the olive-drab water. Twilight was settling over the city. It felt funny and a little sad to be back in Melbourne, a city where I had lived for five eventful years. I scanned its familiar skyline. A shaft of orange sunlight had broken through the clouds, dazzling the mirrored flanks of the Rialto Tower. Black rain clouds formed a dramatic backdrop to the city. The foreshore looked cold and bleak under a melancholy sky, deserted except for two young women in blue lycra, power-walking along the beachfront. Sea gulls wheeled and screeched overhead.

My mind wandered back four years to when I lived a few blocks from here, in a rented 1920s-era bungalow in the bay-side suburb of Elsternwick. I looked over there now. It was curious how drab and small everything seemed, as though I was visiting the setting of a well-remembered novel whose author had very nearly—but not quite—got his details right.

The first lights shimmered on. A stream of commuters headed home to dinner. I lingered against the rail for an hour after we sailed, watching Melbourne slip astern.

We had a millpond crossing by Bass Strait standards: just an hour or two of swells beyond the headlands guarding the mouth of Port Phillip Bay, then a smooth run to Tasmania. I slept soundly. Despite the inauspicious beginnings with my cabin-mate, I got my wish for solitude: Len (for that was his name) evidently got so drunk or seasick—or both—that he never found his way back. I spotted him the next morning, draped over a sofa in one of the lounges, a long strand of drool dangling from his open mouth.

I went out on deck. In the fresh morning breeze, a jagged coastline was emerging from the mist. Tasmania is one of those insular places that it pays to approach by sea, if for no other reason than to get the full measure of its moody isolation. Dark and forbidding, cut off from the rest of the world by the cold currents and furious squalls of the Roaring Forties, it was the place of ultimate banishment in the smelly old days of rum and the lash. Its stormy coast projects Gothic tragedy like a beam from a lighthouse. So much so, in fact, that early mariners marked Tasmania's primeval southwestern coast as "Transylvania" on their charts and gave it a wide berth.

I had seen that wild coast once, years ago, from the heavily pitching deck of an icebreaker returning from Mawson base in Antarctica. It is a brave sight, with its fearsome, serrated cliffs and dense rain forests tumbling down to the sea, virtually unchanged since Dutch navigator Abel Tasman first laid eyes on it in 1642. The approach to Devonport is bucolic by comparison. We docked a little after breakfast. I cleared quarantine and set out along the Midlands Highway for Hobart, Tasmania's capital, on the island's opposite side.

It was a cool and breezy day, the highway rolling through miles of English-style pastureland and historic colonial villages made of honey-colored sandstone. Maybe it was the remnants of the virus still gnawing at me, or memories of covering the 1996 Port Arthur massacre, or simply Tasmania's history of genocide and penal sadism, but I found these picturesque landscapes not soothing at all. Their gentility seemed a smooth and false veneer underlain by violence.

I rolled into the old garrison town of Campbell Town a little before six o'clock, a gentle golden light filtering through the trees, softening the fields and backlighting a flock of sheep grazing near an old stone church. I had covered nearly 100 miles that day, an effort that had left me bone-tired and cold, clammy with chilled sweat, and nursing a headache that hinted at a low-grade fever. I checked into a two-star joint on the southern edge of town, its sign spelling out "M-O-T-E-L" in a turquoise neon ribbon that blinked against the dusk.

The night was cold and clear, with frost in the forecast. I sat up watching TV, shivering beneath a mountain of blankets. The thin curtains failed to shut out the night, allowing that neon sign by the road to flash its blinking despondency on the dingy walls of my room. The effect was so theatrically down-at-the-heels that I had to laugh—a feeble cackle that ended in a coughing fit.

The next day was cold and raw. I pushed on another 80 hilly miles to Hobart, its aggressive rush hour belying its reputation as a laid-back burg. It was late in the afternoon. I was fading fast by the time I rolled over the Derwent River, running a fever and weak at the knees from the last couple of hill climbs. I booked a room in a cheap hostel a few blocks up from Constitution Dock.

I had originally planned a circuitous loop of Tasmania, but that was a pipe dream now. It was well into autumn, the weather was turning, and snow dusted the summit of Mount Wellington, the 4,000-foot-high peak that dominates Hobart's western skyline. I was sick and rapidly running out of go. After a few days' rest and recuperation in town, I headed back toward Melbourne—and the last leg of my journey home.

CHAPTER 45

Memories of Melbourne

BASS STRAIT WAS smooth as glass. The *Spirit of Tasmania* drew up to the dock in Port Melbourne midway through a warm and dazzling Sunday morning. Beaconsfield Parade was bright with cyclists in fluoro lycra. Power-walkers strutted past the ornamental palms along the esplanade. The café at the end of St. Kilda pier bustled with dog-walkers, cyclists out for club rides, and locals dawdling over two-coffee breakfasts and the Sunday paper. I rode out to the end of the pier to take it all in. The bright sunshine dispelled the gloom of the past few days. This was Melbourne the way I liked to remember it, when I had lived along the foreshore and followed this bike path into the city.

As an expatriate New Englander, I had always felt much more at home here in Melbourne than I had in brash, California-style Sydney. Melbourne—with its old-money shadows and school ties and chilly patrician atmosphere—fancies itself a sort of antipodean Boston. Like the more

WASPish Bostonians, Melburnians consider themselves better bred than their nouveau-riche counterparts in other cities. In reality, much of Melbourne's blue-blooded wealth was a lotto win, grubbed out of the mud by strike-it-rich prospectors in Victoria goldfields during the 1850s. Melburnians like to be reminded of this fact about as much as the Cabots and Lowells enjoy having the days of child labor in the cotton mills pointed out to them.

With its gracious Victorian-era bank buildings and green-and-gold trams running along leafy boulevards flanked by plane trees and the lazy Yarra River running through its heart, Melbourne is European. I took a short trip down memory lane, riding into the city along the back streets of Albert Park and South Melbourne—the same route I had followed when I wrote for the *Melbourne Sunday Age* in the 1990s. I could no longer recall the street names, but my wrists turned the handlebars at all the right corners as though I had never been away. Now that I had 9,500 miles of strange Australian roads under my belt, it seemed odd to pedal these once-familiar paths.

With an open and sunny Sunday on my hands, I followed the bike path along the river, through the Botanic Gardens and the leafy yuppie enclave of South Yarra, then meandered around to gritty, working-class Collingwood. I headed back downtown through the raffish inner-city clutter of Brunswick Street and Fitzroy, cut through the Treasury Gardens, and came out onto Spring Street just up from the Windsor Hotel.

The Windsor has been a Melbourne icon since it opened its portals in 1883, an old-style grand hotel with a hushed, clubby air and high teas served in the ornate lobby. Over the decades it has been the haunt of prime ministers, royalty, tycoons, and celebrities. The Australian constitution was drafted in one of its suites. For the past few thousand miles, I had entertained the notion that when I finally reached Melbourne I would treat myself to a night at the Windsor. It had seemed clever then—the prospect of riding up on my bicycle, shaking thousands of miles of trail dust from my shirt, and casually checking into the Windsor. Now, as I squeaked to a halt across the street from the hotel's grand façade, I felt myself go shy. I loitered on the sidewalk, looking at the gleaming brass plaque, the flags snapping by the portico, the green-liveried doorman.

I almost didn't do it. But then I had a rush of blood, said what the hell, and marched across the street. Trying not to look sheepish, I presented myself to the doorman. His name was Neil.

"Good morning. I think I'd like to take a room here."

Neil didn't bat an eye. "Why, certainly, sir. Would you like me to valet-park your pushbike?"

"If you don't mind."

So while Neil escorted my bicycle to the luggage locker, I signed the register of the Windsor Hotel. A bellboy toted my dusty saddlebags upstairs to my room.

CHAPTER 46

The Last Leg

THE FOLLOWING SUNDAY I took the Melba Highway out of Melbourne, through the wine country along the Yarra River Valley, then north toward the Victorian highlands. After a week's rest in Melbourne—not all of it at the Windsor, alas—I was starting to sense that the virus had finally run its course. And even though I pedaled slowly and experimentally to begin with, I felt better than I had in weeks.

I traveled only as far as Yea that first night, Bonnie Doon the second. This was the final leg of my journey—a little less than 500 miles to Sydney. A year ago, when this journey was still just a daydream, I had envisioned myself meandering through the Australian Alps and Snowy Mountains on my way up to Sydney. Now, with the finish line in sight, I merely wanted to push on and get there. Not only was I physically weary, but the last couple of weeks, with their battles against illness and loneliness on the road, had nudged me over some mental edge.

Voyages—like lives—have distinct stages: adolescence, maturity, old age. The raw exuberance I had felt on first heading into Queensland's Gulf Country had given way to cannier knowledge as I rounded the Top End, then to stoical acceptance in the Great Sandy Desert and one last taste of outback freedoms on the Nullarbor Plain. Now I was ready to bring my wanderings to an end.

There was something else, too. Besides laying me low, that virus had thrown a scare into me. I was near the end, with a valuable investment in time and commitment and face, and every additional day on the road made me feel like a gambler foolishly letting his stake ride for another spin of the wheel. Pedaling up to Circular Quay—finishing what I had set out to do thousands of miles ago—now took on supreme importance. That's why I skipped the circuitous back roads in favor of the fast and direct Hume Highway.

At Benalla I saw a sign of hope: "Sydney 672 Kilometres." I skirted the Strathbogie Ranges, where bushranger Ned Kelly and his gang had hidden out in the 1870s, then cranked through Glenrowan, where troopers captured Kelly and killed his gang in a firefight in 1880. Although Glenrowan enthusiastically bills itself as the site of Ned Kelly's last stand, the outlaw's last stand was actually atop a gallows trap in Melbourne Gaol the following November.

I rolled across a bridge over the Murray River and found myself back in New South Wales for the first time since that long-ago morning when I had started up the Gold Coast. I could smell the end of the ride. I made good time, covering the 120 miles from the river towns of Albury-Wodonga to Gundagai in one breezy, hilly, sunburned day. I booked into a seedy motel just up the street from a defunct 1929 movie theater whose premises were now shared by a funeral parlor and novelty shop. I bought myself a couple of celebratory beers in honor of my return to fitness.

The next day was Anzac Day, the anniversary of the April day in 1915 when Australian troops waded into history and a hail of Turkish bullets on a formidably defended beach near Gallipoli in the Dardenelles. The storming of that beach marked the first time Australia had gone to war as a nation, and each year the nation pauses to give thanks to those first "diggers"—and to the generations of Australians who have fought and died in other 20th-century wars. It is a public holiday; unlike any other civic event on a calendar chock-full of extra-long beachy weekends, however, this one is serious. Across the nation—in every city, town, and hamlet—there are well-attended dawn services, wreath layings, and solemn parades of silver-haired veterans marching through the streets in their Sunday suits, regimental ties, and campaign medals, cheered on by thousands of their compatriots. The motto of the day is "Lest We Forget." No one does: This is a day of genuine thanks.

It was still dark, with just a hint of gray in the east, when I set off for the cricket oval where much of Gundagai was gathering for its dawn memorial. The veterans—most in their 70s and 80s—had clustered near the clubhouse. It was cold. Talk came in steamy wisps.

"Ow ya goin', Jack?" a voice asked.

"Aw not bad, mate," the man named Jack replied, forming his words around the stub of a dead roll-your-own-cigarette that dangled from his lips. A prodigious row of campaign medals tugged at his lapel.

Just behind him, another craggy-faced veteran served up coffee at the clubhouse counter. He saw me. "What'll you have?"

"Black coffee, thanks."

He laughed. "You want *black* coffee?"

"Yes."

He nudged his mate, another old codger. "Say, can you believe this bloke? Wants black coffee!"

They laughed. "Say, mate, you sure you want *black* coffee?"

I could tell by the mischievous light in their eyes that something was going on here. "Well, how *should* I have my coffee?"

"With a bit of this in it!" He held up a flagon of rum.

"As you say, it'd be silly to have it black."

"There's the spirit." He poured me a generous slug, a real heart-starter on a cold dawn. Strictly speaking, of course, it was illegal to be serving alcohol at the cricket clubhouse, which had no liquor license. Betting at Two-Up—the classic gambling game among slouch-hatted Australian diggers—was also, strictly speaking, against the law. But where old diggers are concerned, they toss aside the bylaws book on Anzac Day.

They held the memorial service in a copse of 80-year-old kurrajong trees that had been planted in the shape of a cross to commemorate Gundagai's World War I dead. A crusty sergeant nearly as old as those trees barked at his men to fall in, and they marched, stiff and proud, into position. A chaplain read the service. A bugler sounded the "Last Post." There was a two-minute silence, broken only by the distant hooting of a kookaburra in the hills.

I RODE IMPATIENTLY through the farmlands of New South Wales, covering 147 miles in my last full day on the road. I slipped into Sydney early on a Sunday morning. It was bright and clear and warm and sunny, just as it had been 40 Sundays earlier when I set out. Almost 10,000 miles had slid beneath my wheels since then.

As I rode up George Street toward Circular Quay, a stream of memories surged up unbidden: Booming along the Capricorn Highway with a tailwind at my back; the camaraderie in the shearing shed at Fairfield; dealing card games with Mick, Thommo, Terry, and Paul in the back room at Ash Colahan's motel overlooking the croc-infested waters of the Gulf of Carpentaria. Purplish thunderheads and drooping palms in Darwin...blood-red suns sinking into the Kimberley scrub...laughter and barking dogs at the Bidyadanga Aboriginal Community on the fringes of the Great Sandy

Desert. Aching loneliness on the Nullarbor Plain. Rain forests and long, empty deserts. Mountains and coasts.

I had seen almost every sunrise and sunset over the past nine months, owned each day completely. Now it was coming to an end, back where it all began. Although I had been anticipating this moment for the past couple of months, now that it was upon me I found myself slowing down, not wanting to relinquish the delicious freedom I'd found. Memories of the hardships faded. The good things remained.

I rolled up to the ferry landing at Circular Quay just before noon. The harbor looked just as I remembered it, with yachts and ferries plying the sparkling water, the Opera House shimmering in the sun, the quay bright with tourists and buskers. I sat on a bench and looked up at the Harbour Bridge. For one daft moment I considered starting over—crossing the bridge and heading north again, this time with the knowledge and appreciation of Australia that I lacked when I set off in July.

So much had happened since then. I had wondered at the beginning of this adventure whether immersing myself in Australia, which had always seemed just beyond arm's reach, might change the course of my life. As I pedaled up George Street, I realized that these nine months had been a lot like growing up again, this time as an Australian. I had absorbed much from the people I met, and from the land itself. Its history, myths, and legends were part of my story now. And in my own small way, I had become a part of it.

EPILOGUE

I DIDN'T KNOW MUCH about long-haul cycling expeditions when I set out from Sydney. I learned and grew fit along the way. I must have done some things right. I carried enough water on desert crossings, avoided sunstroke in 140° heat, camped safely by the roadside at night, and developed reasonably canny judgment.

But life on the road is straightforward. Needs are basic: food, water, a snug place to sleep. The highway itself provides a steadying and easily understood sense of direction and purpose. The stark simplicity of the outback landscapes and the fragile clarity of the desert light makes plain things that are hard to resolve in the hustle and clutter of the workaday world.

I had set out on this journey to learn about Australia, to try to figure out my future here—if, indeed, I had one. Riding up George Street to Circular Quay marked the end of that journey. I had learned much and seen much. Now it was time for reflection.

Instead, I made what I will always consider my single biggest mistake: I promptly called up an old friend to tell him I was back in town. (Perhaps the bustle and industry around me stirred my long-buried Calvinist instincts; I just had to be up and doing.) We met, and within an hour or so I was sitting on a sofa being brought up to date on the dreary, catty gossip of the Sydney-Melbourne journalism scene: who had been fired, who had walked out, who had been stabbed in the back, who had done the stabbing. It was a melodrama played out before a Greek chorus of the wonderfully sarcastic remarks someone may or may not have actually said.

I grew restive, aware that I should have granted myself a few hours' solitude down at the quay. As I sat there, I could feel the picaresque sunburned freedom that I had found on the road fading away, like one of those pleasurable dreams that dissipate the moment you wake. Taking shape in its place was the gritty reality of the names and faces, tired plots, and emotional baggage I had left behind.

Within a day or so, I had slipped back into my old role of the accidental expatriate. This time around, however, I boxed my bike, packed my bags, and headed back to New England. A couple of weeks later I stepped off a local bus and into the coolness of a White Mountain spring, bright and green and scented with pines. Back to the old farmhouse, its kitchen redolent with familiar smells: coffee, soap, and gas from the slightly leaky old stove.

I was happy that first morning; this was America.

But, of course, it wasn't. It was the incarnation of pleasant memories. I learned something that many expatriates discover: Lives and nations move on. The States had changed a lot since 1982—and so had I. Although I had proudly carried the flag all those years, I suddenly found myself in a big, fast, strange land. I felt like a shy outsider. It wasn't unpleasant—if anything, it was exhilarating—but I never felt settled.

Then came a day a few weeks later when I had to fly back to Australia for a magazine assignment. I'll always remember the relaxing moment I stepped into the Qantas departure lounge at the L.A. airport, picked up that day's edition of the *Sydney Morning Herald*, and began catching up on the cricket season, the weather map, the familiar names and faces and stories of Australia. With a pleasant shock, I realized that I was going home.

GLOSSARY

Apex Club: an Australian fraternal organization similar in purpose and makeup to an American Kiwanis, Rotary, or Lions club

Bilby: a small, rodent-sized marsupial (also known as the rabbit bandicoot) native to Australia. In recent years, this fairly cute endangered creature has been adopted as Australia's homegrown version of the Easter Bunny.

Bivvy bag: essentially a one-man tent, this waterproof covering is not much longer than a sleeping bag. It often has mosquito netting attached to cover the occupant's face.

Black-spot intersection: a crossroads known to be dangerous

Caravan: a towed live-in trailer

Chiko roll: a deep-fried, crispy bit of fast food similar to a Chinese egg roll or spring roll

Cut-lunch: a brace of sandwiches or some other such simple preparation

Doddle: an easy job; a snap

Dole-bludger: a lazy so-and-so who could work but chooses to collect unemployment benefits instead

Doss house: a form of cheap lodging, usually for itinerant workers

Esky: a plastic cooler or ice chest, derived from the brand name "Eskimo"

Hoon: a hooligan; a brawling tough noted for his mastery of swilling beer and squealing the tires of his muscle car

Jackaroo: a cowboy; not to be confused with a jillaroo

Kelpie: an Australian sheepdog

Kip: sleep

Lob in: land, arrive

Milkbar: a combination sandwich counter and hamburger joint (often serving chiko rolls and other greasy offerings), with a few shelves of groceries, magazines, candy, cigarettes, and milk

Muesli bar: a granola bar

Open slather: all-out; full tilt; unrestrained

Poofter: an obscene term for a homosexual

Puggaree: a light scarf wrapped around a sun helmet

Queue: a line

Ringer: a cowboy

Roadhouse: a petrol station with a diner attached. In the more remote corners of the outback, it may also offer a few basic motel rooms.

Roaring Forties: a stormy band of ocean spanning latitude 40 to 50° south, much feared by mariners for its huge seas and extremely violent—and unpredictable—storms

Royal Commission: an Australian court of inquiry roughly similar to a U.S. grand jury

Slab: a case, as of beer

Snags: sausages

Spruik: to advertise, hawk, or otherwise promote

Stubby: bottle of beer

Swaggie: an itinerant worker with his bedroll—known as a "swag"—thrown over his shoulder

Vegemite: a black, strong-tasting, vaguely salty spread made from yeast extract. Although wildly popular with Australians—who spread it thin on toast or crackers, or even make it into sandwiches—most foreigners consider Vegemite to be an acquired taste.

Wheelie bin: a garbage can on wheels

White goods shop: a store that sells household appliances and electronics